TURKEY
IN
CENTRAL ASIA

TURKEY
IN
CENTRAL ASIA

Prof. (Mrs.) Sheel K. Asopa

STANDARD PUBLISHERS (INDIA)
NEW DELHI

First Published 2008

ISBN 978-81-87471-41-7

Published by

STANDARD PUBLISHERS (INDIA)
225, Gupta Place, A-2/42 Rajouri Garden Main Road
Opp. Telephone Exchange (Near Metro Station), New Delhi-110027
Tel. No. 91-011-25415043, 25435043 (O), 91-011-65848273 (R)
Fax No. 91-011-25374397
E-mail: srallbooks3@bol.net.in
sr_allbooks@vsnl.net

Distributed by

GDMK Publishers Distributors
WZ-430-E/1, Naraina
New Delhi-110 028

Laser Typesetting by

The Laser Printers, New Delhi-110027

Printed at

New Elegant Printers, New Delhi-110064

In Fond Memory
of
my Father

Preface

Present study is an outcome of a research project sanctioned to me by the Maulana Abul Kalam Azad Institute of Asian Studies, Kolkata, to work on *Turkey in Central Asia*. Owing to my long association with Turkey, I was keen to work on this subject. As a research scholar working on my doctoral dissertation I studied at the Siyasal Bilgiler Facultesi, Ankara for a year and half in 1966 onward. Today's Turkey, what I could gather by reading about it, is much different from the Turkey of sixties and early seventies. It has made tremendous economic progress and Turkish model of development has evoked considerable interest among several Asian and Latin American countries.

Turkey is a Eurasian country. It belongs to both Europe and Asia but it likes to call itself European ever since Mustafa Kemal Ataturk renounced Ottomanism—Islamism and pan-Turkism and adopted western identity for the nation to become Republic of Turkey. In the final phase of World War II, Turkey joined the allied powers—thus at the end of the War it belonged to the victorious side. In view of the geo-political importance of Turkey it was considered vital to the security of Europe and was covered by the Truman Doctrine and later admitted to the NATO—a purely European-Christian organization established to counter the threat to Europe from the Warsaw Pact countries and the USSR. Notwithstanding, its disappointments with the West over issues of vital interest to Turkey like the Cyprus issue, Turkey continued to be on the side of the west all through the Cold War.

In the aftermath of collapse of the Soviet Union and emergence of the independent sovereign republics in Central Asia and Transcaucsia, Turkey, owing to its early ethno-linguistic and cultural connections with the Turkic people of Uzbekistan, Kazakhstan, Kyrgyzstan and Turkmenistan (Tajikistan is non-Turkic and Persian linguistically) was considered a "model" for the new republics. Turkey's early linkages with the region were seen as a valuable asset, which could help Turkey in winning the Republics' favour. American and western scholars, media and statesmen propagated Turkey's suitability as a leader of Central Asia. Several scholars in the west as well as in other regions have examined this argument bolstered by the West that ethnic and linguistic commonality can help in integration of a region under the leadership of a co-ethno-linguist nation. Even Turkey, at a later stage harped on ethno-linguistic linkages as a basis of relationship between Turkey and Central Asian States.

Turkey's interest in Central Asia has been attributed to different reasons by different scholars. Some have attributed it to the wide spread euphoria which was generated in Turkey at the emergence of Turkic republics as independent states in Central Asia after the collapse of Soviet Union. Now, Ankara was free to interact with them. It aroused the pan-Turkic fervor and Turks started thinking of uniting the world from Adriatic to China as one unit, possibly under Turkey's patronage. Under the impact of initial excitement Turkey started acting as a superior power *vis-a-vis* the new republics and in several ways demonstrated its will to lead the Central Asians, if not to rule over them. The Central Asian states were in no mood to be any body's camp-follower and wanted to steer their destiny independently. They rejected "pan-Turkism" and preferred to base their relationship with Ankara on the ground of mutual benefit. Pan-Turkism as an ideology has been examined by Jacob M. Landau, Gareth M. Winrow, John Glenn, Gennady Chufrin and some others.

Having discarded the ethno-linguistic linkages and pan-Turkism as a basis of relations, Turkey tried to establish relations on mutuality of interests and policies. Ankara's energy needs and its desire to get at least one pipeline (if possible more) pass through its territory made Central Asia a region of great interest to it. The Kirkuk-Yumurtalik pipeline from Iraq to Europe *via* Turkey had economically benefited Ankara. Hence, it wanted the oil and gas pipelines from Azerbaijan and Turkmenistan respectively to pass through Turkish territory.

This could facilitate close relations with Azerbaijan, Turkmenistan and Kazakhstan—the three Caspian Sea Basin states and Turkey became involved not only in the politics of pipelines but also in the politics of the Caspian Sea the legal status of which is yet to be determined. Iran and Russia maintain that it is a lake and prefer to divide it equally among the five user states including Iran and Russia. The Caspian states want it to be treated as Sea because they command more area in the Caspian Sea than they will get otherwise. Turkey finds itself in a situation where it has to support the southern Caucasian Caspian states' stand against Iran and Russia.

In the politics of pipelines Turkey has succeeded in winning the support of the majority of the states interested in the oil wealth of the Caspian Sea for Baku-Tiblisi-Ceyhan pipeline (BTC) starting from Azerbaijan, passing through Georgia to Ceyhan in Turkey to continue the flow of oil in Europe.

Turkey has close relations with the Central Asian Republics but its major interest is in the three Caspian Sea Basin states—Azerbaijan, Turkmenistan, and Kazakhstan only.

It has fairly well developed trade relations with the CARs and is lending all possible support in their struggle against Islamic militancy, terrorism and drug trafficking. Turkey has undertaken several projects in the field of education, banking, finance, management, communication, construction of roads, development of transport, providing technological expertise of the trained personnel in supervising the development work in Central Asia. The newly independent republics are quite handy for organizing the power constellations against the rivals. Turkey has succeeded in getting the support of Georgia and Azerbaijan and Russia has Armenia and Iran and possibly Kazakhstan to its side.

During the past five years some geo-political configurations are emerging although none have taken the shape of an established constellation of states capable of asserting effective influence in the Central Asian oil and gas related matters. Several specialists on Central Asian affairs see the possibility of Russia, Iran, Turkey triangle as a viable configuration as all the three have stakes in the security, stability and territorial integrity of the region as a whole. They are capable of managing the oil and gas affairs together along with the owner states—Azerbaijan, Turkmenistan and Kazakhstan.

Some scholars, including the Turkish as well, have apprehension that at a later stage the United States can also join the Turkey, Azerbaijan, Georgia configuration. The US has prodded Israel too into Central Asian affairs to assist Turkey in its endeavours as it ultimately serves the interests of the west. This "proxy" role of Turkey arouses suspicion about its real objectives in the region. Despite enormous efforts it has not succeeded in winning the trust of the CARs and the Caspian states. Its only success is approval by all interested parties in the Caspian region (minus Iran and Russia) to Baku-Tiblisi-Ceyhan (BTC) oil pipeline, which has become operational from June 2005 and is benefiting Turkey.

It is difficult to answer whether Turkey's major interest is in Central Asia which is the land of its ancestors, or in Europe? Turkey has to make up its mind as to what exactly it wants. Many Turcologists maintain that the Central Asian liberation from the Soviet rule occurred at a time when Ankara was awfully dejected due to European Union's (EU) rejection of its request for membership. Anakra has been dreaming to become a part of the community of European Nations and thus get its European identity recognized by its colleagues in the EU. As an outlet to that frustration and in its need for an alternative to European identity, in case it is further denied by the EU, Ankara looked at Central Asia for asserting its "Turkic Identity" which in fact is more natural, genuine and convincing than the European identity.

Hence how long Turkey would remain attracted to Central Asia depends on: EU's decision on Turkey's membership; possibility of other pipeline proposals and authentic estimation of the volume of oil and gas in the Caspian Sea Basin states.

Some of the Turkish politicians, scholars, writers and foreign policy experts, besides established Turkey-watchers and specialists have been constantly counselling Turkey to maintain a balance in its relations with the West and the East

Turkey belongs to many regions. It is Balkan, Aegean, Mediterranean, Middle Eastern, Black Sea, Caucasian, Central Asian, all at the same time. Besides United States, perhaps Turkey is the only country, which has participated and is still participating in the politics of these regions. Ankara needs to maintain its "international" "synthesized" personality instead of obsessively leaning on the one side—the United States only.

The present study has six chapters. First chapter deals with early ethno-linguistic linkages of the Turkey with Central Asia, the second examines pan-Turkism in its historical and contemporary perspective; the third examines Turkey's interests in southern Caucasian-Caspian States, their oil and gas pipelines' policies and Turkey's stakes in it. Chapter four deals with Turkey's relations with the CARs and the fifth evaluates the strength of emerging geo-political configurations in the Central Asian-South Caucasian region and examines the prospects of the United States and China joining these Asian power constellations. China has already made its presence felt in a substantial way by occupying important position in the oil and natural gas affairs of the Caspian region and undertaking highly ambitious projects of constructing new pipelines and establishing faster rail links with the oil and gas producing states of Central Asia. This changing scenario in Central Asia is discouraging the US from directly entering the power game in the region. Its role in the recent "colour revolutions" and "regime change" operations suggests that the US is likely to remain satisfied with the "proxy" presence only.

Sheel K. Asopa

Acknowledgements

I am indebted to a large number of persons for their help in preparation of this study. In the first place, I would like to thank Maulana Abul Kalam Azad Institute of Asian Studies, Kolkata, for granting the research project on *Turkey in Central Asia* and financing my field trips to Russia and the Central Asian countries which have been highly useful for understanding the complexities of the political environment of the Central Asian states and Russia's policy and role *vis-à-vis* these newly independent states.

It was a pleasure to visit the Russian Academy of Sciences, Institute of Asia and Africa at the Moscow State University, Moscow, the Russian Friendship University, Moscow, and meet the specialists on Turkey, Central Asia and International Politics in general. I am especially grateful to Prof. Belokrinitskii, a well known expert of West Asia and Islam at the Institute of Oriental Studies (IOS); Prof. Urazaeva, an expert on Turkey IVAN (IOS); Prof. Tatiana Shaumian a specialist on International Politics at the IOS; Prof. Michail S. Mejer, Director, Institute of Asia and Africa of the Moscow State University, Moscow; Prof. Evgenia Vanina of the IOS; Prof. Samsonenko of the Russian Friendship University, Moscow; Prof. Victor Krashilchikov, Institute of World Economy and International Affairs for sparing time to have discussions on various aspects of the Central Asian politics, foreign policy and intra-regional relations and some of the outstanding trans-frontier ethnic problems related to Azerbaijan and Armenia and also in Georgia. These meetings were extremely enlightening and helped me in understanding several dimensions of the Central Asian politics and society.

I am greatly benefited by the specialized research and analyses of several foreign scholars and wish to express my sense of gratitude to them. I am especially indebted to John Glenn, Gennady Chufrin, William Hale, Jed C. Synder, Berry Rubin, David Menashri, Patrick Clawson, Graham Fuller, Shirin Akiner, Shirin Hunter, Martha Brill Olcott, Jacob M. Landau, Kenneth Weisbrode, Gareth M. Winrow and several others.

Among the Turkish scholars, I was delighted to read some of the most refreshing unbiased, analytical and informative studies published by Yucel Bozdaglioglu, Bulent Aras, Mustafa Aydin, Kemal Kirisci, Nur-Bilge Criss and Serdar Guner, Yilmaz Bingol and others. My sincere thanks to them for enriching my understanding about the recent developments in Turkey and its foreign policy.

I am extremely grateful to Prof. Devendra Kaushik, former Chairman, Maulana Azad Institute of Asian Studies, Kolkata. Prof. Kaushik is an encyclopedia on Central Asia, Southern Caucasian Republics and Russia. I have heavily drawn upon his knowledge, which is inexhaustible. My meetings with Prof. Warikoo, have also been academically refreshing. I am also thankful to Dr. Nalin Mohapatra for being helpful to me in several ways.

I would like to take this opportunity to thank Prof. Mahavir Singh, former Director, Maulana Azad Institute of Asian Studies for being very helpful all through my tenure as Project Fellow of the MAKAIAS.

My affectionate thanks are due also to my friends Prof.. Girijesh Pant, Chairperson, Center for West Asian Stuties, 'SIS, JNU' Prof. P.M. Kamath, former Head, Department of Political Science, University of Mumbai, Prof. Annapurna Nautiyal, Head, Department of Political Science, HNB University, Garhwal and Mrs. Manjulika Sen for their moral support and constant interest in the progress of my work.

Finally, my profound thanks to my husband Dr. Dev Asopa and daughter Supriya Asopa for their inspiring presence around me.

Jaipur ***Sheel K. Asopa***

Contents

CHAPTER 1

Turks in Central Asia: An Overview of Early Ethno-linguistic Linkages and Political Development in Turkey from Empire to Republic

The collapse of the Soviet Union in 1991 resulted in emergence of five independent sovereign republics, namely, Tajikistan, Uzbekistan, Turkmenistan, Kyrgyzstan and Kazakhstan in Central Asia. The Trans-Caucasian-Central Asian region which was like a forbidden territory for countries of the neighbouring region, suddenly became accessible to each one of them. This unforeseen and unexpected development generated several opportunities as well as challenges for the states situated in the regions adjoining Central Asia.

The four Turkic States of Central Asia offered a fantastic opportunity to Turkey to revive its links with the people of Turkic region and reconstruct the ties based on ethno-linguistic and cultural commonalty with them. In the post-Soviet world order "perhaps no other country outside the Soviet bloc has seen its strategic position more radically transformed by the end of the Cold War than Turkey".[1] During the cold war period, as an staunch ally of the West, the geo-strategic significance of Turkey was determined by its role within the Atlantic Alliance (A.A.) and more narrowly within NATO's Southern flank.[2]

The desovietization of the region liberated Turkey from its limited role in international politics. The advent of five independent states (four Central Asian and Azerbaijan, Tajikistan is not of Turkic origin) in its neighbourhood exposed Turkey to a vast territory inhabited by fellow Muslim Turkic people and presented an unprecedented historical opportunity to utilize for political, economic and psychological gains.[3] The years of clusterphobia suddenly vanished and under the prevailing atmosphere of subsequent euphoria Turkey's common cultural linguistic and religious bonds with the newly independent Central Asian and Caucasian republics were frequently mentioned both within and outside Turkey as a basis for influential position within the region. Turkey was seen as an excellent political and economic role model for the new States.[4] The pan-Turkist ideas were also circulated freely. The friendly response of the Central Asian republics further enboldened Ankara's urge for setting up a pan-Turkist grouping under its patronage in Central Asia. Gareth M. Winrow, an outstanding analyst of Turkish affairs emphatically argued that "Ankara's interest in developing and expanding cultural and educational links as part of its diplomatic campaign in former Soviet Central Asia is strikingly reminiscent of the policies prescribed at the turn of the century by Ismail Gasprinsky, one of the most prominent pan-Turkists.[5] Nevertheless, Turkey's enthusiastic attitude and its willingness to cultivate friendly relations with the new states of Central Asia came as a welcome relief to the latter which have been in dire need for help, assistance and co-operation from the international community. They too, expected Turkey "to help them achieve momentum, consolidate their independence and gain status and recognition in the world".[6]

The pan-Turkism, no doubt, serves as a rational and logical basis of affinity between Turkey and the Turkic states of Central Asia but the new states did not appear in a mood to land into another influential grouping in which they might be placed in a position of secondary importance. Their response to pan-Turkism-based moves of Ankara was lukewarm and some of the Central Asian leaders made it categorically clear that they were not interested in forging a union with Turkey on ethno-linguistic and religious basis. The common cultural bond and history were considered sufficient to generate warmth between the people of Central Asia and Turkey.

The pan-Turkic euphoria subsided as quickly as it had arisen. Turkey also realized that its financial capabilities are much less in comparison to the needs of the Central Asia States. It was also gradually discovered by the government in Turkey that the psychological, emotional and economic bond between the Republics and Russia, forged over centuries and reinforced by need and dependency was far more solid than what the Turks had understood. The pan-Turkist desire had been kindled by the encouraging statements of the western countries, who considered Turkey a most suitable role model for the new states of Central Asia. Its modern-secular-republican profile with Islamic and Central Asian roots could make Turkey easily acceptable as an alternative to 'discredited' Russia. Ankara, however, could comprehend the risks involved in playing a proxy role in Central Asia and gradually eliminated the pan-Turkic reference from its statements regarding the Central Asian Republics.

However, the pan-Turkic debate in Turkey revived the interest of Turks in their early history in Central Asia. The nostalgic memories of their interaction with the indigenous Turkic tribes of the region, enrichment of their culture with the inter-mixing of races, tribes and ethno-linguistic groupings, their dynastic rule and above all memory of the mighty Seljuk Empire made them think afresh on the question of reviving their Turkic identity, as notwithstanding their character as a highly westernized modern-secular Muslim republic, the Turks do not have a well spelled out and widely accepted national identity.

The Westernization-Modernization process had commenced during the Ottoman Empire, but the Islamic character of the state and people's pride in Ottomanism remained intact. However, the humiliating defeat in First World War and the Armistice of Mudros gave a severe jolt to the Ottoman glory. It got eclipsed under the shadow of foreign occupation of the territories of the Ottoman Empire and its subsequent disintegration. Islam, however, continued to be the main driving force. Mustafa Kamal Pasha, the hero of the National Movement for Liberation of Turkey and the War of Independence against the occupying forces, finally negated the universal framework of Islam by abolishing the Caliphate and de-Islamizing Turkey. Pan-Turkism first appeared at the beginning of the twentieth century in Central Asia but in Turkey it surfaced during the Young Turks movement (1908-1918), then again after the end of the First World War (1922), but it could not be recognized as a viable ideology, neither by the Turkic people of Central Asia nor by the Turks.

EARLY LINKAGES OF TURKS WITH CENTRAL ASIA

Prior to the Russification of Central Asia, Persians, Turks, Mongols, Arabs, and several other comparatively less significant ethnic groups held their sway in the region. Persians were the early settlers in Central Asia. The domination of Persians over the region began in the second millennium B.C. However, the region was incorporated into the Persian Empire of Achaemenids (330-550 B.C.) only around the sixth century B.C.[7] It is said that no indigenous state existed in Central

Asia prior to that date.[8] Thus, the original population of ancient Central Asia and of the steppe region was of the same Iranian stock as the Persians. The oldest people known in Central Asia—the Sogdians of the Zarafsan valley and the Khorezmians inhabiting the lower banks of the Amu Darya belonged to the same stock. Their territory formed part of the first world monarchy known to history as the Achaemenid state.[9] The great monarchy of Achaemenid was destroyed by Alexander the Great between 330-327 B.C.

Persian power reasserted itself in the third century A.D. by the Sasanian Empire which spread from Iran through Central Asia to the Caucasus but the Persian influence was again supplanted by an invasion of the Huns (Epthalites) in 425 A.D. The Arabs invaded Central Asia in the middle of the seventh century A.D. and conquered the whole area south of the Syr-Darya by the beginning of the eighth century, bringing the Islamic religion and Arabic script with them. However, throughout this period the earlier Persian influence remained intact and during the Bukhara-based Samanid dynasty (875-999 A.D.) Persian literature attained its full development.[10] The great poets Rudaki and Abu'l-Qasim Firdausi (934-1025 A.D.) wrote their monumental works[11] during that period.

Turks came in Central Asia from the Altai mountains which are considered to be the earliest home of both—Turks and the Mongols. A Turkish Empire emerged in Mongolia in 551 A.D. This led to the presence of Turks during the sixth century A.D. in Kazakhstan and western Central Asia displacing the Ephthalites (White Huns) who had resided there for two centuries. By the eleventh century, Turkic tribes had come to dominate Central Asia to the extent that the region became known as "Turkestan".[12] Their influence, at the same time, had spread to Asia Minor, southern Russia and the Caucasus. The increasing dispersion of the Turks eventually led to the formation of a Western and Eastern branch. The

Western branch was represented by the Oghuz Turks who rose to prominence after the decline of Karakanids who had established the first officially declared Islamic Turkish State in Central Asia.[13] The Oghuz Turks, who are thought to have been composed of 24 clans and initially inhabited north of Aral Sea, spawned the Seljuk Empire (1038-1150 A.D.) that conquered Persia, Syria, Armenia; the Ottomans of Turkey, and the Turkmens of Turkmenistan. The Kipchak branch (Eastern branch) formed the main Turkish component of the Turco-Mongol agglomeration of tribes.[14]

The Turkish encroachments eventually led to general Turkification of the region despite the renewed Persian influence during the Saffavid Dynasty (1502-1736 A.D.) and Nadir Shah's incursion into Central Asia (1740). Although a considerable inter-mixing of the ethnic groups occurred in Central Asia, Turkic influence remained predominant. Besides the Tajiks of Bukhara, Samarkand and Tajikistan represent the areas of Persian influence. Within Tajikistan itself, the Tajiks are divided into two branches—mountain Tajiks or *Pamiris* who speak a 'welter of tongues and dialects' generally placed in the East Iranian group of languages. They are *Ismailis* who follow the Agha Khan sect. The Tajiks of western Tajikistan speak west Iranian language similar to Persian and are followers of Sunni Islam.

The Mongol invasion of Central Asia in the thirteenth century also contributed to strengthening of Turkish cultural influence in the region. The use of Turkish soldiers in the Mongol army and the ubiquity of Turkic culture throughout the area led the two Mongol houses—Ulus of Dzhuchi (ruled by eldest son of Chingez Khan) and Ulus of Chagtai (ruled by the second eldest son of Chingez Khan) to become Turkic States.

With the exception of the Kyrgyzs who migrated to the western Tien Shan mountain range in the twelfth century and the Tajiks who are of Persian stock, the rest of the Turkic states have connections with the Mongols. When Ulus of Dzhuchi began to grow weak, the Uzbeks were united under Abul Khayr (1412/13-1468) a descendent of Dzhuchi's youngest son Shaibani Khan. Initially the confederation was constituted from 24 tribes but by the sixteenth century with the defeat of Timurid rulers of Samarkand and establishment of the Uzbek empire, their ranks had swollen to incorporate about 92 tribes.[15] Uzbeks are known as Shaibanids and it seems that they have taken their present name from Khan Uzbek (1282-1342) of Golden Horde, a section of the Ulus of Dzhuchi.

The ethnogenesis of the Kazakhs has been traced to the break-away group of Uzbek confederation prior to the conquest of the Timurid kingdom. The split perhaps resulted from a dispute between Abul Khayr, the first of the Uzbek Khans and the Kazakh leaders Girey and Dzhanibek which led to the newly formed Kazakh group to migrate north of the Syr Darya river which served a geographical barrier between themselves and the Uzbeks.

The ethno-genesis of each of the ethnic groups is not very clear and it is difficult to identify them as totally distinct from the other. The Kyrgyz were established on the Yenisei river according to Chinese annals of the first century B.C. They migrated to the western Tien Shan mountain in the twelfth century. They are known as the second largest group after the Tajiks. The identification of the Turkmen as a distinctly separate group from the larger Turkic Oghuzs family is not certain. The appellation Turkmen first appeared in the tenth century A.D. to distinguish between those Oghuz who had been converted to Islam and those who had not.[16] The actual consolidation of the Turkmen into a separate entity is placed between fourteenth and fifteenth centuries.[17] This puts the final ethno-genesis of the Turkmen in the same period as the Uzbeks and the Kazakhs.

The ethnic groups are differentiated on the basis of their dress, customs, language, ways of living, myths and culture. Some of the historical epics (*Alpamysh, Dede Korkut* and *Kor Oghlu*) which were traditionally recited orally were in fact common to whole of the region and as such widely known among all Turkic peoples. *Kor Oghlu* is known also to the Iranians and the Tajiks under the title *Gurguli.*[18] There is a message in all epics, in favour of ethnic unity among the inhabitants of the region. The Kyrgyz epic *Manas* which is related to the tribulations of the Kyrgyz warns of possible loss of sovereignty if ethnic disunity continues. Similarly, the Kazakh epics *Koblandy-Batir* (historical accounts of war) and *Kiz-Jhibek* (love stories) are widely known to the people of other ethnic groups as well.[19] The *Oghuz-Nama* of the Turkmen about the legendary Oghuz Khan, mystical predecessor of all Turks is also famous as a great epic. The romantic folklores such as *Kor Ogli, Kissa-i-yusuf* and *Seyid Battal* are also popular Turkic classics.[20] Thus, notwithstanding the presence of different dialects, customs and traditions, the main current of Central Asian culture is full of the "Turkic effect", which had given the region an integrated identity in the pre-Soviet Central Asia.

The linguistic homogeneity has often been questioned by scholars, both in Central Asia and outside. At the one end of the spectrum there are scholars who argue that "it is possible to speak of Central Asian Muslims as possessing linguistic unity: the dialectical differences, significant as they are to the philologist, neither prevent effective communication among the Turkic inhabitants, nor preclude the eventual emergence of a single Turkic literary language of Central Asia".[21] Others believe that "linguistic differentiation had progressed too far among the Turkic peoples to permit them to find a common language suitable for literature a thousand years after their territorial and linguistic unity had been disrupted".[22]

The contention of linguistic unity sprang from the assumption that all dialects progressed simultaneously and were capable to be medium of written expression. In fact, in most cases these languages have assumed a written form quite recently. The two main literary languages employed in the whole of the region were Chagatai[23] and Persian and these acted as the main form of verbal and written communication between the elites of the various ethnic groups.

In terms of emergence of various ethnic groups in Central Asia, the Turkic thread linking them all together is very much visible. Initially the admixture of Europeans, Iranians, and Mongols resulted in the birth of Turks/Tatars, and the Iranian-Mongol inter-breeding created Tajiks. The admixture of Turks and Mongols has led to the origin of Kazakhs and Kyrgyzs and that of Turks and Iranians has led to emergence of Uzbeks. Thus, the "Turkic effect" along with Islam which had been a common faith of the majority people and the Turkic language which is widely used in the region, have been noted as common binding features among all the ethnic units of pre-Soviet Central Asia.

RUSSIFICATION OF CENTRAL ASIA

Prior to the Russian conquest, there existed three Khanates on the territory of Central Asia. Bukhara in the basin of the Zarafshan river and Khiva on the lower Amu Darya were older than Kokand which came into existence towards the close of the eighteenth century. In the beginning of the nineteenth century Kokand annexed Tashkent which was an important trade centre and existed as an independent state. To stem the tide of turbulent Kyrghyz and Kazakh nomads, Kokand Khanate established a chain of forts on the Syr-Darya, Chu and Ili rivers.[24]

The decline of Mongol control over Russia and the rise of Muscovite state in the sixteenth century opened the way for future relations between Central Asia and Russia. The collapse of Mongol empire and the weakness of Iran created a political vaccum giving the Central Asian Khanates opportunity to become independent. Ivan, The Terrible had initiated diplomatic relations with the Khanates of Bukhara, Samarkand and Khiva by sending envoys in the second half of the sixteenth century.[25]

Russia emerged as a major power in the early nineteenth century. Prior to that, there had been two major incursions in the Central Asian Khanates. In 1717, Peter, The Great dispatched troops to Central Asia in order to establish Russian military presence in that region.[26] Despite the failure of the mission, the Russian envoy remained in Bukhara until the death of Peter in 1725. Again in the second half of the eighteenth century, Russia began its penetration into the Kazakh steppes and subjugated the ramnants of the Mongol Small and Inner Hordes in Kazakh lands bordering Siberia.[27] Russian penetration remained limited to Kazakh lands only until the early nineteenth century.

Russia's massive drive in Central Asia began after the defeat of Napoleon. Russia dismantled the Khanates of Inner and Small Horde in 1822 and 1824 respectively and placed them under the Russian administrative and judicial control.[28] In 1847, Russia conquered the Kazakhs of the Great Horde and captured part of the Khanate of Kokand.[29] By 1884, it brought the Kazakhs and the northern Kyrgyzs under its domination.[30] It also improved relations with economically developed Khanates of Kokand, Bukhara and Khiva.

Russia's defeat in the Crimean war (1855) made it realize the importance of Central Asia's natural resources. In a prolonged campaign for annexing Central Asian territories through the use of diplomacy and force, Russia targeted first Kokand, and captured its capital, Tashkent in 1865 and fully annexed it in 1876. Bukhara was taken after a war with the

Emir of Bukhara in 1868, Khiva in 1873, Turkmenistan after series of military encounters in 1869 and 1884 and Kyrgyzia in 1876-77. Thus, by the end of the nineteenth century, the entire Central Asia had become part of Russia. The annexation process led to several administrative and structural changes in the region. However, the areas between Siberia and the Aral Sea and Lake Balkash mainly inhabited by the Kazakh tribes were retained as one unit and the rest—the Turkestan region was also annexed as a separate unit. Hooman Peimani argues that Central Asia, despite annexation, was kept almost intact as a region. Its incorporation into Russia did not affect its geographical and demographic character.[31]

When the Russians arrived as conquerors in Central Asian Khanates they found Samarkand, Bukhara, Khiva, Kokand, Tashkent and Mary (Meris) possessing a rich heritage of historical monuments and functioning of eminent centres of Islamic learning. They refrained from interfering with the traditional way of life of the Muslim community which was governed by the *Shariat*, the Islamic law. The strong religiosity of the traditional Muslim community was well illustrated by the statistics of the nominally independent Bukhara on the eve of the First World War (1914-18). The Emirate of about two million Muslims had 2600 mosques. Girls aged four or more had to wear the *paranja* (veil). Like the rest of their co-religionists in the Czarist empire, especially in the Caucasus, Central Asians considered themselves as Muslims first and foremost. Vasiliy V. Barthold, a leading Orientalist of Russia maintains that the people of Central Asia regard themselves first as Muslims and then as inhabitants of any given town or region; ethnic concepts having virtually no significance in their eyes. This observation has been lent further credence by an Uzbek communist leader who thus described the situation: The working masses of Uzbeks did not recognize themselves as a single nationality. The Farghana Uzbeks usually referred to themselves as Kokandi in accordance with the name of the

Khanate. The Zarafshan, Kashka Darya and Surkan Darya Uzbeks called themselves Bukharans. The Uzbek population of our cities did not consider the nomad population of Kashka Darya and Surkan Darya Uzbeks.[32]

PRE-REVOLUTIONARY RELIGIOUS REFORM MOVEMENTS IN CENTRAL ASIA

The occupation of Muslim territories by Russia led the Muslim community to analyse the causes of their down fall. Either the Christian Russians have devised a system better than Islam or their community has failed to follow true Islam. This realization led to a serious thinking which ultimately resulted in the origin of two schools of thought -*Qadimis* (traditionalists) and *Jadids* (innovators). *Qadimians* favoured the Islamic hierarchy and advocated strict application of *Shariat*. The *Jadidians* proposed innovations and reforms in Islamic practices in view of the fast-changing world from a predominantly westernized perspective.[33]

PAN TURKISM

In the absence of any encouraging response to pan-Islamic drive, the Tatar intellectuals turned to find an alternative to pan-Islamism which could contain the wave in favour of westernization. Ethno-linguistic commonalty appeared an acceptable basis for the new movement. A periodical, *Turk*—established in Cairo in 1902 played an active role in promoting pan-Turkism aspiring for political unity of all Turkish speaking peoples from the Balkans to China. Yusuf Aq Churaoglu in his essay titled "Three Political Systems" published in 1904 in *Turk* claimed to provide "scientific evidence" to prove that "all Turkic peoples from Egypt to China constitute a single nation". Ali Husseinzade, one of Churaoglu's disciples coined a catchy slogan: "Turkification, Islamicization, Modernization" to circulate the ideology of Pan-Turkism among the people of

Central Asia and Ottoman territories. Later, Ziauddin Goek Alp (Ziya Gokalp), the famous sociologist and political philosopher of Turkey also gave a similar slogan which meant: "we belong to the Turkish nation, Muslim religion and European civilization". This philosophy appealed Mustafa Kamal Pasha, the leader of the national movement.

Pan-Turkism was seen by its opponents as a hegemonic drive in the garb of seeking unity on the basis of linguistic commonalty. They were not prepared to accept Turkic (reformed by Gasprinsky) language. They wanted to promote their own languages which had developed considerably. Thus, the pan-Turkism stirred linguistic nationalism, which assumed the form of communal tensions between the Turkic and non-Turkic people and also polluted the region's environment by instigating tensions between the Shias and the Sunnis. The Emirate of Bukhara became a battle ground for the competing ideologies of pan-Turkism and pan-Islamism. The Emir promoted the minority Tajik speaking Shias at the expense of the Sunni Uzbek and Kazakh-Kyrgyz notables and thus created bloodshed between the two sects of Islam. The intra-Muslim violence weakened the *Qadimis* but enabled the *Jadidis* to strengthen and widen their base. They founded an Association for Education of Children called *Tarbiyat* which expanded quickly and by 1914 could claim the loyalty of a large Muslim intellegentia.[34]

The over-enthusiastic *Jadidis* formed an alliance with the heads of *Qadimis* and Kazakh-Kyrgyz tribes on an anti-Russian platform and convened a clandastine congress in Samarkand in June 1916 which resolved to organize an armed insurrection against Russian rule in Turkestan. At the behest of organizers, the clergy issued a call for *Jihad* against the Czar under the pretext of resisting Czar's decree drafting Turkestani Muslims, previously exempted from military service, into non-combatant army units. The anti-Russian insurrection erupted on 13 July 1916. The army promptly crushed it by 20 July.[35]

The Islamic and pan-Turkist developments, however, did not make much impact on the Turks. The Turkish leadership in the early twenties had developed a clear concept about modernization of their society in which religious dimension was almost marginalized.[36] For Turkish modernizers, modernization meant westernization, which meant occupying a place in the civilization of Europe.[37]

The attainment of modernization on these lines required the "negation of the framework of Islam"[38] that had provided the State with political legitimacy and individuals with an identity during the Ottoman Empire. The Islamic identity, in fact, superseded the Ottoman identity although the Turks derived pleasure in asserting Ottoman identity as it filled them with the sense of glory of the Empire. Under the scheme of modernization, the society shifted from the Islamic framework into a newly defined Turkish nation. The religious basis of legitimization was completely rejected and an attempt was made to evolve a secular-national one as the major ideological parameter of the new collectivity ....".[39] This scheme was undertaken in order to achieve "the qualities of nationalism and a modern State in a fundamentally medieval, theocratic Empire and to throw off the pre-existing institutions and concepts.[40]

The credit for modernization of Turkey is predominantly given to Mustafa Kamal Ataturk. He brought a complete break with the past both in terms of Empire and religion. The termination of Caliphate, in a way, liberated Turkey from the institutionalized Islam. However, history of Turkish Empire suggests that the process of modernization—westernization had commenced during the Ottoman period. The Ottoman Empire as a result of continuous interaction with the West underwent a century-long process of preparing the political and social elite of the country, intellectuals and the army for embracing the contents of modernization and westernization. Several western laws and practices had been adopted by the

Ottoman Sultans. Kemalism represented an intensification, radicalization and culmination of that trend.[41] Therefore, prior to explaining the construction and institutionalization of Turkey's western identity through a series of reforms, it would be useful to have an overview of the history of the Westernization-Modernization movement in the Ottoman Empire that had prepared the background for Kamalist revolution in Turkey.

It is also necessary to make anti-Kemalists understand that Kemalism was an outcome of the process initiated much before Ataturk's arrival on political stage in Turkey. Besides, the entire process of westernization was originally initiated by the Ottoman Empire which wanted to take advantage of Europe's progress in the field of science and technology.

Ottoman Reforms: Islam vs. Modernization

The Ottoman Empire was always in contact with the western civilization and interacted in several spheres of state activities. However, during the zenith of its glory, it considered "western civilization" inferior to its own Islamic civilization and ignored the western innovations in the sphere of defence and military technology. Since the western Europe was a rival empire, civilization and religion to the Ottomans, and the *other* in Ottoman self definition "it was the sacred duty of the Islamic Empire to subjugate and convert".[42]

However, the non-hostile channels of communication between the Ottomans and Europe were always active. The European diplomats, scholars, merchants, adventurers travelled in the Ottoman Empire in the fifteenth and early sixteenth century bringing with them "printing, medical and technological knowledge".[43] The Ottomans were too eager to get technological and medical information from the Europeans. They invited the European instructors to educate the army-men of the Empire.

With the gradual decline of the Ottoman Empire after several humiliating reversals at the hands of Austrian and Russian Empires and the treaties of Carlowitz (1699) and Passarowitz (1718), the civil bureaucracy and enlightened elite started debating the causes of these setbacks and felt that "the deteriorating state structure and the military superiority of the West"[44] were the main reasons for the defeat of the Ottoman armies. A programme of westernization-modernization was considered essential to enable the Empire to throw off its weakenesses and once again "become the terror to its enemies".[45]

Damad Ibrahim Pasha, the Grand Vazir (1718-30) undertook immediate steps in the direction of modernizing the army. He sent some missions of high ranking officials to important capitals of Europe with instructions to make a thorough study of the means of civilization and education, and report on those suitable for application in Turkey. These efforts brought good results and their impact could be seen in the realm of army and society. The cultural life of the elite started adopting French life styles and manners.

However, the religious middle classes, the common men and the clergy could not accept the undermining of Ottoman cultural and religious practices. The religious *Ulema* (scholars) and the *Jannissary* corps along with lower and middle classes of the society staged opposition to the policy of Sultan Ahmet III (1703-1730) and forced the Sultan to resign. Several important people of the social elite and the Grand Vazir were killed in the religious rebellion. However, this incident could only delay the implementation of the modernization programme, it could not kill the campaign for westernization altogether.

The outbreak of French Revolution made a serious impact on the Ottoman Empire. This period coincided with the reign of Sultan Selim III (1789-1807) who had great enthusiasm for

European culture and civilization. He launched a programme of reforms known as Nizam-i-Cedid (New order) aimed at increasing the strength of the central state organization, against both external enemies (Russia) and internal ones (the semi-independent *Ayans*—the rural notables).[46] During the period of Selim III several channels of communication with France were established. Establishment of European embassies in the Ottoman capital and the Ottoman embassies in various European capitals, appointment of French military instructors, introduction of education in French language for the army were some of the major steps taken by the Sultan to modernize the military and bureaucracy of his empire.

The process of reforms and the process of outdoing the reforms continued simultaneously. The measures taken by Sultan Selim III were also opposed by the *Ayan* and the Jennissaries leading to deposition of the Sultan in the name of Islam. His successor, Mahmut II (1808-1839) after assuming power embarked on a more ambitious reform-programme which continued to be adhered to by his political successors in the nineteenth and the twentieth century. He destroyed the *Janissaries*, weakened the *Ayan* and the *Ulema*. Sultan Mahmut's reforms in the army, central bureaucracy, provisional administration, taxation, education and communication paved the road for the era of more rigorous and progressive reforms in the form of *Tanzimat* (Reorganization, 1839-1871).[47] The biggest success of Mahmut's reforms was that he could create "a cadre able to execute them". He understood the importance of the knowledge of European sciences and technology and sent groups of students to study modern sciences in 1827. He established a Military Medical School (1827), a Military School (1836) and a Faculty of Administrative Sciences (1859) with secular curriculums. Knowledge of a western language was made an essential pre-requisite for entrance.

The study of modern sciences, medicine, biology, physics inculcated a rationalist and positivist mentality in the students and a number of reformist thinkers emerged out of these institutions which contributed to the creation of a class of secular and materialist minded people who carried the reforms further deep into the society.

These reforms resulted in the drafting and promulgation of the Noble Rescript of the Rose Chamber (3 November 1839), the first of reforming edicts which are collectively known as the *Tanzimat*. The Edict promised the establishment of guarantees for the life, honour and property of the subjects of Sultan, introduced an orderly tax system, a system of conscription for the army and equality before law of all subjects whatever their religion.[48] The second edict, *Hatt-i-Humayun* (Imperial Rescript) was promulgated in 1856 which confirmed the principles of the first one (1839). "This document legitimized the entire process of reforms and outlined the direction it was to take".[49]

The reforms are often attributed to foreign pressure on the Ottoman Empire which was inhabited by a number of foreign minority groups. However, the truth is other way round. It is maintained that reforms were undertaken by the Sultans to avert foreign intervention, gain foreign support on important issues related to the Empire and to help the various ethno-religious communities to get assimilated in the main stream of Ottoman society and willingly adopt the Ottoman identity which would protect the empire from crumbling down.[50]

The impact of reforms started manifesting boldly in the later half of the nineteenth century. The founders of the *Tanzimat* were adopting the military and administrative structure of the west, western culture was penetrating into the day to-day life of the individuals. For reformers, "there was only one civilization and that was European civilization. We must borrow western civilization with both its roses and its thorn".[51] Saffet Pasha (1814-1883) urged Turkey to adopt "the civilization of Europe in its entirety to prove itself a civilized nation".[52] This contention went farther than comparing the technological superiority of the West and "started comparing the two civilizations: Islamic and Christian. Yucel Bozdaglioglu has quoted a few lines from the poetry of Ziya Pasha (1825-1830) in support of this view which read as:

I passed through the lands of infidels,
I saw cities and mansions;
I wondered in the realm of Islam,
I saw nothing but ruins.[53]

ISLAMISM AND THE YOUNG OTTOMANS

The impact of the half-hearted reforms undertaken by the Sultans and their followers lost lusture and impact by 1870. They failed to produce concrete results and save the empire from declining. During this period *Young Ottomans*—a political opposition came to the fore as an influential pressure group.[54] It was a movement against the policies of the *Tanzimat* and the way they were implemented. The members of the Young Ottoman group came from the administrative and governing elite that had emerged as a result of Mahmut II and his successors' reforms.

The Young Ottomans, Namik Kemal and Sinasi being the most prominent of them, were both pious Muslims and Ottoman patriots, who looked back nostalgically both to the Golden era of Islam and the era of Empire's greatness.[55] According to Young Ottomans the politics of Ali Fuat Pasha was superficial imitation of Europe which undermined the traditional Ottoman and Islamic values, and made the Empire submissive to the western interests. To them, *Tanzimat* was a cultural imitation of Europe which deteriorated the foundations of Muslim society.[56] It was a one-sided bureaucratic despotism and led to destruction of the State.

The Young Ottomans wanted to defend liberal values with Islamic arguments,[57] aimed at creating an "Ottoman Consciousness" among all the subjects of the Empire. The Young Ottomans did play an important role in the drafting of the 1876 Constitution.

The Young Ottomans succeeded in establishing the importance of Ottomanism "and defended the liberal values without offending the Islamists. But this sanction did not satisfy the Islamic groups. In the course of time they gathered strength and emerged as a powerful organized group to oppose the Young Ottomans whose impact had already started declining.

The Islamic opposition emerged and intensified during the period of Abdul Hamid II (1876-1909), who ruled the Empire as an absolute monarch for thirty years. The *Tanzimat* were introduced during his tenure and he had opted in favour of the western model of administrative reforms. Abdul Hamid II while supporting the import of western technology and political and bureaucratic institutions had great inclination for retaining the high status of Islam. He took great pride in the Islamic character of the Empire and enjoyed the glory of Caliphate.[58]

The emergence of pan-Islamism is often attributed to Islamic policy of Abdul Hamid who wanted to create Muslim solidarity on the one hand and gain loyalty of outside Muslims to Caliphate on the other.[59] It is also argued that his Islamic policy known as Pan-Islamism was in a sense a reaction to western ideologies that had been gaining momentum in Europe after 1870s. Abdul Hamid ignored the growing "nationalism" in the empire's subjects and the multi-ethnic and multi-religious character of the Ottoman society which was highly vulnerable to such an ideology. Hence, pan-Islamism failed to make much impact on Ottoman society. The Civil Service Academy (*Mulkiye*) and the War Academy (*Harbiye*) continued to instil liberal values and constitutional ideas.[60]

YOUNG TURKS AND CONSTITUTIONAL REFORMS (1908-23)

The first organized opposition to Sultan Abdul Hamid II was put up by a new generation of elite trained in military academy and other secular institutions of learning in the field of science and technology. The core group known as the *Ittihad-i-Osmani Camiyeti* (Ottoman Unity Society) was founded by four students of the military medical college in 1889 to reinstate the constitution and the parliament. Some of its members were arrested by Sultan's police and some fled to Paris where they formed a small committee called *Ittihat ve Tarakki Cemiyeti* (Committee of Union and Progress, CUP). In France, it was known as *Jennes Turcs* (Young Turks).[61]

The Young Turks movement grew rapidly and in 1908 resulted in a revolution which initiated the second constitutional era in Turkish history. The CUP occupied central position and became the major ruling power in the Ottoman Empire between 1908-1918. According to a Turkish scholar, "the official ideology of modern Turkey as shaped during this period by early Young Turks has continued to exert its influence even today on Turkey's intellectual and political life ...The founders of modern Turkey, including the first three presidents, were former CUP members.[62]

The Young Turks movement was certainly a link in the chain of the Ottoman modernization–westernization programme. Its leaders honoured the previous reforms and demanded the Ottoman state establish western institutions. For them relations with the western civilization was the beginning of the enlightenment era in the Ottoman Empire. As Sabahattin Bay, a well known young Turk leader had argued: "Since we established relations with the western civilization, an intellectual renaissance occurred; prior to this relationship our society lacked any intellectual life".[63]

The Young Turks were deeply affected by the European sciences and materialism. They gave no credit to efforts of the Young Ottomans "to reconcile western civilization and sciences with Islam and traditional values".[64] They secularized the judicial and educational systems and undermined the status of *Ulema*. The study of European languages was made compulsory. As Ali Kazancigil maintains, "The Young Turks' modernization was not only confined to education, they infilterated into every sphere of life. Young Turks' ideology envisaged several of the socio-cultural reforms that Mustafa Kemal implemented later on: abolition of polygamy, replacement of Fez by European headgear, rights for women, introduction of common Ottoman language".[65] Thus, hardly anything was left untouched. They, not only affected the political system, but also tried to refashion the society.

The Young Turks' era is also known for the ideological evolution of Turkey. The openness introduced by the Young Turks movement, public debates on all aspects of political and social issues commenced. Political debates largely centered around three competing ideologies: Ottomanism, the ideal of the young Ottomans to unite the different communities in the Empire around the Ottoman throne; (Pan) Islamism, which tried to create solidarity within the Islamic community; and (Pan) Turkism which sought the union of the Turkic peoples under the Ottoman flag.[66]

Westernism, the other significant ideological current was a constant factor in the middle of these ideologies that could be differentiated by their approach to the degree of westernization. While Ottomanism and Islamism were not against the idea of borrowing western science and technology, they wanted to keep them in tune with the Islamic principles and protect the society from the harmful effect of the western culture. Their main concern was how "to become modern while remaining oneself".[67]

ADVENT OF TURKISM

The Young Turks movement introduced another component—the Turkism to the ideological debate. Prior to the advent of Young Turks, there existed two traditional forms of identification in the Ottoman society: Ottoman and Muslim. By the turn of the nineteenth century, many educated Turks had started identifying themselves as "ethnically Turkish". The accelerated process of conversion to Turkism prepared the ground for Kemalism.[68] The rise of nationalism in various ethnic units of the Empire, especially the Arab nationalism intensified the Turkist fervour in the Ottoman Empire. The CUP too defined Ottomanism as Turkification of the non-Turkish elements of the Empire.[69]

The most outstanding promoter of Turkism was Ziya Gokalp, a poet, political thinker and sociologist whose ideas deeply influenced the minds of the founders of modern Turkey. He is known as the founder of Turkish nationalist doctrine which guided the leaders of the National Movement for Independence of Turkey. Gokalp often tried to find answer to the most piercing question of the time: "who is a Turk and how ought his national identity be understood in relation to Islamic identity on the one hand, and modern scientific rational identity on the other".[70]

Ziya Gokalp's "Turkism" assumed the form of "Turanism" which regarded the Turkic people of the Russian Empire as part of the larger Turkic group. Their inclusion was to facilitate pan-Turanism or Greater Turkey. For this Gokalp emphasized upon the revival of pre-Islamic Turkish civilization.[71] He maintained that Turkish civilization is not in conflict with western civilization but the former needs to be purified from the harmful effects of Islam through secularization. However, emphasis on "Islamization" along with "Turkeization" and "Westernization" were thought essential to save the Empire.[72]

Ziya Gokalp's perception of Islamization meant introducing reforms in religion and religious practices and translating *Quran* into Turkish language to make it understandable to the common man. Turkeization meant purification of Turkish culture not only from the effects of Islam and Islamic traditions, but also to liberate Turkish culture from the influence of mixed culture of the Ottoman Empire. To him, Westernization meant reforms in Turkey's socio-cultural life to enable the Turks to understand and absorb western culture and get oriented to western civilization. With the decline of Ottomanism, Zia Gokalp thought that Islamization, Turkeization and Westernization would provide an alternative source of corporate identity. It would enable a Turk to declare: "I am of Turkish race, Islamic religion and western civilization".[73]

Nevertheless, the Young Turks, in spite of having introduced large number of reforms on western model could not save the Empire from decaying. It is argued that the biggest drawback of these reform movements was that they only introduced new reforms and did not abolish the old ones. This dualism created confusion in society as both reforms and the radical reactionaries continued to exist at the same time.[74]

The Ottoman Sultans and the Young Turks undertook the programme of westernization without deciding as to what will be done to Islam and the Islamic identity of the Empire. The westernization too, once undertaken overshadowed the Ottoman culture and resulted in the creation of western identity of Turks in addition to the Islamic and Turkish identities. The emergence of three fundamental identities in the country eventually turned into a struggle between the three to capture the state power. The Kemalist revolution ultimately succeeded in eliminating this ideological conflict by declaring the western identity as the national identity of modern Turkey.[75]

The history of the national liberation movement in Turkey and its war of independence suggest that in the process of carrying on the struggle against the occupying forces and enemies of empire even Ataturk made use of all these ideologies in mustering support of the Muslim countries in favour of his campaign. He discarded them all after attaining independence and stabilizing reforms in the new Republic of Turkey.

THE INDUCTION OF WESTERN IDENTITY

After the victory of nationalist forces in the war of national liberation, a debate over the nature of polity and society cropped up afresh. The argument centred around oriental and western civilizations. According to Ataturk: "if we are going to be westernized let us go to the fundamentals of the west".[76] Modernization cannot succeed by combining the old and the new aspects of Turkish society. It would have to assume a radical character to affect all aspects of Turkish society, and to sweep away most, if not all, of its traditional beliefs and institutions. Ataturk wanted the revolution not only in the institutions but also in thoughts, and determined the agenda for the new Republic of Turkey focusing mainly on westernization, modernization, secularization and Turkish nationalism as the guiding principles as well as the main objectives to be attained.

Kemalism (named after Mustafa Kemal Ataturk) and the Kemalist principles are the product of the Turkish revolution and denote the basic character and the ideological format of the Turkish Republic. The six principles of Kemalist ideology, namely, nationalism, republicanism, populism, secularism, statism and revolutionism were unveiled in 1931 at the Congress of the Republican People's Party (RPP). These principles are an integral part of the Constitution of Turkey. Among these six principles, republicanism, nationalism and secularism are most important. They occupy an important place in the construction of modern Turkey and symbolize "the rejection of the Ottoman dynasty, Caliphate and Ummet (*Umma*) ideology.[77]

Kemalism is aimed at placing Turkey at the level of "contemporary civilization" which meant European civilization. To replace the religion and religious culture as basis of individual's identification, Ataturk embarked upon a movement of cultural westernization, which is equated with civilization. In creating a new national identity, Ataturk had to stand against the Muslim concept of political identity which had been the legitimate basis of polity of the Ottoman Empire.[78] To many Turkish scholars, the westrernization movement constituted the scientific basis of the Turkish revolution and the basis of the identity of the new Republic of Turkey.[79]

At the end of the World War I, Turkey had been totally overpowered by the Allied forces and the Sultan-Caliph had become a virtual prisoner of the occupation forces. Ataturk after attaining independence and forming the government at Ankara abolished the Sultanate but retained the Caliphate for sometime. It was argued that retention of Islamic linkages would be helpful in seeking the support of the Muslim countries of the world in getting the Ottoman territories vacated by the occupation forces. Soon after the defeat of the Greek and the British forces, Ataturk abolished the Caliphate and announced the secular character of the Republic of Turkey. This total break with Islam and Islamism necessitated a new and increased emphasis on Turkish nationalism and "Turk" identity of the people. During the Ottoman period "Turk" was a derogatory term of addressing a person but in the post independence republican period, it became an honourable expression. Ataturk himself argued that:

The Turks were a great nation even before they had

> accepted Islam. However, after they had accepted Islam it loosened their national ties and numbed their national feelings. That was a natural outcome because the purpose of Islam as laid out by Mohammad was an *ummet* policy".[80]

Similarly, discrediting the Caliphate, Ataturk maintained that the Caliphate represented Turkey's unnecessary attachment to the past and to Islam. He said:

> The Caliphate had never enjoyed universal jurisdiction over the Moslem world, as had the papacy over the Catholic world. The office was an Arab institution adopted by a former Turkish Sultan, whom millions of Moslems had never acknowledged as their spiritual ruler. The new Turkey was not irreligious but needed a religion stripped of artificiality which implied nothing contrary or hostile to progress.[81]

Ataturk rejected the Ottoman and the Islamic past of Turkey, introduced western dress code, removed *Fez* (which was a symbol of Ottoman identity) and switched over to the western calendar and social norms of behaviour. He described *Fez* as something that "sat on the heads of the nation (people) as an emblem of ignorance, negligence, fanaticism and hatred of progress and civilization".[82]

However, with the passage of time resentment against total rejection of the Ottoman history and glory of the Empire picked up momentum specially after the death of Ataturk in 1939. The Democratic Party (DP) in fact came to power in the elections in 1950 by making the negation of Ottomanism and Islamism by Ataturk, an electoral issue. The process of transforming a traditional society with a cultural background different from that of Europe "into a modern one with considerable European elements"[83] created political, economic and social crises and paved the way for the emergence of new political parties and groups calling for a radical revision of

Turkish foreign policy and a change in the principles governing the policies and structure of the state[84] throughout the sixties and the seventies. The revival of Islam as a political force in post Ataturk Turkey again called into question the continued validity of Kemalism.[85]

It is argued that the nature of the process of modernization in Turkey created a society, which is neither new nor old, began to search for a definite cultural identity. This search coupled with the failure of modernization, created an anti-western segment and led to polarization of society.[86] The westernized elite—army, bureaucracy and intellectuals on the one hand are deeply committed to Kemalism and westernism and on the other hand, the rural masses and urban middle classes which have retained their Islamic roots are constantly striving for a cultural identity which can be representative of their Islamic and traditional mindset and give psychological satisfaction to them.

The new political parties that emerged in post-Ataturk Turkey—the Democratic Party (1950) and the Justice Party (1961) tried to use anti-Kemalism as the basis of their electioneering. The Democratic Party formed the government in 1950 and the Justice Party (a reincarnation of the discredited Democratic Party) which emerged as a large political group in the Turkish Grand National assembly participated in the coalition governments formed between 1961-1965 and finally formed the Government independently after the 1965 elections of the GNA. The Communist Labour Party and the Islamic National Order Party (later National Salvation Party and finally known as the Welfare Party) thrived on anti-westernism which eventually diluted the principles of Kemalism.

The debate between the Kemalists and anti-Kemalists concerning the identity of the Turkish state and society has hampered the process of modernization.

The Kemalists argue that the modernization has derailed

because the nation has deviated from its secularist path under the influence of reactionary forces bent upon asserting the primacy of religion in Turkish society.[87] The Islamists take just the opposite view. They maintain that failure of the modernization process can not be attributed to just going adrift of Kemalism but in fact sticking to it for too long.[88] In their opinion, "Kemalist modernization is not compatible with Muslim culture".[89] They maintain that:

> Under Ataturk, Muslims in Turkey were cut off from their religious tradition by force ...once the restrictive cloak of Kemalist ideology is removed, Turks will rejoin the Islamic world and be perfectly capable of creating a society that is not only modern (which they take in the technological sense of the word) but also more equitable and 'just' than the one created by the Kemalist elite after the Western image.[90]

This debate has entered into the arena of foreign policy as well. The Kemalists argue that the best course for Turkey is to retain its relations with the western camp and follow a west-oriented foreign policy. The Islamists hold the view that Turkey's interests are in the Muslim world to which it originally belonged. The Islamist Prime Ministers and their governments like Islamic Welfare Party (IWP) in 1995 and their short term presence in the office again from 1996 to 1997 attempted to revive links with the Muslim countries of West Asia, the Gulf, South and South-east Asia and the newly emerged republics of Central Asia. The Prime minister and head of the Islamic Welfare Party, Necemettin Erbakan paid official visits to the radical Islamic countries like Iran and Libya even at the cost of provoking widespread resentment in Turkey and the western world.[91]

This continued conflict between the Kemalists and the Islamists and Turkey's consistent search for identity suggests that the Kemalist victory although transformed a traditional

Ottoman state into a modern westernized secular one, Kemalism has yet not fully taken roots in Turkish society which has large segments of people who are deeply religious and believers in Islam. It has been noted that whenever a critical situation questioning Turkey's national identity arises, Turkey's traditional groupings tend to turn to Islam and the Islamic world. In the post-Soviet period, Kemalism and Islamism have been joined by a freshly revived ideology of pan-Turkism. After the collapse of the Soviet Union in 1990 the emergence of independent republics in Central Asia and Trans-Caucasia revived the pan-Turkist aspirations in Turkey. This added a third component to the debate centering around Turkey's search for identity.

Notes

1. Edward Mortimer, "Active in a New World Role", in *Turkey: Europe's Rising Star: The opportunities in Anglo-Turkish Relations* (London, 1993, published by Embassy of the Turkish Republic), p. 44.
2. Sukru S. Gurel, "Turkish Foreign Policy in a Changing World" in *Turkey in a Changing World* (Tokyo, Institute of Developing Economics, 1993), p. 1.
3. *Ibid.*, p. 3.
4. Even before the actual collapse of the USSR. President Turgut Ozal (1991) in his opening speech in the Turkish Grand National Assembly (TGNA) on 1 September 1991, described the situation as an "historic opportunity" for the Turks in Central Asia and urged the TGNA not to throw away this opportunity which has come for the first time in 400 years. Also, the then Turkish Prime Minister, Suleyman Demirel put it "we share common history, a common language, a common religion and a common culture. We are cousins cut off from each other for over hundred years, first by the Russians under the Czars, and then by the Communist regime". See Mushahid Hussain, "Iran and Turkey in Central Asia: Complementary or Competing Roles", *Middle East International*, 19 February 1993, p. 19. Also see "Turkey: Central Asia's Dominant Power", *Newsweek*, 28 January 1992, "Turkey: A Guarantee for Soviet Muslims", *Los Angeles Times* cited in the *Newspot*, 12 December, 1991, pp. 2, 6.

5. Gareth M. Winrow, "Turkey and Former Soviet Central Asia: National and Ethnic Identity", *Central Asian Survey*, Vol.11, No.3, 1992, p. 101.
6. Paul B. Henze, *Turkey: Towards the Twenty-First Century, A RAND Note*, 1992, p. 2.
7. Richard N. Frye, "Pre-Islamic and Early Islamic Cultures in Central Asia", *Turco-Persian Historical Perspective*, ed. Robert L. Canfield (Cambridge, Cambridge University Press, 1991), p. 37.
8. Ali-Reza Sheykh-Attar, *The Roots of Political Behaviour in Central Asia and the Caucasus* (Tehran, Institute for Political and International Studies, 1992), pp. 146, 161, 182.
9. Devendra Kaushik, *Central Asia in Modern Times: A History from the Early 19th Century* (printed in Soviet Union, 1970, 1st edn.), p. 15.
10. Govin Hambly (Ed.), *Central Asia* (London, Weidenfield and Nicolson, 1969), p. 72.
11. Firdausi's epic poem *Shakh Name* or *Shahnama* (Book of Kings) enjoys a high place in the classical literature of the Tajiks.
12. Richard Frye, *Bukhara: The Medieval Achievement* (Oklahama, Oklahama University Press, 1965), p. 112. Also Lawrence Krader, *Peoples of Central Asia* (Bloomington, Indiana University Press, 1971), p. 76.
13. C.E. Bosworth, *The Islamic Dynasties* (Edinburgh, Edinburgh University Press, 1967); See John Glenn, *The Soviet Legacy in Central Asia* (Macmillan Press, 1999), p. 52.
14. *Ibid.*, p.52. Also see, Olaf Caroe, *Soviet Empire: The Turks of Central Asia and Stalinism* (New York, St. Martin's Press, 1967), pp. 42-53, Mehmet Saray, *The Turkmens in the Age of Imperialism* (Ankara, Turkish Historical Society, 1989), p. 14.
15. Edward Allworth, *The Modern Uzbeks: From the Fourteenth Century to the Present* (California: Hoover Institution Press, 1990), p. 36. The 24 tribes were the Barak, Bayly, Durman, Imchi, Jat, Kengaz, Kitay, Kiyat, Kungrat, Kurlaut, Kushchi, Mangyt, Min, Naymam, Qarluq, Tangut, Taymas, Tubay, Tuman, Ugrish-Nayman. Utarchi, Uyghur, Uyshun and Yiyjan/Alman. Some of the later tribes were also part of the Kazakh Confederation—e.g. Qirq, Jalayir Qongrat, Alchin, Argun, Nayman, Kipchak. See John Glenn, *op.cit.*, p.162 (Notes).
16. Shirin Akiner, *Islamic Peoples of the Soviet Union* (London, KPI, 1986), p. 303.
17. *Ibid.*

18. G. Wheeler, *The Modern History of Soviet Central Asia* (London, Weidenfeld & Nicolson, 1964), p. 209.
19. *Ibid.*, also for Epics of the Region see, Zev Katz, *Handbook of Major Soviet Nationalities* (London: Collier Macmillan Publishers, 1975), p. 21.
20. John Glenn, *The Soviet Legay in Central Asia*. (Macmillan Press Ltd., 1999), p. 54.
21. Richard Pipes, "Muslims of Soviet Central Asia: Trends and Prospects", *Middle East Journal*, 9 (spring, 1958) p. 159.
22. Serge Zenkovsky, *Pan Turkism and Islam in Russia* (Massachusetts, Harvard University Press, 1967), p. 33.
23. Chagatai now-a-days called "old literary Uzbek" which was first promoted by Timurid Dynasty (14th century) and had become literary language of the whole region, was aided much by the writings of Emperor Babur (1482-1530). See John Glenn, *op.cit.*, pp. 54-55 also p. 163, note 39.
24. Devendra Kaushik, *op.cit.*, p. 29.
25. Hooman Peimani, *Regional Security and the Future of Central Asia* (Praeger Publishers, Westport, C.T., 1998), pp. 25-26.
26. Michael Rywkin, *Moscow's Muslim Challenge: Soviet Central Asia* (Armonk, N.Y. M.E. Sharp, 1990), p. 4.
27. Habibollah Abolhassan Shirazi, *The Nations of Central Asia* (Tehran, Institue for Political and International Studies, 1991), p. 48.
28. *Ibid.*, p. 49.
29. *Ibid.*, p. 51.
30. Edward Allworth, "Encounter", in *Central Asia: 120 Years of Russian Rule*, ed. Edward Allworth (Durham, Duke University Press, 1989), pp. 47-53.
31. Hooman Peimani, *op.cit.*, p. 27.
32. John Glenn, *op.cit.*, p. 69.
33. Dilip Hiro, *Between Marx and Muhammad: Changing Face of Central Asia*. (Harpe, Collins Publishers, London, 1994), pp. 3-4.
34. Dilip Hiro, *op.cit.*, p. 6.
35. *Ibid.*
36. Sibel Bozdogan and Resat Kasaba, "Introduction", in *Rethinking Modernity and National Identity in Turkey*, ed. Sibel Bozdogan and Resat Kasaba (Seattle: University of Washington Press, 1997), p. 3.
37. Caglar Keydar, "Wither the Project of Modernity: Turkey in the

1990s" in Sibel Bozdogan and Resat, *op.cit.*, p. 37.

38. S.N. Eisenstadt, "The Kemalist regime and Modernization: Some Comparative and Analytical Remarks" in *Ataturk and Modernization of Turkey* (ed.) Jacob M. Landau (Boulder, CO: Westview Press, 1984), p. 9.
39. *Ibid.*, p. 9.
40. Enver Z. Karal, "The Principles of Kamalism" in *Ataturk: Founder of Modern State*, (ed.) Ali Kazancigil and Ergun Ozbudun (Hamden: Archan Books, 1981), p. 12. n. 25, p. 12.
41. Ergun Ozbudun and Ali Kazancigil, "The Principles of Kemalism" in *Ataturk: The Founder of a Modern State*, ed. Ergun Ozbudun and Ali Kazancigil, (Hamden: Aschon Books, 1981), p. 3.
42. Bernard Lewis, *The Emergence of Modern Turkey* (London, Newyork, Toronto ; Oxford University Press, 1961), p. 43. Also see Iver B. Neumann and Jennifer M. Welsh, "The Other in Eruopean Self-Definition: An Addendum to the Literature on International society", *Review of International Studies*, vol. 17 (1991), pp. 327-348. The authors maintain that Christians held the same view and considered Ottoman Empire as a rival culture that had to be destroyed.
43. Bernard Lewis, *op.cit.*, p. 43.
44. Yucel Bozdaglioglu, *Turkish Foreign Policy and Turkish Identity: A Constructive Approach* (Routledge, Newyork, London, 2003), p. 36.
45. Bernard Lewis, *op.cit.*, p. 45.
46. Erik J. Zurcher, *Turkey: A Modern History* (London and New York, I.B. Tauris & Co. Ltd., 1995), p. 23.
47. Zurcher, *op.cit.*, p. 59.
48. Zurcher, *op.cit.*, p. 53.
49. Serif Mardin, "Religion and Secularism in Turkey", in *Ataturk: Founder of a Modern State*, ed. Ali Kazancigil and Ergun Ozbudun (Hamden: Archon Books, 1981), p. 196.
50. Zurcher, *Turkey: A Modern History*, *op.cit.*, p. 59.
51. M. Sukru Hanioglu, *The Young Turks in Opposition* (New york and Oxford, Oxford University Press, 1995), p. 17.
52. Serif Mardin, *op.cit.*, p. 197.
53. Bernard Lewis, *op.cit.*, p. 122.
54. Feroz Ahmed, *The Making of Modern Turkey* (London and New York, Routledge, 1993), p. 28.

55. Zurcher, *op.cit.*, p. 71.
56. Serif Mardin, *Turk Modernlesmesi*, 5th ed. (Istanbul: Iletisim Yayinlari, 1997), p. 10.
57. Zurcher, *op.cit.*, p. 71.
58. Serif Mardin, *Turk Modernlesmesi*, p. 93.
59. *Ibid.*
60. Zurcher, *Turkey: A Modern History, op.cit.*, p. 90.
61. *Ibid.*, p. 91.
62. M. Sukru Hanioglu, *The Young Turks, In opposition* (New York & Oxford: Oxford University Press, 1995) p. 3.
63. *Ibid.*, p. 17.
64. *Ibid.*, p. 18.
65. Ali Kazancigil, "The Ottoman-Turkish State and Kamalism" in *Ataturk: Founder of Modern State*, ed. Ali Kazancigil and Ergun Ozbudun (Hamden: Archon Books, 1981), p. 50.
66. Zurcher, Turkey: *A Modern History, op.cit.*, p. 132.
67. *Ibid.*, p. 132.
68. David Kushner, "Self Perception and Identity in Contemporary Turkey", *Journal of Contemporary History*, Vol. 32 (1997), p. 221.
69. Zurcher, Turkey: *A Modern History, op.cit.*, p. 133.
70. Andrew Davison, "Secularization and Modernization in Turkey: Ideas of Ziya Gokalp", *Economy and Society*, Vol. 24 (May 1995): 189-224, p. 190.
71. Enver Z. Karal, "The Principles of Kemalism", in *Ataturk: Founder of a Modern State*, ed. Ali Kazancigil and Ergun Ozbudun, *op.cit.*, p. 26.
72. *Ibid.*, p. 26.
73. *Ibid.*, p. 27.
74. Zurcher, Turkey: *A Modern History, op.cit.*, p. 48.
75. Yucel Bozdaglioglu, *Turkish Foreign Policy, op.cit.*, p. 45.
76. Enver Z. Karal, *Principles of Kemalism, op.cit.*, p. 13.
77. *Ibid.*, p. 28.
78. Takeshi Hayashi, "The Modernization of Japan and Turkey: Some Comparisons", in *Ataturk: Founder of Modern State*, ed. Ali Kazancigil and Ergun Ozbudun, *op.cit.*, p. 228.
79. Enver Z. Karal, *Principles of Kemalism, op.cit.*, p. 12.
80. Levent Koker, *Modernlesme, Kemalism ve Demokrasi* (Istanbul, Iletisim Yayinlari, 1995), pp. 152-53.

81. Patrick B. Kinross, *Ataturk: A Biography of Mustafa Kemal, Father of Modern Turkey* (New York, William Morrow and Company, 1965), p. 438.
82. Ataturk quoted in Bernard Lewis, *op.cit.*, p. 263.
83. Osman Okyar, "Ataturk's quest for Modernism" in *Ataturk and Modernization of Turkey*, ed. Jacob M. Landau (Boulder, Co., Westview Press, 1984), p. 52.
84. David Kushner, "Westernism in Contemporary Turkey", in *Ataturk and Modernization of Turkey, op.cit.*, p. 234.
85. Yucel Bozdaglioglu, *op.cit.*, p. 54.
86. Okyar, *Ataturk's Quest for Modernization, op.cit.*, p. 52.
87. *Ibid.* Also see Resat Kasaba, "Kemalist Certainities and Modern Ambiguities", in *Rethinking Modernity and National Identity in Turkey, op.cit.*, p. 17.
88. Resat Kasaba, *op.cit.*, p. 17.
89. *Ibid.*
90. *Ibid.*
91. Yucel Bozdaglioglu, *op.cit.*, pp. 54-55.

Chapter 2

Pan-Turkism: Historical and Contemporary

The pan-Turkism reasserted by Turkey in post-Soviet Central Asia is not an unprecedented phenomenon. It has been around for at least a century but circumstances did not favour its implementation. The eclipse of the Soviet Union which had always been the biggest obstruction in the way of reaching out to the Turkic people in the past, aroused the pan-Turkic euphoria afresh in Turkey. Turks started looking at the collapse of the Soviet Union and emergence of independent States in Central Asia as a "historic opportunity" which has come to them most unexpectedly and which they must utilize in their interest. The history of Central Asia suggests that the Turks arrived in Central Asia from the Altai mountains and the existing Turkic people of Central Asia have much in common with the Turks of Anatolia—ethnically, culturally and linguistically. Turkey wants to revive its old linkages with the Central Asians. They maintain that circumstances had compelled them to leave their brethern in Central Asia and remain cut off from them for such a long time though at the back of their mind they always cherished the dream of uniting with them.

Turkey's desire to make pan-Turkism a basis of relations with Central Asia is motivated by several factors. In the first phase, it had always been a dream of the Turks to get united with the Turkic people at least emotionally if not politically and with time and circumstances favouring them now it needs to be materialized. Secondly, the emergence of independent sovereign states in Central Asia provided an unprecedented opportunity to expand its sphere of influence in the "extended neighbourhood" and establish an economic and political grouping of Turkic States on the pattern of European community or European Union under the leadership of Ankara. Thirdly, with the end of the Cold War, Turkey was feeling a little insecure as its strategic value for the West and importance of its role in NATO had declined. It was expected that its new found prominence in Central Asia would revive Turkey's importance for its western allies. Here, Turkey was not mistaken. In fact, the United States and its allies in NATO considered Turkey a most suitable role model for the new republics in Central Asia. With its democratic secular republican character Ankara can easily cultivate good relations with the modern secular republics of Central Asia and also save them from falling prey to fundamentalist encroachments from Iran, Afghanistan, Pakistan, Saudi Arabia and the Gulf States. Emboldened by the encouragement given by the US and its European friends, Turkey initiated its "ostpolitik" and launched a vigorous campaign to bring the Turkic states of Central Asia under its protective wings. Pan-Turkism was considered the best vehicle to commence its sojourn in Central Asia.

ORIGIN OF PAN-TURKISM

Pan-Turkism which became a prominent ideological trend in the political life of the Ottoman Empire in the early twentieth century, initially originated in the Crimean-Volga region of the Czarist Russia. The waves of Westernism and Islamism which have been stirring the neighbouring Ottoman Empire had a spill over effect on the Turkic people of Trans-Caucasia and Central Asia as well. The zeal of Ottoman Sultans to modernize their armed forces and equip them with western technology and art of warfare had given the Turkish army men, bureaucrats and the social elites opportunity to come in contact with western culture, civilization ard achievements of the West in the field of military and modern sciences. They started thinking in terms of transforming the Ottoman governance too, on the pattern of the West.

The modernization efforts of the Ottoman Sultans which in fact were tentamount to westernization of Turkish polity, army and society, were faced with widespread resentment from the Islamic groups of the country which have been powerful enough to derail the entire process of modernization-westernization. The Islamists in Turkey were not opposed to the import of science and technology and western military skills but they desired to have all this within the broader framework of Islam practiced through *Shariat* and *Holy Quran*. The Islamists took pride in the glory of the Ottoman Empire as it was the symbol of their faith. The Caliphate represented the magnificence and honour of the Islamic community of the world. The rivalry between the modernists and Islamists for influence over the Ottoman Sultans and the power of the state could continue but the heavy reversals faced by the Ottoman Empire in the wars with Austria and Russia and the treaties of Carlowitz (1699) and Passarowitz (1718) forced the Ottoman elite in both Islamist and the modernist camps to think about the causes of the decline. The modernists turned to a vigorous campaign for initiation of large-scale political reforms in the Empire and the Islamists to explore the reasons which made Islam succumb to the power of the western countries.

In Central Asia, the occupation of Kokand, Khiva and Bukhara by the Russians under Czar Alexander II brought the entire Turkestan under the control of the Russian Empire. The Trans-Caspia, the land of Turkmen tribes also fell into Czar's hands in 1881. Five years later, Czar Alexander III named the entire region as Turkestan Territory of the Empire. The Russians, however, refrained from interfering in the religious and social life of the Muslims of Turkestan and they continued to be governed by the laws of the *Shariat* and *Quran*. The economic activity undertaken by Russia drew the Muslim masses to work with the Russians and their living style and standard started getting transformed. The traditional people in the Caucasus and Central Asia who consider themselves "Muslims first" were disturbed with the alien influence on their lives. They started analysing the decline of their community in the religious context and pondered over the causes of strength of the Christian Czarists. This process of self introspection resulted in the emergence of two schools of thought in Central Asia—*Qadimists* (Traditionalists) and the *Jadidists* (Innovators) which tried to redefine the relationship of the Muslim community as a distinct religious grouping with the rest of the society in Russia.[1]

The *Qadimists* advocated strict application of the *Shariat*, while the *Jadidists* proposed innovation in view of the fast changing world around them. The *Qadim-Jadid* debate highlighted the Islamism in Central Asia and generated an atmosphere for a serious debate among the Islamists of all shades about the nature and extent of reforms in Islam.

Qadimists too acknowledged the need for reforms in Islam but they wanted it to be within the framework of Islamic tradition and not under the impact of alien ideas. They were opposed to the Russian rule of the territory of the Muslims but refrained from giving a call for *jihad* or resorting to radical methods of opposing the Russian rule. Since their ranks were filled with clerics and *ishans* (guides) of the Sufi order (mystical Islam) who were scattered throughout the country side, *Qadimists* had a mass appeal.[2]

The *Jadidists* were graduates of Quranic schools and Islamic colleges. They were well-versed in foreign languages, western political theory and practice. They focussed on social and cultural reforms and demanded better rights for women. They were not opposed to the Russian rule over Turkestan and supported spread of western technology and modern sciences in their territory. The pan-Turkist thinkers emerged out of the *Jadid* school of thought. They wanted to forge and strengthen the unity of the Turkic people on the basis of common ethnicity and language in place of religion. Their leaders Sheikh Shahabuddin Mirjani (1818-1889), Ismail Gasprinsky (1851-1914) whose real name was Ismail Hasbarali developed the ideology of pan-Turkism on these lines.[3]

In the late 1890's, some Tatar intellectuals from the Crimean and Volga regions had begun advocating pan-Turkism as an alternative to both Islamism and westernism and sought unity on the basis of ethno-linguistic and cultural commonalties. *Turk* a periodical established in Cairo in 1902 propagated pan-Turkism—political unity of all Turkic-speaking peoples from the Balkans to China. The journal's founder, Yusuf Aq Churaoglu in his essay "Three Political Systems" published in 1904 claimed to own "scientific evidence" to prove that all Turkic people from "Egypt to China" constituted a single nation. Ali Hussainzade, a disciple of Churaoglu, later coined a popular slogan: "Turkicization, Islamicization, Modernization". Zia Gokalp, the well known political philosopher and great sociologists of Turkey also provided a similar slogan: "We belong to the Turkish nation, Muslim religion and the European Civilization".[4]

The efforts to forge a common version of Turkic—a sub-family of the *Ural-Altaic* languages to be used by all Muslims of the Czarist Russia, Ismail Gasprinsky established a newspaper called *Terjuman Perevodchik* in 1893 and proposed a new language constructed by him. It was based on Ottoman Turkish which was purified by eliminating the words of Persian and Arabic languages. This Turkic language was made simple and "easily understandable to a boatman of Bosphorus and a cameleer of Kashgar equally". *Terjuman* stressed the politico-cultural commonalty of all Turkic peoples and gave a catchy slogan "Dilde, fikirde, ishte birlik" (Unity of Language, Unity of Thought, Unity of Action). Gasprinsky wanted to forge cultural-political and ethno-linguistic unity of all Turkic people of the Russian Empire with the Turkic people of West Asia, Balkans and China. However, his effort, although a very thoughtful exercise, was seen as a devise to establish cultural domination and superiority of Turkic language over other languages of the region. In disgust Gasprinsky closed down his newspaper in 1905 and gave up the campaign for pan-Turkism based on linguistic unity. Emir of Bukhara raised Islamic bogey against Pan-Turkism which created communal tension between the supporters of the two groups. *Jadids,* however, continued their reformist drive in Central Asia and by 1914, they could claim the loyalty of most of the Muslim intellegentsia.

Some members of the intellectual elite of Muslims had become interested in socialist ideas as well. Muhammad Amin Rasulzadeh, a journalist from Baku (Azerbaijan), Nariman Bey Narmanoglu (later Narimanov) and Ahmed Azizbekoglu formed *Himmat* (Effort Party) linked to the Social Democratic Labour Party (Bolshevik).

The nationalist and pan-Islamic trends in some of the Muslim sections led to emergence of *Musavat* (Equality Party)—an organization with Islamic overtones in 1912. *Musavat* called for the unity of all Muslims irrespective of nationality or sect, restoration of independence of all Muslim nations and assistance to all Muslim peoples and countries "in offence and defence". However, in the absence of any clear ideology and agenda, the *Musavat* turned out to be a small time venture.[5]

During the period of Provisional Government in Moscow, some political organizations appeared which had roots in the *Jadidists*. The *Turkestan Jadidists* formed a political party in 1909 which in 1917 convened the Congress of Muslims of Turkestan in Tashkent. It appointed a National Committee which during the October Revolution tried to seize power from the Provisional Government. The *Young Bukharans* and *Young Khivans*—groups formed on the line of Young Turks also appeared in the Emirate of Bukhara and Khiva.[6] A revival of interest in Gasprinsky's Turkic language was also witnessed during that period. The Congress of All Muslims (1917) reiterated its support to introduction of Gasprinsky's Turkic language as a medium of instruction in the higher schools, but at the primary and secondary levels, national language of the region to be the medium of instruction. This relegated a secondary place to Gasprinsky's Turkic language.[7] The rising wave of linguistic nationalism again undermined the chances of reappearance of "new Turkic" language in the social-cultural and educational life of the Turkic people. Notwithstanding this aspect, the urge for pan-Turkism remained alive in the minds of those who wanted to attain unity of all Turkic people on the basis of common language—which was seen as a "key" to forge unity of ideas, thought and action.

PAN-TURANISM OF ZIA GOKALP

The Young Turks movement in Ottoman Turkey made a deep impact on the poltiical thinking of the Turkic people of Central Asia. The Pan-Turkism propagated by the Young Turks was different from the pan-Turkism envisioned by Ismail Gasprinsky and his followers in Central Asia. In the company of *Jadidists,* they had thought of uniting all Turkic peoples in one state and claim autonomy within the Russian State. To assert their claim with justification they decided to base their campaign on ethno-linguistic unity of the Turkic people. In contrast, the Young Turks envisoned an expanded Ottoman state that would comprise of all the Turkic territories of Central Asia and some parts of the territory of the Czarist Russia which was to be ruled under the Ottoman flag. The author of this philosophy was Zia Gokalp who entertained a grandoise dream of eventual establishment of a Turan or Greater Turkestan which was to unite politically in the form of an empire of Turkey and the Turkic peoples of the Soviet Union.

The history of the Russian Turkish relations throws light on expansionist ambitions of both the Empires at the cost of each other. The Ottomans wanted to acquire territories in Caucasus and Central Asia and Russia aspired to secure its trade routes through the Bosphorus and the Dardanelles (the Black Sea Straits), which was an essential condition for developing its trade with the countries of the Mediterranean and southern Europe.

The competition and hostility between the Ottoman Empire and the Russian Empire was often exploited by the Europeans. By the end of the nineteenth century, the Ottoman Empire had become a "sickman of Europe" whose survival or end was in the hands of the powerful states of Europe. Notwithstanding the decline in its political and military power, the Sultan enjoyed the title of Caliph and was the Head of the Muslims of the world. The religious power of the Ottoman Sultans was resented by Russia as the latter suspected the role of Sultan in instigating the Muslim population of Russia against the Russian government. Zia Gokalp, a leading sociologist and pan- Turkist theorist who had enunciated the national doctrine of modern Turkey, viewed Pan-Turkism as a device for creating a "Great Turan" which would include all

Turkic speaking nationals of Caucasia, Central Asia, China, Balkans and some other regions of Asia owing allegiance to the Ottoman throne.

The pan-Turkic sentiment flourished among the descendants of the outside Turks (Dis Turkler) who had migrated to the present Turkish Republic in stages since the last quarter of the eighteenth century. Pan-Turkism had become the key ideology of the Young Turks when they came to power in 1908: "According to their views, every thing in the world should be considered in the light of the role of the "Turks"[8] meaning all Turkic nationals.

> The history of civilization should be seen as the history of the Turks, the forefathers of human civilization; the science of language should recognize the primacy of Turkish language as the parent language for the whole of mankind; geography should be studied from the point of view of geo-political concept of the habitation of the Turks, culture should be valued from the standpoint of the grandeur of Turkish culture and its guiding influence on all world cultures. Pan-Turkism thus embraced practically every sphere of human activity and reflected larger than life.[9]

Gennady Chufrin argues that pan-Turkism was an important factor behind the Turkish leaders' joining Germany and its allies in the World War I in a hope that Germany would help the Ottoman Empire achieve the occupation of Russian Armenia which was to be a step towards the creation of "Greater Turan"—a Turkic state from the Adriatic to the Pacific.[10]

The loss of European territories in the Balkan war (1912-1913) rendered a severe blow to the Ottoman Empire. Germany, taking advantage of the vulnerability of the Ottomans approached the Young Turks with proposals which could make them amenable to Berlin. The Young Turks triumvirate of Enver Pasha, Jemal Pasha and Talat Bey after assuming power in 1913 stressed pan-Islamism (to rally the Islamic countries round the Caliphate in the war) and pan-Turkism (to draw the Turkic people of Central Asia and Caucasia in favour of the Young Turks). Out of these, Enver Pasha (1881-1922) was most articulate and effective. He commanded tremendous power over the administration and people of the Empire. It is maintained that the renowned French writer, Andre Marleux's father, then posted in the German Embassy in Istanbul, had collaborated with Enver in strengthening the idea of "Turan". Enver himself had set views on "Turanism" and already co-opted Muslim activists from among the Turkic groups in the Czarist Empire into the young Turks' circles. He had envisaged a union of all Turkic peoples from Edirne (Adrianople) to the Chinese Oases along the "Silk Route" (the Silk Road).[11] As soon as peace had been secured in the Balkans, Enver's emissaries contacted the Emir of Bukhara and Afghanistan as well as Khans of Turkestan to revive the project. Before the outbreak of the World War I, Enver set up the *Teskilat-i-mahsusa*, a secret service whose agents, all volunteer officers, carried out the Pan-Turkic and Pan-Islamic propaganda beyond the Ottoman frontiers, amongst the Turkic people. During the war several agents were sent to Afghanistan, Iran, India and Trans-Caucasia. It appeared that Germans were greatly interested in exploiting Pan-Turkism and pan-Islamism both in order to weaken Turkic Russia and to secure some hold over the valuable natural resources of Caucasia and Central Asia.

The pan-Turkist fervour, however, got dampened by the revolutionary developments in Russia. Initially, the Islamic clergy and the religious organizations in Turkestan opposed the Russian revolutionaries and tried to strengthen their religion-based unity against the Bolsheviks. But military and political ascendancy of the Bolsheviks to power led the members of the major Muslim parties from the *Himmat* in

Azerbaijan to *Alash Orda* in Kazakh-Kyrgyz regions to the *Young Bukharans* and the *Young Khivan* movements enroll themselves into the communist party and start propagating its political and economic policies among the rural masses. This *volte-face* unnerved the pan-Islamists to a great extent.

THE BASMACHIS MOVEMENT

The situation was further made complicated by the outbreak of the *Basmachi* movement which discredited both pan-Turkism and pan Islamism. This armed movement had emerged in the winter of 1919-1920 when, following the sixty two percent drop in the cultivated area of Turkestan ASSR and the government's policy to feed the armed forces at the expense of civilians nearly half of the population was faced with starvation. The *Basmachi* movement was led by prominent sections of Kokand Autonomous Government. They operated from the mountains and attacked the Red Army's supply convoys and outposts. This movement had drawn inspiration from Islam and by 1920, succeeded in gaining support of the people of the Farghana Valley, a traditional *bastion* of Islam.[12]

However, by combining the military campaign with socio-economic reforms and concessions in matters of faith, religious beliefs and practices the Russian government succeeded in putting down the radical groups and overpowering the entire *Basmachi* Movement by 1921.

The defeat of Germany in World War I placed the Young Turks specially Enver, Jemal and Talat into difficult position. They fled the country. Enver came to Central Asia and found the region in the midst of the *Basmachi* movement. He, somehow succeeded in convincing the Russian government that he would conciliate the warring groups in Turkestan. However, after his arrival in Bukhara in the spring of 1921, Enver developed an ambition to become a monarch himself.

This led him to forge an alliance of conservative and liberal Muslim leaders and the mountain tribal chiefs under the twin slogans of "pan-Turkism" and "pan-Islamism" with the objective of creating a single "Islamic" Turkic state in the region.

Enver assumed the title of "Emir of Turkestan" and took over the command of the *Basmachi* movement against the Red Army. However, in one of the military campaigns during his attempted escape to Afghanistan, Enver was killed in an ambush on 5 August 1922, and with him ended pan-Turkism too, at least for some time. The legend of pan-Turkism he left behind keeps reappearing in the minds of Turks every now and then.

The pan-Turkic campaign led by Enver Pasha made a deep impact on the then political situation of the world. The Kaiser of Germany had encouraged Enver in 1914 to liberate fellow Turks and fellow Muslims from the yoke of the Russians in Central Asia. This motivated the Ottoman Turkey to support Germany in the World War I.

Under the leadership of Enver Pasha, the Ottoman War Minister Sultan Mehmet VI (1909-1923) urged the Muslims worldwide to launch a *jihad* against the foreign rule. This call found resonance in India during the British Raj in the Khilafat Movement launched by Ali brothers. Indian nationalists collected funds to liberate the Sultan Caliph from the occupying forces and mobilized political support against the foreign powers' strategy to occupy Turkey. However, the money sent to save the Caliphate was used by Mustafa Kemal Ataturk in the construction of the building of the old Grand National Assembly in Ankara which later housed the office of the CENTO—a US sponsored military organization for collective security in the northern tier.

TACTICAL USE OF PAN-TURKISM AND PAN-ISLAMISM DURING THE WAR OF INDEPENDENCE

Mustafa Kemal Pasha had no love for Islam (although he had earned the title "Kemal" for his non-stop and faultfree recital of Quran at the age of eight only), nor did he intend to form any pan-Turkic group of states under the leadership of Turkey. In fact, after the successful termination of war of independence, Ataturk renounced Turkey's claim over the overseas territories of the disintegrated Ottoman Empire and the sovereign jurisdiction of the Republic of Turkey was confined to Turkish mainland only. Nevertheless, during the War of Independence and the movement for the national liberation Ataturk used both pan-Islamism and pan-Turkism as strategic tools to win the support of the Muslim countries of the world including the Turkic peoples of Central Asia and Trans-Caucasia. He even befriended Russia which was treated by the Ottoman Empire and the Young Turks as an eternal enemy of the Empire.

In view of the developments in the Ottoman Empire, the Balkans, Caucasia and Central Asia and the acquisition of territories by the British in the regions bordering Turkey, Ataturk needed support of Russia in withholding the British forces on the one hand and keeping the Turkic Muslim peoples favourably inclined towards the survival of Turkey as an independent state on the other. The friendship with Russia could end Turkey's isolation in international politics and enable it to seek political and military support from the Bolshevik government of Russia.

The end of the First World War resulted in political turmoil creating a vacuum in the region from the Balkans to Central Asia. The entire area fell prey to the British and their allies after the defeat of the Ottoman and German armies. At the time of the Armistice at Mudros (30 October 1918) Mesopotamia, Palestine, Syria and other Arab provinces had already been occupied by the British. What complicated the situation further was the British occupation of the Caucasian lands which made borders of Turkey further vulnerable from the standpoint of security.[13]

As a result of the armistice agreement, the defeated Ottoman army was to withdraw from the north-west Persia, Baku, Batum and the rest of Trans-Caucasia. The Trans-Caucasian railway was also put under the control of the Allied forces.[14] No favour was given to the Turks regarding the straits either. Allied access to the Black Sea was considered of supreme importance as the command of the Black Sea would make it possible for the Allies to secure positions in the Caucasus, the Caspian and the South Russian regions.[15]

To implement the Armistice Agreement British forces immediately occupied Baku and its surrounding oil fields. Three British divisions arrived in Constantinople and settled on both sides of the Bosphorus, Sea of Marmara and Dardanalles. A British naval squadron was sent to the Ottoman capital to secure direct control of the Sea routes and the straits.

The Ottoman armies had won control over large areas in the Caucasus in the last year of the war but the Turkish armistice put the Caucasian lands also at the mercy of the British troops. It opened the way not only to the Turkish lands of Anatolia and the Thrace but also the Caucasian lands in the north-east. The British troops quickly went to Baku and Batum and the entire line of Batum-Baku Railway was captured by them. This enabled the British to form a "cordon" across the Caucasus from the Black sea to the Caspian.[16]

Russia was watching the turn of events in its neighbourhood. The British control over the Caucasus troubled Moscow. Knowing the increasing strength and influence of Mustafa Kemal Ataturk on Turks of Turkey and the Turkic peoples in Central Asia, Moscow envisioned some kind of understanding with Ataturk—together they could weaken Britain's position in the Caucasus to the Caspian Sea region.

At the end of the World War I, British wanted to control as many territories as possible and appear as the sole power in the region but soon they realized that to manage all the territories occupied by them was much costlier and more difficult task than what they had envisaged. In the months following the end of the war, the nationalist Turkey gained an unexpected momentum and reached a crucial stage by late 1919 as the resistance groups developed into a strong army to wage the war of independence against the Allied Powers. It appeared that the "sick man of Europe" was hardly ready for his deathbed. In Nicolson's words, "The victim recovered overnight".[17]

However, the trouble for Britain was related not only to the Turkish affairs. There have been even more serious difficulties with the Caucasian affairs. After the defeat of Turkey Britain was entitled to a dominant position in the Caucasian region because it were the British who had snatched back these lands from the Turks.[18] The Trans-Caucasian republics, Armenia, Azerbaijan and Georgia had all declared their independence in May 1918. By September the same year they all had come under the partial occupation of Turkey and Germany. Following the defeat of the Ottoman Turkey and Germany, they attempted to regain their independence. They expected the British to help them in attaining independence instead of keeping them under their prolonged occupation.

The situation in Trans-Caucasia demanded more involvement on the part of the British than they were willing to give. The relations between Georgia, Armenia and Azerbaijan were far from harmonious, mainly because of their long standing territorial aspirations. As soon as the Turkish armies left the region an armed struggle broke out between Armenia and Georgia over Borchalo region which both sides claimed as their own. The conflict between Azarbaijan and Armenia was even more serious. Many Azeri and Armenian villages were located side by side and used the same common land for the cattle and sheep grazing. The rival claims on Zangezur, Nakichevan and Karabakh demanded immediate attention from the British who had no directives from the home government and no experience of tackling the territorial disputes between these countries.

The British government had been supporting the anti-Bolshevik white Russian armies as early as December 1917 and the British soldiers had been in Russia from March 1918 when they landed at Murmansk together with other allies. The military intervention was initially thought necessary to defend the eastern front against the Central powers but after the war, the rationale for military intervention was no longer valid. The anti-Turk and anti-German objective behind the Allied expeditions in the Caucasus and Russia lost its significance.[19]

By March 1919, three months after the dispatch of British troops to Caucasus, British government decided to withdraw from the region. All the troops were called back with the exception of a garrison at Batum. The British forces were to be confined to the control of the Black Sea and the Straits, bordering the sensitive southern flank of Russia. It provided a coherent framework to Britain's strategic interests in the region as all roads to the Mediterranean and the Middle East passed through the Straits.[20] However, the situation for Russia and Turkey continued to be alarming.

Britain had made this move to avoid a direct confrontation with the Bolsheviks. They considered control over Turkish Straits more important to safeguard their interests in the region. However, the emerging situation made confrontation with Russia inevitable as the increasing warmth between the Turkish nationalists and the Bolsheviks enhanced the prospects of formation of an anti-British alliance between the two.

TURCO-RUSSIAN RAPPROACHMENT

The British withdrawal from Caucasus offered Russia an opportunity to fortify its sensitive southern flank against the tightening grip of Britain in the Black Sea and the Turkish straits. The rapproachment with Turkey provided an extra bonus to the Bolsheviks in their Caucasian campaign, to mobilize a significant part of the Turkic Muslim population of the Caucasus on their side.[21]

The Caucasian region acquired a renewed importance for Turkey as well as Russia. The nationalist in Turkey and the Bolsheviks in Russia were convinced that the region would provide vital links in their struggle against the British. Bolshevik campaign to "Sovietize the Caucasus" and diffuse the movement for independence was supported by Turkey because the Turkish nationalist believed that an independent Caucasus would be an obstacle in receiving the war materials sent to them by Russia. Bolshevik control over the Caucasus would enhance the military position of Turkey vis-à-vis its enemies—the British and the Greeks.

The Turco-Russian friendship proved useful to the Bolsheviks too. By the end of October 1919 the white armies were facing reversals and the anti-Bolshevik forces were driven back on almost all fronts by the winter (1919-20). On 6 February 1920, Mustafa Kemal in a telegram to his colleagues elaborated that "if three Trans-Caucasian states could constitute a pro-western barrier, this would be an end of the dream and all hopes for establishment of an independent Turkish state. Therefore, Turks should do every thing possible in the Caucasus to facilitate the Bolshevik control of the region".[22]

The Bolsheviks taking advantage of Turkey's strategic compulsions initiated the processes to establish a grip on the political groups and organizations in the three Caucasian states. The Turkish nationalist wanted to give a formal status to their agreement with Russia. During the negotiations, the Bolsheviks drew the attention of their Turkish counterparts to the importance of Erzurum-Baku railway line in transporting the military equipment and other supplies from Russia to Turkey. The greater part of this railway line was controlled by the independent Armenian Republic. On July 28, the Polit Bureau declared the decision to give material support to Turkey in terms of weapons and gold. Within a fortnight of formalization of Turco-Russian Agreement, the Treaty of Severes[23] was signed (10 August 1920) by the Istanbul government under the Sultan. Ataturk immediately dispatched a letter to Moscow to form a joint front against the British and on his part, confirmed that, "the Turkish Government accepts the responsibility .... of compelling Georgia and Azerbaijan to enter into union with the Soviet Russia".

The draft Turkish-Soviet Accord called for both sides to make every effort to open unobstructed avenues between the two countries for the flow of men and material. The Bolshevik forces appeared ready to pounce on the Caucasian front with all their might. In September 1920, soon after the Turco-Soviet Treaty, unfortunately a full scale war broke out between Turkey and Armenia. Since the summer of 1919, there was a dispute between the two sides over the eastern provinces of Anatolia. An independent Armenia was seen by the Turkish nationalists as an obstacle in reaching to Turkic people of Azerbaijan and wanted to occupy this Caucasian republic. Turkey still holds the grudge for not being able to capture Armenia. Just a little strip of territory could get Turkey direct access to Central Asia, especially to the oil rich Azerbaijan which would have turned the fortune of Ankara.

The Turkish offensive caused great anxiety in Armenia and it sought Russian assistance in countering the Turkish attack. The Bolsheviks, however, initially refrained from intervention. The Turks moved in Armenia without much opposition and took over Kars on 30 October 1920. In November, Russia took an unexpected step by pressurizing the independent Armenian Government to transfer the authority to the Revolutionary Committee of Armenia. This was followed by armed intervention by the Red Army. The Russian intervention caused the first crack in the Turkish-Russian rapproachement. It became clear that the co-operation between the two sides was more like a business partnership than a unity of principles. Turkey did not attempt to move into historically Russian held parts of Armenia and the Russians did not move further down into Turkish Armenia. Surrounded by the Bolsheviks from the north and the Turkish nationalists from the south, the independent Armenia was divided into two.[24]

Russia repeated the Armenian mode of occupation in Azerbaijan and Georgia as well. They fomented political trouble against the autonomous governments of these countries and then compelled them to transfer power to the Revolutionary Councils to meet the situation and finally assumed total control of the state concerned.

Mustafa Kemal Ataturk resented the Russian *volte-face* but maintained the sanctity of the Truco-Russian Treaty. Unlike the Young Turks, he was not interested in pursuing the pan-Islamist and pan-Turkist ambition in Central Asia. After winning the War of Independence against the Allied forces and restoring the sovereignty of Turkey Ataturk buried the ideology of pan-Turkism and steered the nation on the path of modernization, westernization and secularization. Pan-Turkism had no place in his scheme of things. Commenting on pan-Turkism Ataturk maintained: "We wish the communities set up in different countries by the believers in our God to live independently, on their own... But to rule and guide the whole of Muslim society from a single centre as an 'empire', one big empire is fantasy. This runs counter to science, knowledge, logic".[25] However, soon after Ataturk's death in 1939, his successors went adrift and fell prey to the rut of pan-Turkism during the World War II—once again at the insistence of Germany.

The climate in favour of revival of pan-Islamism and pan-Turkism started warming up slightly before the outbreak of the World War II in 1939. The twin movements for pan-Islamism and pan-Turkism which had officially been rejected by the Kemalists were eventually revived in the post-Ataturk Turkey. The members of the émigré Union of Turkestan Youth which had been disbanded in 1937 became active. The pan-Turkist publications—books, periodicals with articles on pan-Turkism commenced quickly. The government of Sukru Saracoglu also lent full support to the pan-Turkic moves made by intellectuals, officials and political leaders of Turkey.[26]

Some western studies note that after invading the USSR, the German ruling circles cleverly used pan-Turkic aspirations to form military units of Soviet war prisoners of Turkic descent.[27] Turkish emissaries drove about the German camps for the Soviet prisoners of war and tried to urge Turkic speaking Soviet citizens to commit acts of treason against their homeland.[28] In the autumn of 1942 Turkey stationed large military forces near the border with the Soviet Union.[29] In his talk with the German Ambassador on 27 August 1942, Saracoglu ardently desired the destruction of Russia. "The destruction of Russia is a feat of the Fuehrer, which can only be emulated once in a century, is also a life-long dream of the Turkish people. However, with the tables turned against the Germans in the later part of the war, Turks gave up pan-Turkish ambition and switched on a pro-American campaign for rest of the period till the end of the war.

The study of pan-Turkism in its historical perspective reveals that it had not been a spontaneous, original or indigenous ideology in Turkey. The pan-Turkism propagated by the Tatar intellectual Ismail Gasprinsky was aimed at uniting all Turkic speaking people as an integrated unit within the Czarist Russia. He also had a dream of bringing all Turkic people residing in various regions like Balkans, Egypt, China, Turkey and elsewhere together as a cultural-linguistic unit through a common language constructed by him. But this was more of a fantasy—a distant dream. Similarly, the pan-Turanism or pan-Turkism of Zia Gokalp was motivated by super patriotism and nationalism. He proposed to bring all Turkic territories of Russia under the Ottoman flag by advocating the cultural and linguistic commonalties between them and the Ottoman Turkey. The Young Turks while seeking modernization and westernization of their society, polity and army also nourished the dream of pan-Turkism. They tried to attain its fulfillment with the support of Germany. To a great extent, Germany had encouraged the pan-Turkist fervour in the mind of the Young Turk leaders, especially Enver Pasha who had been the "key figure" in the echelons of the Young Turk organization. Mustafa Kemal Ataturk simply made a tactical use of pan-Islamism to win the support of the Islamic countries during the war of national liberation waged by him against the Allied forces which had occupied Turkey at the end of the First World War. The pan-Turkist sentiments were used to keep the Turkic people of Central Asia inclined towards Turkey during the days of its war against the occupation forces. He had two objectives: (1) to develop solidarity with the Turkic people and keep them interested in the freedom and sovereignty of Turkey; (2) and giving an impression to Russia that the nationalists had a hold over the Turkic population of Caucasia and Central Asia. Turkey's friendship would enable Russia to establish control over the Turkic states as Ataturk himself did not cherish any territorial designs. He dumped both pan-Turkism and pan-Islamism as soon as independence was attained In the post-Ataturk period, an attempt was made under pressure from Germany, to revive to pan-Turkic ideology to destabilize the Soviet Union. This was a temporary feat which ended with the defeat of Germany in the war.

The revival of pan-Turkism in the post-cold war Turkey has given rise to a debate on how genuine is Turkey's desire to cultivate, relations with the Turkic states of Central Asia? What are its credentials and what are its capabilities in shouldering the responsibility of fulfilling the needs of the newly independent republics of Central Asia? Turkey's insistence on its historical, ethno-cultural and linguistic linkages with the Turkic people of Central Asia does not carry weight as modern republics of Central Asia do not appear inclined to going back to the pre-Soviet Central Asia. They wish to embark upon a programme for economic development, political stability and security instead of getting tied down to any ethno-linguistic Union of States or Commonwealth of Turkic States under the leadership of Turkey which in fact, in matters of development is not ahead of the Central Asian republics.

In view of the shifting objectives and emphasis of pan-Turkism as a policy, philosophy or ideology, it is difficult to define it. Gareth M. Winrow, a specialist on Turkey believes that "pan-Turkism has become a pejorative term, immediately associated with expanisonism and irredentism, dream of Empire and overt racism—certainly the pan-Turkists of the 1930s were impressed by Nazi racists beliefs".[30] Basking in the warmth of international praise for the Turkish model of political and economic development, democracy and secularism, Turks appeared eager to promote pan-Turkism in Central Asia. However, the lukewarm response of the Central Asians and their total and categorical rejection of the idea of Turkism—based union of the Central Asian republics dampened Turkey's spirits. Turks were seen contradicting it. President Turgut Ozal and Prime Minister Suleyman Demirel who have been the main exponents of contemporary post-

Soviet pan-Turkism themselves stressed that "Turkey harbours no pan-Turkist ambitions in Central Asia."

J.M. Landau, a well known scholar and expert of Turkish affairs thinks that pan-Turkism as a term needs to be used with caution on account of its emotive overtones. He has referred to the need to distinguish between the two types of pan-ideologies and pan-movements—one cultural and other political.[31] Political pan-Turkism according to Landau in the nineteenth century (Gasprinsky era) and the other phases did not embrace irredentism as desire to forge cultural unity among the Turkic speaking ethnic groups of people with a sense of belonging to the Turkish nation.

However, a variant of cultural pan-Turkism pursued by the government of Suleyman Demirel in the post-Soviet Central Asia with the support of leaders of the new republics in the region succeeded in gaining momentum in the initial phase of the desovietized Central Asia. Its impact, although feeble, was noticeable in the Turkish-Central Asian interactions.

CONTEMPORARY PAN-TURKISM

The renewed interest of Turkey in the post-Soviet Trans-Caucasia and Central Asia is attributed to several factors. The Turkish scholars consider end of cold war and emergence of a new world order an encouraging scenario which inspired Turkey to revive its contacts with the Turkic republics of Central Asia. Throughout the Cold War, Turkey as a distant outpost on the European periphery and a barrier to Soviet ambitions in West Asia based its foreign policy exclusively on its relations with the West, particularly with the United States. As an active participant in the cold war, Turkey's geo-strategic 'value', was then largely limited to its role within the Atlantic Alliance and more narrowly, its place within NATO's southern flank.[32]

The end of the cold war altered the international scenario altogether. New zones of conflict which appeared on three sides of Turkey enlarged its role in the world affairs. The emergence of six independent Muslim states to its north-east opened Turkey's eyes to a vast territory inhabited by fellow Turkic speaking Muslims which presented Turkey with an unprecedented historical opportunity, at least politically, to utilize for political, economic and psychological gains.[33] The clusterphobia of years suddenly ended and the atmosphere of euphoria highlighted the common cultural, linguistic and religious bonds with the newly independent Central Asian and Caucasian republics. The pan-Turkic ideas came to the fore and more frequently mentioned both within and outside Turkey.[34]

Secondly, the resurgent pan-Turkism is also attributed to the emergence of a new and extremely welcome alternative to the western identity of Turkey forced by the Kemalist revolution and reforms on Turks. The western identity had alienated Turkey from the Muslim countries of West Asia, North Africa and South and South-East Asia. The westernization, secularization and modernization influenced their life style, thinking on national and international issues and their attitude towards the world around but it could not curb their yearning for remaining associated with the Muslim world. The sudden appearance of Central Asian Turkic republics in the immediate neighbourhood of Turkey filled the psychological and emotional vacuum which they have been feeling ever since their alienation from the community of Muslim nations in the early twenties.

The newly surfaced pan-Turkist fervour was of course taken with caution by the Turkish government which was conversant with the fate of pan-Turkist policies adopted by Turkey in the past. Hence, they categorically denied any interest in the so-called "outside Turks", especially those who have been within the Soviet Union. Gorbachev's *glasnost* and *perestroika* policies, in a way opened, the gates of Central Asia for Turkey but Ankara maintained a detached profile until the final break-up of the Soviet Union in December 1991.

The collapse of the Soviet Union and independence of Turkic republics generated a widespread euphoria in Turkey in which all sections of society persuaded the government to take immediate initiative to initiate contacts with the Turkic republics and extend all assistance in their stabilization.

Within the first year of their independence, Turkish leaders paid official visits to every Central Asian republic and the Heads of State of the Republics also visited Turkey. About 1170 official delegations from Turkey visited the region.[35] Turkey established the Turkish International Cooperation Agency (TICA) to coordinate the flow of financial assistance to the region.

Turkey's initiative was supported by the West which feared that the vacuum left by the collapse of the Soviet Union could lead to emergence of Islamic fundamentalism among the Muslim republics of Central Asia. A secular, democratic Muslim Turkey was seen as the best "role model" for the Central Asian Muslims.[36] President Demirel of Turkey maintained that he will prove how Islam, democracy, human rights and market economy go together hand in hand.[37]

Following the various visits of Central Asian leaders to Ankara they were offered $ 1.1 billion import credits and loans. Cultural co-operation protocols were exchanged. To promote economic co-operation Prime Minister Demirel spoke of the possibility of establishing a Union of Turkic States and advised them to quit the Ruble Zone.[38]

Turkey also discussed the possibility of providing military training to Central Asians, advocated building gas and oil pipelines through Turkey to market the Central Asian energy, encouraged the adoption of Latin alphabets for the Turkic languages in Central Asia and introduced several programmes for Central Asians on its television.

Thus, Turkey while denying having intentions toward reviving pan-Turkism on earlier pattern, began to promote cultural pan-Turkism with political and economic undercurrents under the state's patronage. Emboldened by the enormous praise showered by the western countries for its secular-democratic model and progress through market economy Turkey started pursuing its agenda of bringing up Central Asian republics under its influence vigorously. In its missionary zeal, Ankara overlooked the fact that the republics may be new states but they are old nations, highly modern, educated and developed under the Soviet Union and are capable of handling their economic and political affairs independently.

The "big brother" or "patron" type attitude of Turkey irked the Central Asians, and they rejected the idea of pan-Turkism based association with Turkey. However, the plans and projects introduced by Ankara and the programme undertaken for promoting economic and cultural co-operation are continuing.

Turkey's aggressive moves in the region to forge closer relations with the Central Asians were seen as hegemonic designs by its neighbours. The Turkish leaders repeatedly expressed the view that such apprehensions are baseless and Turkey has no intention of extending its hold over the region under the pretext of ethno-linguistic commonalties between Turkey and the Central Asian republics.

However, Greeks, Arabs, Iranians and Soviet Union continued to believe that Turkey is applying the "racial criterion" for increasing its presence in Central Asia. The earlier utterances of Turkish leaders of forming a belt of Turkic speaking communities from Adriatic to China were used to substantiate their apprehensions. It was also suggested that any talk of pan-Turkism may also trigger the feelings of pan-Slavism and pan-Iranianism which may lead to further disintegration of the region. President Nursultan Nazarbaev of Kazakhstan while visiting Turkey in 1991 said:

> In this part of the world pan-Turkism became a political current only as a reaction to the Soviet role and 70 years of neglect...I am against the idea of putting people into solid frames by espousing the cause of pan-Turkism or pan-Islamism. These have no chance of success..."[39]

Notwithstanding the rejection of pan-Turkism based relationship by the Central Asian republics, a sizeable group consisting of a political elite continues to insist on Turkey's economic, cultural and even political thrust in Central Asia. To them the region appears receptive and favourble for carving out a "sphere of interest" for Turkey which would bring massive economic gains and open several new opportunities for them in the region.

Turkey's ambitions in Central Asia do not match with its capabilities. When Suleyman Demirel visited the Turkic republics along with Alparslan Turkes who is well known for his pan-Turkish views, gave assurances that Turkey harbours no "pan-Turkish ambitions" but added that "there is nothing wrong in Turks declaring that Central Asia was the land of their forefathers and that their history and culture originated there. He even referred to Central Asia and Azarbaijan as a new community "Eurasia", populated by Turks. While Turkey could not administer this community of Turks, "it would lead them to the world". President Turgut Ozal was exponent of Turkey's post-Soviet Central Asia policy and he actually initiated the Turkish drive for gaining access to the region. He argued at the first Turkic Summit convened on December 30-31, 1992 that "Turkey and Turkic republics should work together to make the 21st century a Turkish century".

This zealous outburst was an outcome of some setbacks that Turkey received in its relations with the European countries. Turkey, ever since its signing of the Association Agreement with the European Community (EC)—later European Union (EU) in 1963, has been trying to get full membership in the organization of European states.

The European countries are not happy about Turkey's demand for membership in the EU on the plea that "civilizationally" it is a European country. The membership question has become an emotional issue in Turkey because inclusion or exclusion presents Turkey with the greatest problem concerning its identity.[40]

Turkey has always had something of an identity problem with regard to its position within the European states system. It does not share the Judeo-Christian cultural tradition, nor does it belong to the predominantly Arab Islamic culture. Ataturk-led revolution uprooted Turkey from the Islamic world and it could not successfully transplant it in Europe. In late forties, when the NATO was formed, similar problem had arisen as Turkey wanted to become member of the NATO. The NATO was a strategic alliance and Turkey's geo-strategic location at the southern periphery of the Soviet Union qualified it to NATO's membership. The case of EU is different.

Ankara had enthusiastically welcomed its associate-member status in the EC in September 1963 as a step in the direction of full membership at some later stage. Turhan Fevzioglu, the then state-minister and the Vice-Premier declared that:[41]

> The efforts Turkey had been making for a long time to be a European state reached a new victory by the Agreement. Turkey's desire to participate in the European Economic Community (EEC) as an associate member was not based only on short term and simple foreign trade calculations. It confirms that Turkey shares the same destiny with the

free West that European borders are drawn through Eastern and southern Turkey.

The membership in EU requires three basic conditions to be met by the aspiring state. First of all, in theory, for a country to be eligible for membership of the EU, the country must be European, be a democracy, and have a market economy. Turkey was made an associate member at a time when cold war was at its peak and Turkey's strategic importance for the security of western Europe made the Europeans ignore the issue of Turkey's "European character". Walter Hallstein, the then President of the EU, said: "Turkey is part of Europe".[42] Turkey was seen as a loyal ally and they wanted to bind Turkey closer to the west because for them it was an indispensable ally in countering the strategic threat from the east.[43]

Turkey's belief in its "Europeanness" and inclusion in European Union was emboldened by the attitude of western statements and declarations. Vahit Halefoglu, then Foreign Minister of Turkey while putting in the application for Turkey's full membership in the EU in April 1987 said that "it was a natural result of our foreign policy goal to integrate Turkey with western civilization since the establishment of the Republic".[44]

Notwithstanding the adverse effects of the association on Turkey's economy and the multiplying difficulties with implementing the terms of agreement, Turkey continued to abide by the commitments undertaken. The Justic Party government signed an additional Protocol on 23 November 1970 to make Turkey European not only politically but also economically. Suleyman Demirel the then Prime Minister observed:

> For many years, Turkey had implemented a closed and introverted economic policy. Turkey can not afford to continue with such an economic policy any longer ... it is

compulsory to change the identity of the economy and open it up to the rest of the world.[45]

The dilemma of Turkish politics has always unfolded in the outbursts of the various political parties and intellectual elite groups whenever debate over Turkey's "Europeaness" commenced. Several opposite views, to the extent of violent reactions came forth when Turkey made an application for full membership of the EU, the leftist and Islamist parties came out with vehement criticism of such moves.

Turgut Ozal, leader of the Motherland Party, turned out to be an influential Prime Minister in early eighties and a highly imaginative, forward looking ambitious President in the late eighties and early nineties. Ozal's economic reforms made Turkey a developed and prosperous country and qualified it to demand full membership in the EU.[46]

However, the EU was still evasive on full membership issue. Several new conditions were put forth which included solution of conflict with Greece over Cyprus dispute over the use of continental shelf of the Aegean Sea islands; responsibility for the Armenian 'Genocide' committed in late 19th century and the early twenties; solution to Kurdish problem and improvement in the Human Rights record of Turkey. This hardened attitude of the members of the European Union disillusioned Turkey with the West. The political elite and the people of Turkey started thinking afresh about their "Europeaness" and regretted the steps taken for seeking membership in the EU. Prof. Korkut Boratav argued the impossibility of full membership in the EU:"Turkey's approach to Europe is not healthy and often carries schizophrenic and paranoid characteristics. The EU's rejection will contribute to the development of fascist and fundamentalist ideologies in Turkey. Therefore, it would have been better if Turkey had never made this application in the first place.[47]

This is especially true for Turkey because Turkey's European identity was created within the country without acceptance by others. This self image is dependent on the possibility of being supported by the other states. The identity crisis manifested itself most clearly in the split between secularist, westernized Kemalists and the Islamists. The disillusionment with the EU's attitude brought Islam back into politics and occupied a central place in the ideology and programme of the mainstream conservative parties in Turkey.

The end of cold war and the EU's constant rejection of Turkey's full membership on the one hand and the increasing power of nationalists and Islamists on the other put an end to the westernized Kemalist elite's monopoly on political power as became clear in the electoral victory of the Islamist Welfare Party in 1995 and the Nationalist Action Party in 1999. Turkey's failure in getting membership of the EU generated a debate on the validity of Kemalist modernization project and the identity envisioned by it. The EU's rejection on the cultural basis was also considered as failure of the Kemalist reforms.

However, the emergence of five Turkic-Muslim republics in Central Asia and the Caucasus came as a Godsend to the Turks and they were saved from falling into the rut of Islamic fundamentalism. The Turkic identity of Central Asia aroused nostalgic memories of early linkages of the Turks with Central Asia and led them to rediscover their Turkic identity, which was lost in the 'illusion' of "Europeanization". Thus, the pan-Turkism based moves of Turkey in the early years of Central Asia's independence from the former Soviet Union were motivated by Turkey's urge to reassert its Turkic identity by searching roots in Central Asia. The development in post-Soviet Central Asia and Trans-Caucasia were seen as a great opportunity for Turkey which was to give a great boost to its status in the western world as well as in the region. Owing to its own Turkic ethnicity and origin in Central Asia Turkey could envision an ambitious role for itself in the region.

At all stages of its occurrence and recurrence, the manifestation of pan-Turkism in Turkey was caused by external factors. Gasprinsky sought linguistic-cultural unity of all Turkic people within the Czarist Russia and thought of linking the Turkic people outside Russia also emotionally with the Russian Turkic inhabitants. Zia Gokalp, using ethno-linguistic and cultural identity with the Turkic people of Central Asia, rather with the people from Adriatic to the Far-East thought of forging a "Greater Turan" under the Ottoman flag. Pan-Turkist waves during the First and the Second World War caused at Germany's instigation were dangerous and remained ineffective and short-lived.

The contemporary wave of pan-Turkism which swept over Turkey in the immediate post-Cold War years, was primarily caused by Turkey's disillusionment with the EU and the hard conditions imposed by it for Turkey's full membership in the European Union. The contemporary pan-Turkism has proved irrelevant to today's Central Asia. It has been categorically rejected by the independent Central Asian-Caucasian republics as a basis of relations with Turkey. However, one positive outcome of the recent pan-Turkism can be seen in Turkey's growing interest in Central Asia which ultimately may lead to correcting Turkey's foreign policy imbalance. Its excessive slant in favour of the West although it brought some benefits to Turkey, took Turkey too far away from Asia—the region it actually belongs to.

Notes

1. Dilip Hiro, *Between Marx and Muhammad: The Changing Face of Central Asia*, (Harper Collins Publishers, 1994), p. 3.
2. *Ibid.*, p. 4.
3. *Ibid.*, p. 4.
4. *Ibid.*, p. 5.
5. *Ibid.*, pp. 7-8.

6. John Glenn, *The Soviet Legacy in Central Asia* (Macmillan Press Ltd., London, 1989), pp. 66-67.
7. Sergei Zenkovsky, *Pan-Turkism and Islam in Russia*. (Massachusetts: Harvard University Press, 1960), quoted in John Glenn, *op.cit.*, p.66.
8. The word "Turk" was regarded in the Ottoman Empire as almost a term of abuse. It was used to depict an uncouth peasant figure in contrast to the sophisticated Ottoman gentleman. But influenced by the new European science of Turcology and ironically, by writings of pan Turkist thinkers in the early twentieth century referring to the "Turks" and "Turkism", Ataturk fashioned a new Turkish nation within a greatly reduced territory following the collapse of the Ottoman Empire. Gareth M. Winrow, "Turkey and the Former Soviet Central Asia: National and Ethnic Identity", *Central Asian Survey*, Vol. II, No. 3 (1992), p. 108.
9. Gennady Chufrin, *Russia and Asia: The Emerging Security Agenda* (Sipri, Oxford University Press, 1999), p. 172.
10. *Ibid.*, p. 173.
11. *Spotlight on Regional Affairs*, Vol. XIX, No. 4, (April 2000), p. 5.
12. *Ibid.*, Also Dilip Hiro, *op.cit.*, p. 18.
13. Bulent Gokay, "Turkish Settlement and the Caucasus, 1919-1920", in Sylvia Kedourie (ed.), *Turkey: Identity, Democracy, Politics* (Frank Cass, London, 1998), p. 45.
14. E. Parkes (Comp.), *British and Foreign State Papers* (London, 1921), CXI (1917-1918), pp. 611-12.
15. Sylvia Kedourie, *op.cit.*, p.46. See also H.R. Rudin, *Armistice 1918* (New Haven, 1944), p. 294.
16. Bulent Gokay, *op.cit.*, p. 45 and p. 53.
17. Sylvia Kedourie, *op.cit.*, p. 53.
18. *Ibid.*, p. 54.
19. *Ibid.*, p. 58.
20. *Ibid.*
21. *Ibid.*, p. 61.
22. *Ibid.*, p. 62.
23. For the text of the Treaty of Severs, see: H.W.V. Temperley (ed.), *History of the Peace Conference of Paris* (London, Henry Frowde and Hodder and Stoughton, 1924), Vol. VI, pp. 70-74 (A Royal Institute of International Affairs Publication). For Ataturk's negotiation—a *quid pro quo* see Sylvia Kedourie, *op.cit.*, p. 65.

24. *Ibid.*, p. 68.
25. Ataturk's speech on 1 December 1921, *Selected Speeches and Presentations*, (Progress Publications, Moscow, 1966), p. 187.
26. Gennady Chufrin, *op.cit.*, p. 173.
27. Landau, J.M., *Radical Politics in Modern Turkey* (C.J. Brill, Leiden, 1974), p. 193.
28. Novichev, A.D., *Turtsiya: Kratkaya Istoriya* (Turkey: A Short History), (Nauka, Moscow, 1965), p. 192.
29. Miller, A.F., *Ocherki Noveyshey Istorii Turtsii* (Essays on Modern History of Turkey), (Academy of Sciences publishing House, Moscow and Leningrad, 1948), p. 206.
30. Gareth M. Winrow, *op.cit.*, p. 108.
31. Jacob M. Landau, "The Fortunes and Misfortunes of Pan-Turkism", *Central Asian Survey*, Vol. VII, (1988), No.1, p. 2.
32. Mustafa Aydin, "Turkey and Central Asia: Challenges of Change", *Central Asian Survey* (1996), p.158; also see, Sukru S. Gurel,"Turkish Foreign Policy in a Changing World" in *Turkey In a Changing World*, Tokyo Institute of Developing Economies, 1993, p. 3.
33. The Turkish President Turgut Ozal, in his opening speech at the Grand National Assembly (TGNA) on September 1, 1991,described the situation created by the end of the cold war and the breaking up of the former Soviet Union as an "historic opportunity" for the Turks to become a "regional power" and urged the TNGA not to "throw away this change which presented itself for the first time in 400 years". See *Minutes of the TNGA*, Vol. 1, No. 3, p. 25.
34. Mustafa Aydin, *op.cit.*, p. 158.
35. Mushahid Hussain, "Iran and Turkey in Central Asia: Complementary or Competing Roles", *Middle East International*, 19 February 1993, p. 14.
36. *The Time*, 17 February 1992.
37. Newspot, 21 My 1992, p. 7.
38. *Turkish Daily News*, 30 April 1992; Also *Newspot*, 21May 1992, p.2.
39. *Cumburiyet*, 16 December 1991.
40. Meltem Muftuler-Bac, *Turkey's Relations with a Changing Europe*, (Manchester and New York, Manchester University Press, 1997), p. 11.
41. Yucel Bozdaglioglu, *op.cit.*, p. 68.
42. Muftuler-Bac, *op.cit.*, p. 5.

43. Heinz Kramer, "Turkey and the European Union, A Multi-Dimensional Relationship with Hazy Perspective" in *Turkey Between East and West*, ed. Vojtoch Mastny and R. Craig Nation (Boulder: West View Press, 1966), p. 204.
44. Esra Ceyhan, *Dunden Bugune Turkiye—Aurupa Birligi: Iliskileri ve Siyasi Partilerin konuya Bakisi* (Istanbul, Boyut Kitaplari, 1997), p. 294.
45. Suleyman Demirel quoted in Selim Ilkin, "A History of Turkey's association with the European Community", in *Turkey and European Community*, ed. Ahmet Evin and Geoffrey Denton (Opladen: Leske and Buldrich, 1990), p. 35.
46. See Ozal's profile in Erik Cornell, *Turkey in the 21st Century: Opportunities, Challenges, Threats* (Curzon Press, Richmond Surrey, 2001), pp. 61-69.
47. *Cumhuriyet*, January 8, 1998.

CHAPTER 3

Turkey's Interest in the Caspian Sea Region: Relations with Azerbaijan, Turkmenistan and Kazakhstan

Turkey has been among the few states that have shown a great interest in the Turkic republics of the former Soviet Union after their emergence as independent political entities. The collapse of the Soviet Union and advent of new republics on the north-eastern frontier of Turkey opened a floodgate of abundant opportunities to Turkey. Owing to its historical, ethno-linguistic and cultural linkages with the Central Asian republics, Ankara envisioned an absolutely new role in the region. It tried to encash the ethnic and linguistic commonalties by bringing the new republics into some kind of loose Commonwealth of Turkic States under its patronage. However, in course of time it became apparent that fulfilment of these ambitions involved a complex pattern of relations rather than simply undertaking efforts to expand influences and register presence afresh therein.

Turkey was seeking a sphere of influence abroad for the first time in its republican history. As stated earlier the liberation of Central Asian republics from the Soviet rule generated a widespread euphoria in Turkey. For more than seven decades Turkey's entry into that region was totally forbidden. It had lost all contacts with the people of Turkic origin inhabiting the territories to its north-east. The people, political parties of all shades and ideologies, intellectuals, political analysts, Islamists, liberal and leftists—all persuaded the government to initiate communication with the Central Asian republics and extend all possible assistance to them in getting stabilized as the new states. The then government of Suleyman Demirel in Turkey enthusiastically prepared agenda for economic and cultural cooperation with the new republics, although Turkey was cautious in its moves as it did not want to provoke Russia and Iran against its initiatives in the region.

Turkey's over-enthusiastic attitude towards Central Asia was caused by other factors too, related to the new developments in international politics. With the end of cold war and ideological bi-polarization of the world, the military pacts and alliances of the post-World War II period were rendered irrelevant. This made Turkey feel insecure as its importance for the west was now on decline. Owing to its geo-strategic location connecting three continents, controlling important waterways—the Turkish straits, Dardanelles and Bosphorus, entrance to the Mediterranean Sea and access to the oil rich regions of West Asia, it was given a central position in the southern flank of the NATO. As a security bulwark to Europe, Turkey was hopeful of getting full membership in the European Union and thus recognition of its European identity but the collapse of the Soviet Union frustrated all its dreams.

The emergence of Central Asian Trans-Caucasian republics on its North-East, inhabited by fellow Muslim—Turkic speaking people offered a unique opportunity to Turkey. Ankara perceived this development as a source of potential opportunity as well as challenge. It projected itself as a secular-democratic model for the new republics in their struggle to free themselves from the Soviet legacy and integrate with the international world order. The new republics opened new vistas for Turkey to carve out a sphere of influence and secure access to Central Asia's energy resources. The ethno-linguistic and cultural affinity with the Central Asian republics appeared as a great asset, which would bring good dividends in the long run. Turkey wanted to use these new possibilities for making its importance felt by the west especially by the Untied States which wanted to safeguard the Central Asian republics against any possible reversal of the situation. Turkey's leaders, Prime Minister Syleyman Demirel and President, Turgut Ozal were already marketing Turkey's ethno-linguistic homogeneity with the Central Asian republics as a basis of its future relations with the region. Some 'kind' of 'pan-Turkic' fervour was also witnessed in their statements. As explained in the preceding chapter the west was too eager to buy this thesis and offered to promote Turkey in Central Asia as a shield against fundamentalist encroachments from Pakistan-Afghanistan, Iran and Saudi Arabia and as a best suitable model of political governance and development for the new republics of Central Asia.

Turkey's drive for influence in Central Asia on pan-Turkic lines generated adverse reactions not only in Iran and Russia but several western nations also saw "racism" on the Nazi pattern of Hitler's Germany in it. It was expected that with the dissolution of Russia, the 'power vacuum' created in the offing will generate regional competition for power and influence in Central Asia. Turkey by harping on its ethnic ancestral ties was seen as trying to fill the vacuum in Central Asia. Bulent Aras, a well-known Turkish scholar has come out openly in defence of Turkey's overtures in Central Asia in the period following the collapse of the Soviet Union. He argued that:

> This idea of "filling the vacuum" in the Caucasus and Central Asia was not generated in Ankara's 'think tanks'. It was the result of a handful of articles and papers penned by well-known American specialists (such as those at the

> Rand Corp. and Heritage Foundation) which were quickly picked up and reproduced by influential press organs (*New York Times, Washington Post,* etc.). This new strategy—which had a multitude of objectives, such as rewarding Turkey, acknowledging the role of history and language and thwarting a 'mythical' Islamic threat to the region—was embraced in Europe, the United States and, of course, Turkey itself. Official Ankara grabbed onto it and ran as fast and as far as it could, hoping and expecting that the rhetoric was going to turn into cold cash, not to mention long-term influence.[1]

However, Turkey could liberate its foreign policy especially towards Central Asia from emotional euphoria and nostalgic memories of their early linkages with the region within a short span of time. The rebuff given by the Central Asian leaders to pan-Turkism based statements and official moves of Ankara made Turkey to learn that new republics are new states but old nations and having lived under a strong, highly disciplined and technologically advanced Soviet state, they are capable of handling their affairs independently, and not prepared to accept any body's patronage. This realization steered Turkey's Central Asia policy on a more pragmatic course. Ankara has tried to strike a workable understanding with Iran and Russia—the two rivals in Turkey's drive in Central Asia. Today Ankara is importing natural gas from Iran and Russia and at the same time trying to workout a pipeline from Turkmenistan to Turkey to take its natural gas to European markets. In the Azeri oil affairs too, Ankara has earned an influential position, notwithstanding Tehran and Moscow competing for the same.

Central Asia as region is 'blessed' with certain complexities which are unique in several respects. It is inhabited by diverse nationalities divided in several states which make them ethnic minorities nourishing a perpetual desire to get united with their kith and kin. There are Turkic and non-Turkic states. The Turkic States—Azerbaijan, Kazakhstan are rich in oil resources and Turkmenistan has abundant reserves of natural gas. All the three are situated in the Caspian Sea Basin region and share it with other two—non-Central Asian—non-Turkic States—Iran and Russia.

The three Turkic-Caspian Sea states have been a part of the former Soviet Union. Moscow has been the sole exporter of the Azeri and Kazakh oil and Turkmen gas to the world outside the region. Hence, all pipelines traverse via Russian territory. The Caspian oil and gas producers, despite their political independence, still depend on Moscow for the export of their natural resources.

The regional contenders (Turkey and Iran) for power and influence in the Caucasia-Central Asia want to acquire substantial control over the production and export of oil and gas from the region. For this, construction of new pipelines passing through their territories is essential. Iran has well developed and well maintained pipelines to carry Turkmen gas and Azeri oil to international markets but owing to American intransigence they are unable to use the Iranian facility. The other route passes through Russia. Prior to the operationalization of Baku-Tiblisi-Ceyhan (BTC) oil pipeline in 2005, Russian pipelines have been the only way to export Azeri and Kazakh oil to Europe.

TURKEY'S INTERESTS

Geopolitically Turkey is placed in an envious position. In Trans-Cancasia it has access to Armenia and Georgia and has close ethnic and linguistic ties with Azerbaijan which is a rich oil producing state of the region. Turkey's interest in the region emanates firstly, from its early ancestral linkages with the Turkic people of Caucasia-Central Asia and secondly, from its growing requirement of oil and natural gas. During the past three decades, Turkey has made tremendous progress economically and its energy needs have increased with the growing affluence and development.[2] The availability of oil and gas in its immediate neighbourhood has made it actively involved in the affairs of the region.

Turkey's major interest is in the southern Caucasia—in particular Azerbaijan. It is a crossroads among land masses; Trans-Caucasia offers Turkey access to Central Asian republics. Serving as a bridgehead to the east is Azerbaijan, important to Turkey due to its large oil reserves and its 7.5 million population of Azeri Turks, the closest relatives to the Anatolian Turks of all the Turkic peoples of the former Soviet Union.[3]

In the early years of their independence Turkey took active interest in the politics of Azerbaijan and supported the pan-Turkic candidate Abulfez Elchibey for the post of President in the elections. In its dispute with Armenia over Nagorno-Karabakh, Turkey supports Azerbaijan's point of view and wants to get the dispute settled in favour of Azerbaijan. Ankara is keenly watching the process of identity determination (lake or sea) of the Caspian Sea to safeguard its own interests in the resources of the Caspian basin.

Turkey's quest for new markets has also attracted it towards Central Asia. During the cold war period, Turkey could draw tremendous benefits out of its alliance with the Untied States and close relations with the countries of Western Europe. As a country threatened by the Soviet Union it was given aid under the Truman Doctrine (1947) and Marshall plan (1947). Later after joining the NATO (1952) Turkey could develop its economy along with development of its war machinery. In the post cold war world it is seeking opportunities to capitalize on the establishment of ties with the republics of the former Soviet Union. These opportunities include guaranteed access to vital energy resources, lucrative oil transport revenues and new potential markets for Turkish goods as well as increased diplomatic clout and strategic importance. The benefits are mutual. For the new republics Turkey offers them the prospect of attractive investment and technological expertise, as well as establishing a secure route for the distribution of their products to the West. Thus, among the newly independent states, Azerbaijan, Turkmenistan and Kazakhstan—the Turkic speaking former Soviet republics of the Caspian region—have attracted the greatest interest on the part of Turkey.[4]

Turkey's interest is no less in countering the fundamentalist forces operating in the Central Asian region. Turkey's secular profile was projected as an ideal model for the new republics by the West. At the outset of their independence from the former Soviet Union, the western media predicted that Central Asian republics being Muslim would be vulnerable to the maneuverings of the fundamentalist forces in the region. Here, the Islamic threat was to be 'mainly from Iran' (and not from the Taliban and *Al Qaida* forces active in Central Asia's immediate neighbourhood). The West encouraged a number of Islamic countries notably Turkey, Pakistan, Egypt and Saudi Arabia to establish relations with the Central Asian republics and support them in countering the "Islamic impact of Iran". On its part Turkey had no objection to playing this role as it was in conformity with the national ideology of the country. However, Turkey's proxy role behind the anti-fundamentalist activities, had an adverse effect on Turkey-Iran relations in Central Asia.

Turkey is constrained to endorse the exaggerated version of Iran's Islamic thrust in Central Asia. Ankara knows it fully well that Islamic drive of Iran has hardly been able to make any impact on the people of Central Asia except Tajikistan which even otherwise belongs to the Persian stock and Tajiks speak Persian language. Instead of engaging Iran in this meaningless confrontation, Turkey is seeking areas of co-operation and mutual benefit with Iran, notwithstanding the rivalry between the two for control over the natural resources in Trans-Caucasia.

Turkey's US designed foreign policy in Central Asia has influenced its domestic politics in a different way. Initially, the policy makers concentrated on constructing the Turkic identity and in order to thwart fundamentalist onslaughts on Central Asian states, Turkey tried to appear a 'better Muslim state committed to non-fundamentalist, non-radical Islam'. The domestic policy also had to take note of this role of Turkey and shape itself accordingly. Turkey sent several thousand copies of *Quran* to Central Asia and introduced religious programmes through means of mass communication. This policy-shift on the one hand facilitated better understanding with the people of Trans-Caucasia-Central Asia, on the other, this Islamic image of Turkey distanced the Europeans from Ankara. Europeanization of the country and seeking membership of the EU has been and is the foremost objective of Turkey's foreign policy which is partially marred by its role as an adherent of Islam in Central Asia.

Turkey is trying to correct the imbalance caused by excessive tilt towards the US and support to the US' interest in the Central Asian region by engaging Russia and Iran economically. The realization, which has come after the experience of having dealt with the Central Asian States, that neither Turkey nor Iran can occupy the place which was and is occupied by Russia in the Central Asian region. Hence, their rivalry for exclusive control over the natural resources of the region and policies of the countries inhabiting the region is meaningless. Iran and Russia too, owing to Turkey's continuous dependence on the United States and its unfailing loyalty to Washington, see Ankara as a 'Westoxicated' regime subservient to the interests of the United States in the region.

It is well known to Iran that 'Turkish-Iranian competition' for power and influence is prompted by America. It has been made a vanguard against the spread of Islamic fundamentalism (only the Iranian brand) among the Central Asian-South-Caucasian States.

A proper assessment of Turkey's Central Asia policy, its fall out for the region and its success in achieving the desired objectives especially in the field of oil and natural gas, construction of export-lines via Turkey, enlargement of trade in Central Asia and forging a proper understanding with the Trans-Caucasian States, Azerbaijan, Armenia and Georgia need to be analysed at length. In the post-cold war period Turkey has forged closer ties with Israel and is trying to develop workably good relations with Greece as both the countries have developed substantial stakes in Central Asia and both are close to the United States as well.

POLICY TOWARD THE CASPIAN-CAUCASIAN STATES

Azerbaijan, Turkmenistan and Kazakhstan—the three Turkic speaking former Soviet states of the Caspian region have generated great interest in Turkey. The reason for its interest is not only linguistic, ethnic, religious and cultural affinity shared by Turkey and these States but also the tremendous oil and gas reserves possessed by the Caspian States. According to some estimates Turkey will be importing about 22 million tons of oil annually by the year 2010.[5] Ankara views oil resources of the Caspian Sea States as a source of peace and stability in the region as the European community had seen coal as a source of peace and stability in post-Second World War Europe. Harmonised oil policies may be helpful in preventing local disputes among the ethnically and religiously diverse states that are inhabiting the South Caucasus and Central Asia.[6]

Ever since the States of Central Asia—Trans-Caucasia attained independence and planned to utilize the natural resources of the region in their own interest, several controversies and conflicting claims over the resources and export lines have been put forth by interested parties. The export of oil and natural gas from Caucasian-Caspian states is held back due to these tangling controversies.

THE CASPIAN SEA CONTROVERSY

The determination of legal status (lake or sea) of the Caspian Sea is one of the most important of the major controversies. Besides the three Caspian-Sea Central Asian states, the other states involved in the controversy are Iran and Russia. Prior to the dissolution of the Soviet Union except Iran, all other states as part of the Soviet Union were sharing the resources of the Caspian Sea basin as an integrated single unit. Thus, Caspian Sea was shared only by Iran and Russia. With the emergence of new states in south-Caucasia and Central Asia legally more than two states are claiming their legitimate share in the Caspian Sea. The legitimate share could be determined only after the legal status of the Caspian Sea is decided and all concerned parties arrive at a mutually agreed upon solution of the problem.

Before the collapse of the Soviet Union the Caspian Sea was under the joint ownership of the two regional powers—Russia and Iran—based on two separate treaties of 1921 and 1940. The division of the sea between the two was mainly for defining the fishing rights rather than oil, and for preserving the cavier-producing sturgeon found in these waters.

In the post-Soviet period new states bordering the Caspian Sea are laying claim to the large oil deposits that lie under its waters. The Caspian is a relatively shallow water body and is the size of Japan. Caspian, in fact, is probably the world's largest landlocked body of water which is hiding about 200 billion barrels of oil (estimates are on a much higher side).[7] The more realistic estimates place it at about 27.5 billion barrels of proven reserves with an estimated 50-60 billion barrels of estimated reserves.[8] Even this figure is not final.

If the Caspian is to be given the status of a sea, it would be divided into territorial zones with each country bordering it being allowed control over their own portions. This would allow the three Central Asian-Caspian states a major share in the Caspian Sea's hydrocarbons and right to develop their own portions of the sea-bed.

If the Caspian is to be given the status of a lake, as Iran and Russia have been maintaining so far, it would be a common property of all the five littoral states which means that any exploitation of its waters as well as navigation rights would have to be subject to agreement by all the five. The objection to laying of sub-sea pipeline, however, is based on ecological reasons rather than on any political reasons. Now, the three Caspian states want it to be declared 'Sea' which would give them bigger share. Iran and Russia want it to be a lake in which all the five can have equal share. Turkey is closely watching the developments as its major interest lies in what the three Central Asian states get as a share in Caspian basin's oil wealth. These controversies are by no means limited in their implications to Turkey and the Caspian states alone. Several other players in the oil arena stand to benefit or lose from the successful exploitation of the 'Caspian Sea resources'.

TURKEY—AZERBAIJAN OIL PIPELINES AND THE KARABAKH DISPUTE

Owing to its small size and comparatively low level of economic development Azerbaijan appears more concerned about the outcome of the Caspian Sea controversy. Its prolonged dispute over Nagorno-Karabakh with Armenia has taxed its economy a great deal. The Azerbaijani Government asserts that development of the Caspian shelf deposits will provide a boost to its economy and enable it to alleviate the suffering caused by the ongoing conflict which began in the early 1990s with the neighbouring Armenia over the Nagorno-Karabakh region. Azerbaijan hopes that the ownership of massive energy deposits will bring it into a position of greater strategic significance and improve its weak diplomatic bargaining power vis-à-vis energy hungry states around the globe including the United States and members of the European Union. The ideal outcome from the perspective of Azerbaijan would surely be to induce these countries to pressurize Armenia into settling the Nagorno-Karabakh dispute in a manner favourable to both—end occupation by Armenia of some 20 percent of its territory.[9]

Azerbaijan, with its burgeoning confidence in the country's future as a major oil producer has vigorously set about trying to realize the country's oil ambitions. As a first move, it began negotiations in the very first year of its independence with a group of foreign oil companies through the State Oil Company of the Azerbaijan Republic (SOCAR) which led to signing a deal on 4 June 1994 that has been widely acclaimed as the "Contract of the Century", worth around $ 8 billion.[10] It is officially named as "Agreement on the Joint Development and Production Sharing for the Azeri and Chirag Fields and the Deep Water Portion of the Guneshli Field in the Azerbaijan Sector of the Caspian sea". The contract called for the establishment of a business entity known as the Azerbaijan International Operating Company (AIOC) whose purpose is to exploit some of the richest oil reserves over which Azerbaijan claims sovereignty.[11]

The shares of the AIOC consortium are currently divided between the SOCAR and the foreign companies. Originally the SOCAR had a 20 percent share which was to give it a majority interest, but Azerbaijan subsequently transferred 5 percent share to Turkish Petroleum, Turkey's state oil company. Turkey also has 9 percent stake in the consortium developing the Shah Deniz field.

NAGORNO-KARABAKH CONFLICT AND TURKEY

Turkey wants to have a major share in Azeri petroleum but its hopes were dashed by the AIOC's refusal to a Turkish proposal made in February 1996 to finance the Baku-Batumi pipeline project with very advantageous conditions because it had to be under Turkish control.[12]

Nagorno means 'mountainous' in Russian and Karabakh is a territory in Azerbaijan populated predominantly by the Armenians. The origin of the Nagorno-Karabakh conflict dates back to the era of Sovietization of Central Asia in early twenties. Soviet Union, in 1923 placed Nagorno-Karabakh autonomous *Oblast* although largely populated by the Armenians, within Azerbaijan partly in an effort to maintain good relations with Ataturk's Turkey. This separated the Karabakh Armenians from Armenia and made them dependent on Moscow for protection, in case *Oblast's* autonomy was infringed. Azerbaijan also relied on the Moscow's support to ensure that the Armenians in Karabakh remain passive.

Tension between Armenians and Azeris broke out in Karabakh and rapidly spread to Armenia and Azerbaijan where nationalists began to challenge the pro-Soviet leadership in both the republics. To curb the uprisings, Moscow took over Baku in January 1990 and a state of emergency was declared in the Karabakh capital, Stepanakert. In August, the Armenian Supreme Soviet declared its intention to annex Karabakh. It led to a full-scale war between the two States. Azerbaijan imposed energy and transport blockade against Karabakh and the Armenian capital, Yerevan. After a prolonged war, cease-fire agreement was signed on 12 May 1994 to be followed by a negotiated settlement.[13]

A number of outside forces such as the Conference on Security and Co-operation in Europe (CSCE), United States, Russia, Iran, Turkey are involved in this conflict for various reasons of their own. The CSCE wants Karabakh to be fully autonomous within Azerbaijan, refugees to be allowed to return back and "autonomy" and peace in Karabakh to be guaranteed by outside powers. Russia apprehending escalation of such conflicts in the entire Caucasia which is inhabited by multiple ethnic units in each state prefers a solution to the problem almost on the CSCE lines. Iran, which shares a common border with the belligerants sent military units to form a buffer zone for restraining entry of refugees in its territory. Tehran, however, remained restrained all through the five year long conflict. United States, which is greatly interested in the Azeri oil, has a soft corner for the Armenians as well which have a powerful lobby in America. The United States' role was dubious. It did not allow support to reach the Armenian side, and did not strongly discourage those who sought to help the Azeris keeping in view Turkey's sensitivity and expectations.

The Armenian lobby in the United States wields some influence in American Congress. It succeeded in forcing the Congress to reject proposals to repeal section 907 restrictions on US assistance to Azerbaijan, commenced according to the Freedom Support Act of 1992. It also forced on to the agenda legislation condemning Turkey for its massacre of Armenians in 1915—a resolution which was only dropped under the most intense pressure from the White House, the State Department and the Pentagon in 2000. The resolution caused outrage in Turkey and its relations with the US remained deteriorated for quite sometime. Recently once again a Bill introduced in the US House of Representatives wants to recognise Turkish atrocities against its Armenian populating in the early twentieth century as genocide. Turkey is outraged at the US meddling in its internal affairs. It might disturb the currently prevailing peaceful relationship between Turkey, Armenia and Azerbaijan. All the players in the Caspian region realize that peace in Karabakh is a pre-requisite for development of the "Eurasian Energy Corridor". A new war between Azerbaijan and Armenia would certainly call for greater attention from the US government particularly if the Baku-Tiblist-Ceyhan oil pipeline has to be made safely operative. Although not passing through Karabakh the route runs close to its border, putting it at risk of sabotage in the event of conflict.

Turkey's interest in the Azeri oil prompts it to acquire access to the domestic policies of Azerbaijan and wield some kind of pressure on the political elite of this Caucasian country which shares ethnic affinity with Turkey. The foreign policy of Turkey, especially in Central Asia concentrates on finding ways to facilitate a negotiated settlement of the Karabakh problem because Turkey's own interests are at stake on account of this dispute between Armenia and Azerbaijan. Turkey has no love for Armenians but owing to the influence of the Armenian lobby on the American administration, Ankara is mindful of Armenia's reactions and responses. Even the European Union is concerned about the interests of the Armenians.

Recently, the EU has asked Turkey to own responsibility for the massacre of the Armenians in 1915 during the First World War and demanded its apology to the Armenians as a precondition to Ankara's membership in the European Union.

TURKMEN GAS AND TURKEY

Bringing Turkmen gas to Turkey has been one of the most important objectives of its Central Asia policy. Ankara is importing gas from Russia and Iran. It wants to diversify its sources in order to attain energy security. The desperate need for gas in newly industrialized central and eastern Anatolian region is another motivation for increasing the gas imports.

Turkmenistan is equally eager to take its natural gas to the European markets via Turkey by laying a Turkmenistan-Turkey-Europe gas pipeline via Iran. The US administration also seems amenable to this project. The pipeline plan was coordinated by the inter-state council involving Turkmenistan, Iran, Russia, Turkey and Kazakhstan in 1994. At the same time international companies, including the Turkish BOTAS had prepared blueprints for several routes for the pipeline to Turkey including along the bottom of the sea and *via* territories of the former Soviet republics. But the Deputy Minister for Turkmen Oil and Gas Industry, Gochmurad Nadzhanov said that "we will be loyal to the understanding reached and back the Iranian version". The capacity of Turkmen-Iran pipelines will amount to 28 billion cubic meters of gas a year, out of which 15 billion cubic meters will belong to Turkey and 13 billion to the European countries.[14]

A joint Turkish-Turkmen group—consisting of the representatives of BOTAS and Turkmen Oil and Gas Ministry was formed in February 1996 to evaluate options to reach a decision. According to MOU signed between the two countries on 14 February, "Turkey will purchase 2 billion cubic meters of natural gas in 1998, 5 billion cubic meters between 1999-2004, 10 billion cubic meters between 2005-2009 and 15 billion between 2010-2020.[15]

In December 1996, the Iranian, Turkish and Turkmen oil ministers met in Tehran to discuss the ways of exporting Iranian and Turkmen gas to Turkey. The Ministers agreed to meet Turkey's gas requirements and transfer of Iranian and Turkmen gas to Europe through Turkey. A letter of understanding was officially signed at this meeting.[16]

Hashemi-Rafsanjani, the then Iranian President on 26 December 1996 stated that national interests dictate that Iran,

Turkey and Turkmenistan co-operate in practice so the gas transfer project can be implemented as rapidly as possible. Recai Kutun, reiterated Ankara's determination to co-operate towards the construction of pipeline carrying Turkmen and Iranian gas to International markets *via* Turkish soil. He emphatically told that Turkey will carry out such projects decisively in tune with its own national interests regardless of foreign pressure. Turkmenistan also reiterated its commitment to co-operate in the construction of pipeline and export of gas *via* Turkey to Europe.[17] On 14 May 1997, Niyazov, Rafsanjani and Suleyman Demirel, the leaders of Turkemenistan, Iran and Turkey signed a memorandum in Ashgabat on issues concerning construction of a gas pipeline—from Turkmenistan to Europe.[18]

At a meeting between Turkmen President Niyazov and the Turkish Prime Minister Mesut Yilmaz held at Ashgabat in December 1997, the decision to build the pipeline from Turkmenistan to Turkey was confirmed and it was decided that the memorandum on mutual understanding (MOU) to build a Turkmenistan-Turkey-Europe gas pipeline which was signed by the Energy Ministers of the two countries should be legalized. In this document two routes were suggested to pump Turkmen gas to the markets of Turkey and Europe.

Yilmaz suggested that a possibility should be studied to pump gas from Turkmenistan both on the bottom of the Caspian and then across Azerbaijan and Georgia as well as across the territory of Iran. Niyazov, agreed in principle to various versions of export pipelines and insisted on recording necessary conditions in the memorandum in order to start work on the Trans-Caspian route.[19]

The French Sofregaz Company also presented a study on proposed gas pipeline from Turkmenistan to Europe in January 1998. It suggested two possible routes and several options for gas transportation. The starting point is the Turkmen gas deposit of Shatlyk. The route will go from east to west of Turkmenistan and then continue in parallel with the operating Turkmen-Iranian-Korpeje-Kord-Kuy gas pipeline which was commissioned in December 1997. There are two options for the route in Iran—either along the Caspian coast or to the south of Tehran. Iran prefers the latter. If the route goes to the south of Tehran the construction of pipeline will cost $ 3.1 billion, if the gas is to be delivered to Turkey at Dogubayazit, and if the predicted volume of 15 billion cubic meters is recovered. If the route is extended to Erzurum, the construction cost will be $ 3.6 billion, and if extended to Ankara $ 4.8 billion.[20] Regarding the Turkish-Turkmen natural gas project Ashgabat wants to transit between 16 and 28 billion cubic meters of gas annually to Turkey and thence to Europe. For this, the Turkish-Turkmen natural gas purchase agreement has been signed in Ashghbat by the Turkmen State Minister Saparmurat, Turkmenbashi and Ziya Aktas, Turkish Energy Minister in May 1999.[21]

Turkey has succeeded in striking proper understanding with Azerbaijan and Turkmenistan on oil and gas exports via Turkey. However, for both the projects, the most important challenge is to find necessary funds. Turkey, however, is determined to see the pipeline constructed and for that it might be prepared to contribute a major share or if necessary, to meet the entire cost of construction of the Turkmenistan-Turkey gas pipeline. After the death of Turkmenbashi the progress in this matter has gone a bit slow.

THE KAZAKH OIL AND TURKEY

In Kazakhstan, Turkey's main ambition is related to build an extension to the BTC pipeline to carry Kazak oil through its territory. In addition to northern routes, Kazakhstan and the Caspian Pipeline Consortium's (CPC) foreign participants have kept alive the possibility of alternative projects for pumping Kazakh oil for export. In June 1996, an official of the Azerbaijani oil consortium stated that a 'common' Azerbaijani-Georgian or Azerbaijani-Gerogian-Turkish route for pumping Trans-Caspian oil from Azerbaijan and Kazakhstan need not be ruled out. In the autumn of 1995, Kazakhstan and Turkey had signed an agreement on the transit of Kazakh oil through the Turkish Mediterranean port of Ceyhan. There are two stages in this project's implementation—*via* Mangyshlak-Baku undersea Iran-Caspian oil pipeline and then *via* the Azerbaijan-Georgia-Turkey route.[22]

Kazakhstan is interested in seeking new exit points for its oil. It wants to reduce dependence on Russian pipelines and find new avenues for the export of its oil to international markets in Europe and elsewhere.

Nursultan Nazarbaev, President of Kazakhstan during his various visits to Tiblisi and Baku during 1996 discussed the possibility of construction of new pipelines through their territories. Out of a dozen proposals, Kazakhstan finds two options more realistic—*via* Novorossisk or *via* the Trans-Caucasus across the Caspian Sea. Kazakhstan's reluctance to transport its oil through Russian land exposed the impact of restrictions on the passage of big tankers through the Bosphorus and Dardanelles straits.[23] Bulent Aras argues that if one considers the construction of pipelines leading to Novorossisk, the Turkish route will be unlikely to be considered in the short or medium term. Kazakhstan preferred the Turkish option in the long run given the fact that by the year 2005 it was expecting to export up to 25 billion tons of oil. However, the construction of any new pipeline in the region is not free from geo-political constraints. Besides, it would not be possible to construct the Trans-Caspian oil pipeline before resolving the problem of legal status of the Caspian Sea. It is also maintained that a "go slow" attitude in the pipeline construction matter is caused by uncertainty about the actual volume of oil and gas deposits in the Caspian. The general impression is that the early estimates were not so accurate. They were exaggerated by the oil producing states in order to appear important to the western oil companies.

TURKEY AND THE POLITICS OF PIPELINES

The Caspian Sea oil reserves even if one goes by modest estimates will necessitate construction of new pipelines for the export of oil to consumers in Europe and elsewhere. It would require substantial financing and guarantee of security of the new routes. As far as Azerbaijan is concerned the AIOC consortium suggested to transport its oil to Western markets *via* existing pipelines to the Russian port of Novorossisk, then by tanker through the Black Sea and into the Mediterranean via Turkey's Bosphorus straits.[24] However, Turkey is not prepared to allow increased shipping *via* Bosphorus in view of environmental hazards created by the oil shipments.[25] According to Turkish figures, nearly 45000 vessels pass through the straits each year and there are frequent accidents. In March 1994, the Cypriot tanker *Nassia* collided with another ship, killing 30 seamen and spilling 20,000 tons of oil into the sea. If the accident had occurred a few miles to the south, Istanbul itself would have faced a major urban disaster. There is no technology which can avert the possibility for an oil spill. Some 19 miles long and a mere 700 meters wide at its narrow point, the Bosphorus is one of the most difficult, water ways in the world to navigate with tankers having to change their course at least 12 times due to abrupt shifts in topography.[26]

The International Maritime Organization (IMO) had also warned in 1994 that, "Navigation through the Bosphorus straits ... presents an increasing potential risk to shipping, safety, the environment and the well being of the local communities.[27]

The Montreux Convention (1936) which still regulates the passage of cargo ships through the Bosphorus requires the straits to be kept open to merchant ships of all nations, regardless to the nature of their cargo. This restricts Ankara's capacity to control the shipping through Bosphorus. On 1 July 1994, Ankara issued a new set of regulations to restrict the excessive shipping through Turkish straits but it was opposed by the regional users—Iran and Russia. This controversy over Bosphorus made the AIOC to contemplate alternative routes. One such route is BTC on the Mediterranean near Syrian border.[28]

Some other options were also examined. The first of these was that of shipping oil from Azerbaijan to the Black Sea port of Poti in Georgia, then on to Odessa in Russia and then Ukraine and on to Europe.[29] The Turkish Minister of Economy, Gunes Taner proposed yet another alternative called the Novorossisk-Samsun route, which would involve shipping oil by tankers to Turkey's Black Sea Port of Samsun and then transporting it south across the Anatolian Peninsula to Ceyhan via a pipeline that would have to be constructed in part. Turkey's argument is that since there is already a pipeline from Kirkkale—a city in Turkey to Ceyhan, construction costs would be manageable for Ankara.[30]

However, of all the suggestions offered the Baku—Tiblisi-Ceyhan was seen by all interested parties, including the United States as most feasible, viable, and generally accepted route for export of Caspian oil to the world outside.

In the pipeline game both Russia and Turkey are fervently advocating the route passing through their respective territories. Ankara favoured the direct Baku-Ceyhan alternative because this route saves Bosphorus from the dangers of tanker shipping and still allows Turkey to reap the financial rewards of being a conduit for Caspian oil. Since Turkey has no border with Azerbaijan, a stretch of connecting pipeline through a neighbouring country would have to be constructed to make the Baku-Ceyhan pipeline viable. This neighbouring country could be Armenia. However, Azerbaijan's Nagorno-Karabakh conflict and Turkey's involvement in the conflict from Azerbaijani side made the idea of Baku-Ceyhan route via Armenia unrealistic. Even if Armenia permitted the use of its territory under some external pressures, the security of the route and the cargo passing through could not be guaranteed at all times.

Another neighbouring country could be Iran, but the United States objected to the transport of oil through Iranian territory "pursuant to its general policy of limiting the international trade and investment prospects for the fundamentalist republic". It is well known how United States differentiates between Iranian fundamentalism and the Saudi fundamentalism. Its own national interest and illogical superpower obstinacy nourished by the "neocon" lobby in the US Administration makes it undermine the interests of the Caspian States' oil prospects. However, in 1997, the White House announced that it would not oppose transportation of oil from Turkmenistan through Iran to Turkey",[31] which was taken as an indication that the Iranian route through Azerbaijan is also not to be ruled out.

Turkey was putting hopes in another comparatively tension-free and more viable alternative route for the Caspian oil to Turkey for further exportation to Europe. If the US opposition to Iranian route remains inflexible then Azerbaijan-Georgia-Turkey route could be taken into consideration. This would be a deviation from the earlier Novorossisk-Samsun route proposad by Gunes Taner. This new route would take oil from the fields of Azerbaijan to Georgian ports and from there by tankers to Turkish ports on the Black Sea, then by pipeline across Turkey to Ceyhan.[32] Yet another route proposed with slight variation was to be from Baku directly across Georgia then down through Turkey to Ceyhan thus bypassing the Black Sea too. The estimated length of the pipeline from the Georgian border to Ceyhan was 1900 kilometers and the cost of construction of pipelines to be about $ 3 billion. The Turkish government declared its readiness to finance the entire cost of any pipeline that would pass through its territory.[33]

Georgia was very happy about the prospects of Azerbaijan (Baku)—Turkey pipeline *via* its territory which would give a boost to its economy and also bring it closer to Turkey and the United States. It will be able to get some benefits directly from Azerbaijan by co-operating with the latter in other areas too. Ankara has pointed out that Ceyhan will be able to handle many times the capacity of the Russian port of Novorossisk. Besides, Ceyhan is workable all through the year due to warms climate of the Mediterranean, whereas the Black Sea ports need to close down in winter due to weather conditions.[34]

Ahat Andican, a State Minister who played a highly influential role in shaping the Turkish policy towards the Central Asian Republics in the initial period of desovietization of Central Asia, maintained that "the total output from the Caspian and Central Asia will eventually be 50 to 60 million tons a year, but Baku-Novorossisk and Baku-Supsa routes have a combined capacity of 16 million tons a year. Hence, the BTC pipeline is the most inevitable and stable option".[35] One possible threat to BTC pipeline may be Kurdish uprising in eastern Turkey. It may cause threat to the security of oil transportation through this route. However, in view of Iraqi scenario in Turkey's neighbourhood, the Kurdish problem has acquired some new dimensions and perhaps in coming times it may not remain too unmanageable for Ankara.

Turkey's assertion on Baku-Tiblisi-Ceyhan pipeline was emboldened by the favourable stand taken by several influential and knowledgeable people active in the field of oil industry, trade and transportation. Terry Adams, the former President of the AIOC, Jim Norosky, Vice-President of the US Company AMOCO (holding 17.0 percent stake in the AIOC) expressed preference for Baku-Tiblisi-Ceyhan pipeline as a most viable route for carrying the Caspian oil to European markets.[36] Azerbaijan's President Heyder Aliyev also favoured the Baku-Tibilisi-Ceyhan oil pipeline.[37] Turkey, Georgia, Kazakhstan, Turkmenistan and Azerbaijan held a meeting at Istanbul in March 1998 to review the work that was underway on Baku-Tiblisi-Ceyhan pipeline. Russia and Iran were not invited to this meeting. Iran was perhaps excluded from the consultations on the pipeline in view of United States' hostility towards Tehran but exclusion of Russia, in view of its focal position in the entire oil export business in the region, and it being a Caspian sea basin state is not justified. It provoked severe criticism from Moscow.[38] Turkey argues that Russia has a deep-seated fear that if any route for transporting Azerbaijan oil bypasses Russian territory, Russia will not only lose a lucrative source of revenue but also experience a decline in its economic and political influence in this resource-rich region. It is for this reason the Turkish decision to restrict tanker passage on the Bosphorus was opposed so vehemently by Moscow.[39]

However, the foreign policy makers in Ankara have realized that the US backing alone is not helpful in furthering Ankara's economic interests. The regional countries need to be given proper recognition and their interests have to be taken into account while serving its own interest. Mutual benefit may lead to more viability in relations than rivalry and revengeful confrontation. Turkey has shown accommodation to Iranian and Russian interests in Azerbaijan and diversifying its economic relations with the two countries in areas of mutual interest. Anakra's trade with Iran and Russia is on an upswing mark.

TURKEY AND IRAN IN THE CASPIAN SEA BASIN

Iran has been one of the most influential players in the Azerbaijan oil controversy and a formidable obstruction in the way of Azerbaijan's ambition of becoming one of the world's greatest energy producers. Turkey's own energy stakes are high in the Caspian Basin States. It wants to play important role in the extraction and exportation of the Azeri oil through participation in international consortium and get at least one significant pipeline pass through its territory to carry the Caspian oil to Europe. Turkey has been keenly watching the negotiations between the Caspian Sea oil States regarding the determination of the status of the Caspian—whether it is a Lake, as Russia and Iran claim or a Sea, claimed by the Caspian oil producing states. Some recent changes in the attitude of Russia and Kazakhstan suggest that a final solution to the Caspian Sea's legal status problem is not far.

Iran's Central Asia policy is not entirely driven by an ideological-Islamic fundamentalist urge as claimed by the West. Tehran's first priority is to protect its own oil interests in the region, maintain its traditional rights in the Caspian Sea and safeguard peace in the region by promoting goodwill among the countries inhabiting Central Asia. The United States is seen by the Tehran as biggest obstruction in the way of accomplishing these objectives in Central Asia. Iran is opposed to increasing interference of the US and the continuously growing dependence of the Central Asian Trans-Caucasian states on America and its allies like Turkey, Israel, Pakistan, Egypt, South Korea and also Greece.

The Central Asia policy of the United States is aimed at curtailing the power and influence of Russia in the region, 'liberating' the Caspian and Central Asian oil and gas producing states from the monopoly of Moscow on the export of these two vital sources of energy by curtailing the use of Russian pipelines. This can be achieved only when new pipelines are constructed. The US wants the new pipelines to bypass Russia and Iran leaving no room for them to play any role in the Caspian-Central Asian oil and gas business.

However, it has been realized by the concerned parties that Russia is comparatively a lesser evil than the small countries of South-Caucasia plagued with several trans-frontier ethnic disputes like Nagorno-Karabakh between Azerbaijan and Armenia, Kurdish problem in eastern Turkey, Dagestan, Chechnya, Lezin, Abkhazia and several others owing to their geo-political and strategic location which make construction of new pipelines difficult. In case, they have to pass through their territory possibility of a threat to the safety of pipelines will always be there.

Degestan is associated with Russia's economic interests related to transportation of oil from Azeri oil fields under and near the Caspian Sea because the pipelines from Baku to Novorossisk run via Dagestan. Similarly, Lezin national movement, *Sadval* has sought the unification of its people living on both sides of Russian-Azeri frontier since 1991. The continuation of conflict causes problem to any foreseeable pipeline project through this area. Similarly, the ambitious project of "Great Chechnya" stretches from Georgia to the Caspian Sea which further endangers oil transport through these troubled territories. Abkahzia, North and South Ossetia and several such pockets of conflict discourage the new pipeline projects in the Caucasian-Caspian region. It is being realized that Russia alone is capable of keeping the ethnic fervour in control and its participation in the Caspian oil deals may prove beneficial and not a hindrance.

However, until this realization dawns on the United States and George W. Bush, President of America approves the Russian participation in the Caspian oil's export, the local players and the regional interested parties are likely to remain passive—no matter how much loss in oil revenues occurs to them.

Turkey's Caspian ambitions are backed by the United States because Ankara is seen as the primary geo-strategic player in the Turkic speaking belt. From Turkey's perspective Azerbaijan is the key to Ankara's oil ambitions. As far as Azerbaijan is concerned its freedom to make independent strides in initiating and implementing oil-related decisions is constrained by the Iranian and the Russian attitude to some of the measures taken by Baku to enhance its oil prospects. An analysis of Turkey-Iran and Turkey-Russia relations will reveal the exact scenario and help in understanding how much involvement of the US in safeguarding Turkey's interests in Trans-Caucasia is beneficial to the latter.

TURKEY'S RIVALS: IRAN AND RUSSIA

In South-Caucasus, Iran has the longest border with Azerbaijan, a relatively short border with Armenia and no border with Georgia.

During the Second World War, Russia wanted to occupy Iran's two north-western provinces of Azerbaijan and Kurdistan and establish communist governments in the 1940s. However, Iranian resistance frustrated the Soviet designs.

The relations between Russia and Iran have become very cordial after the developments that had taken place in the Soviet Union during Michael Gorbachev's period. The desovietized Russia and post-Khomeini Iran's interests in South-Caucasus, especially in Azerbaijan and Armenia converge and they share identity of interests in the Caspian basin region too. Contrary to its established image as a fundamentalist state, Iran avoided using Islam in its relations with Azerbaijan and other Muslim states of Central Asia. However, this did not inhibit Iran from seeking sphere of influence in post-Soviet Azerbaijan. Turkey, also in the race with more substantial ethno-linguistic claims pursued its interest in this Caucasian state. Nationalists and communists in Azerbaijan also contributed to creation of political instability which could easily be exploited by Turkey and Iran had Russia not intervened militarily.

AZERBAIJANI OIL AND TURKEY AND IRAN

The Russian intervention in Azerbaijan for the sake of keeping the territorial integrity of the state intact and restraining the irredentist ambitions of Azerbaijan's western neighbours—Turkey and Iran proved beneficial to Tehran in the long run.

In the post-Soviet Caucasus the major threat to Iran was from the nationalists with pan-Turkist fervour in Azerbaijan and also in Turkey. The Azerbaijan Popular Front (APF) not only propagated the idea of unification of two Azerbaijans (Iranian and Caucasian) but also provoked the Iranian Azeris to rise against the Iranian government. Thus, the developments in South-Caucasia created a potential security threat to Iran.

During the Soviet period too, Iran had relations with Azerbaijan. Its autonomous republic of Nakhicheven which is cut off from rest of Azerbaijan by the Armenian and Iranian territory could communicate with Azerbaijan main land through the land and rail linkages provided by Iran and for energy supply too it depended on Tehran. This economic complementarity somehow maintained the continuity in Iran-Azerbaijan relations which further improved after Abulfez Elchibey's coming to power in June 1992.

The Nagorno-Karabakh conflict also provided an opportunity to Tehran to win the confidence of both Azerbaijan and Armenia as it enjoyed the trust of both the states. In 1992, Iran negotiated a number of ceasefires between the two belligerents which however, did not last long. In fact, the Nagorno-Karabakh problem, in the course of time became so enmeshed with Azerbaijani domestic politics and with regional and international competition for power, that its solution became almost impossible unless issues related to these rivalries were settled.[40]

Owing to these regional and international rivalries, certain elements in Azerbaijan, notably the pan-Turkist nationalist Azerbaijan Popular Front (APF) did not want to see Iran having any role in the peace making between Azerbaijan and Armenia. Turkey, Russia and the West—all the three, for reasons of their own desired to exclude Iran from Azerbaijani affairs. For similar reasons, Iran did not want others to succeed. In fact, Iran because of its acute vulnerability to instability in Azerbaijan was more eager to see the conflict resolved than the other three, which were not so vulnerable to its disruptive effects. Commenting on the increasing closeness of Turkey with Azerbaijan, Iranian ambassador said: "Azerbaijanis, for now have found their cousins, but in time they will turn to their brothers". The geo-political realities, no doubt, forced the two countries—Iran and Azerbaijan—to revive some degree of co-operation. The Elcibey government came to believe that an overly antagonistic attitude towards Iran was not in Azerbaijan's best interests. He sent the Azerbaijani Foreign Minister, Towfiq Qasimov to Tehran to express his willingness to have cordial relations with Iran in the light of developments that were taking place in the Caucasus. The war in Karabakh and the Armenian blockade of Azerbaijan's road and rail connections with parts of its territory, notably with Nakhichevan combined with the turmoil in Georgia increased Azerbaijan's economic dependence on Iran. Thus, mitigated the impact of ideological and political difference between the two neighbours. However, the production and export of oil—and the status of Caspian (Lake or Sea) remained in prominence threatening the relations any time.

Iran is basically averse to Turkey's involvement in the Caspian affairs as Ankara becomes a convenient vehicle to bring western investments in the Caspian oil, especially of the

American companies. Ali Akbar Nateq Nouri, the speaker of Iran's Parliament is quoted as saying that: "the United States should be restricted from participating in the Caspian ventures since any involvement by the US companies would simply represent an effort by the US government to satisfy its "historical dream" of establishing influence in the region.[41] He criticized Azerbaijan's President Haider Aliev for "making a historic mistake by laying grounds for US interference".[42] In August 1997, without naming the country, Iran's Vice-President Mohammad Vaezi openly stated that "certain states have caused unrest in the sensitive region by signing unilateral contracts with foreign countries",[43] indirectly targeting Azerbaijan. Obviously Iran does not want external powers using the Caspian resources.

The idea of joint regional and western collaboration in the Caspian oil's production and exportation was appreciated by Iran and it had expressed willingness to join whatever arrangement evolves for that purpose. When the AIOC came up, Iran offered to obtain a 5 percent share in the consortium known as the "contract of the century". But the United States blocking Iran's share in the consortium frustrated its oil ambition.[44] The official excuse given by the United States was that the US law forbids American companies from doing business with the Iranian companies owing to its fundamentalist ideology. It threatened to quit if Iran is not excluded from the consortium.[45] This triggered Iran's opposition to the AIOC and American involvement in the Caspian Sea's oil affairs.

On the issues of determination of legal status of the Caspian Sea, Iran sides with Russia which treats the Caspian as a "Lake" rather than a "Sea". If it is accepted as "Lake" than the waterbody's resources will be divided equally among all the Caspian States—Azerbaijan, Turkmenistan, Kazakhstan, Iran and Russia. By endorsing this stand Iran will be greatly benefited.

In fact, Iran and Russia both stand to benefit from the "Lake" classification. This convergence of interests provided an incentive to join hands with Russia and align Iran to its overall regional policy. Tehran's stand on Nagorno-Karabakh issue also underwent some change under the influence of its increasing understanding with Moscow. It supported Armenia in its conflict with Azerbaijan. In 1995, it virtually closed its border with Azerbaijan and for sometime cut off electricity to Nakhichevan—the Azeri enclave dependent on the Iranian power supply.[46]

The Iran-Azerbaijan relations suffer on account of three factors. The first is the obvious fact that Azerbaijan refuses to accept the Russian-Iranian position with regard to the legal status of the Caspian. Second, Azerbaijan's continued association with the AIOC deal. Third, Iran's fear that a prosperous independent Azerbaijan would be an unwelcome role model for the enormous Azeri minority which makes up a quarter of Iran's population and which constitutes a majority in several northern Iranian provinces.[47] Iran believes that increased affluence and international strategic clout will certainly embolden tiny Azerbaijan and give it courage to incite nationalistic sentiments in its ethnic brethern across the border.[48]

Azerbaijan, conscious of adverse impact of Iranian hostility on its pipeline prospects, land and rail links etc., is trying to placate Tehran by offering it some share in its oil resources, notwithstanding the American disapproval of such moves. It granted Tehran a 10 percent share in a separate oil venture to develop fields in the "Shah-Deniz area" where no American Company is directly involved as yet. However, such efforts can not change Iran's attitude towards Azerbaijan's policy of involving western companies in its oil and also for not endorsing the Iranian-Russian stand on the status of the Caspian Sea.

Ankara, in a way, stands benefited by the lukewarm relations between Azerbaijan and Iran but knows that Iran's involvement in oil exporting arrangement will be necessary if the Caspian oil is to be taken to Europe via its territory. Tehran needs to be given its due share.

TURKEY AND RUSSIA

Turkey has always been taken as a country which works to further the interests of the United States in the Central Asian–Caucasian region. Its early moves (1990-1992) were also seen as pan-Turkist designs to seek "sphere of influence" on the basis of ethno-linguistic commonalties and thus dividing the region between the Turkic (all oil producing) and non-Turkic States. However, Ankara moved cautiously and tried not to provoke Moscow by its Central Asia policy.

Turkey's revived interest in Azerbaijan and its increasing involvement in the oil consortium and planning for construction of new pipelines (some through its own territory) is also not liked by Russia. Prior to collapse of the Soviet Union, Moscow controlled the natural resources of the Caspian basin states and exported them to international markets through its pipelines. In the post-Soviet period, several outside forces from America, Europe, South-East Asia and West Asia are vying with each other for establishing the areas of influence and acquiring control over the oil wealth of the region. Obviously, Moscow can not easily tolerate the Caspian wealth slipping into the hands of the western companies and the new pipelines (when constructed) depriving it of its privileged position of being the sole exporter of Caspian oil and gas to Europe. As discussed above in the section on "Turkey and Politics of Pipeline", Turkey has succeeded in making the major competitors agreeable to its proposal on Baku-Tiblisi-Ceyhan oil pipeline through Georgia instead of Armenia which owing to Nagorno-Karabakh conflict is hostile to Azerbaijan. It excludes both Iran and Russia. Moscow is also sometimes accused of feeding the Karabakh problem by supplying weapons to Armenia.

Russia has tried in the past (1992-1995) to put pressure on Azerbaijan for not allowing the western companies any share in its oil business. It interfered in the internal affairs of Azerbaijan by seeking removal of its President Haider Aliev who is known for his pro-West policies. Russia also increased its troops enforcement in the Caucasus as a security requirement. In 1995, Russia had closed its border virtually cutting off trade between Azerbaijan and Russia.

However, it is being realized by several analysts in Russia that its continued hostile stance in the Caucasus is likely to harm its own oil interests in the region. Russian Government's policy is depriving private oil companies of profitable oil deals in Azerbaijan. For example, the Russian government in August 1997 forced the cancellation of a contract signed by the LUK-OIL and *Rosneft* companies, asking them to renounce participation in an international consortium organized to develop the Kyapaz offshore oil field.[49] The Kyapaz field is claimed by Turkmenistan which views its exploitation under Azerbaijan as an illegitimate appropriation. Russia thought that by cancelling the Kyapaz deal it would win the Turkmen goodwill and later on seek its support to the Russian stand on the status of Caspian as a "Lake". Moscow's high handed approach alarmed Turkey and turned it to look for some pacifying means which could make Moscow less hostile to Turkey's endeavours in the region. Russia's upper hand in Caspian Pipeline Consortium (CPC)—the body charged with constructing an export pipeline from Kazakhastan's giant Tangiz oil field is the primary obstacle to Turkey's plans to transport Kazakh oil through Turkish territory.[50]

The aggressive policy of Russia is likely to push the south Caucasian states farther from their historic trading partner to the north, into the eager embrace of the capital-rich western countries and comparatively more developed Turkic state—Turkey which is too eager to have a foothold in the Caucasus.

The private oil interests in Russia are increasingly becoming disenchanted with Moscow's strong arm approach to the Caspian issues. The Kyapaz Consortium episode bewildered the LUKOIL.[51] The oil interests of Russia seem mindful of the risk of alienating other republics south of Russia's borders. Yuri Federov, observes, "the oil people want to respect national aspirations of other new independent states, while at the same time expecting that those states would decide to make maximum use of the scientific, technological, human potential still possessed by Russia".[52] The official Russia is still not receptive to these ideas. By and large Kremlin's stand is putting the Russian private sector to loss.

Russian stand on oil issues related to Caspian States has placed Turkey in an advantageous position. It has already gained access to development of Azerbaijani oil reserves, as the state-run Turkish oil Company (TPAO), has earned a 6.75 percent stake in the consortium developing the Azeri, Chirag and Guneshli oil fields and a 9 percent stake in the consortium developing the Shah-Deniz field.[53] Any other shares in future projects are also likely to come in Turkey's hands if the Russian intransigence continues.

The Turkish Companies have already set up operations in Azerbaijan including such industrial giants as TPAO, Bayraktar Holding, Koc's Ram Division and Borusan Makina's Caterpillar Division, not to mention many other smaller firms.[54] Interestingly, notwithstanding the differences of opinion on several issues and conflicting aims in various matters, the trade between Turkey and Russia is flourishing to the tune of several billion dollars and the prospects of enhanced economic relations appear bright.

TURKEY'S EXPECTATIONS FROM THE UNITED STATES

The United States is certainly a counterweight to the ambitions of Iran and Russia in the Caucasus. It is a great support to Ankara's ambitions in Azerbaijan and Central Asia. Washington is helping Ankara to become an effective actor on the energy map in Central Asia and the primary geo-strategic player in the Turkic world with the support of Israel. The United States is encouraging Turco-Israeli co-operation in the Caucasus and Central Asia and relations between the two have improved tremendously during the last decade.

The oil interests of Turkey are also protected by the United States, which is propagating the need for multiple pipeline routes from Caucasus to the world outside. Washington has been advocating the selection of Baku-Ceyhan pipeline as a most viable route to carry Azeri oil to Europe. It is maintained that President Clinton personally lobbied Azerbaijan's Presidetn Haider Aliev to consider the Turkish pipeline.[55] The Baku-Ceyhan pipeline is not only likely to prove viable and secure but would also bring significant revenue to Turkey. From Washington's perspective this is in the interest of American foreign policy, because strong Turkey represents a positive, secular model for the new republics in Central Asia. To minimize the prospects of Iran, Clinton encouraged Aliev to consider the northern route through Russia in addition to the Turkish route.

Turkey wants that Washington lifts section 907, a provision of US law enacted in 1992 as part of Freedom Support Act. It forbids direct US aid to Azerbaijan including humanitarian assistance.[56] It was passed by the US Congress at the insistence of the powerful Armenian lobby active in America. Owing to this law, Armenia has the upper hand in the conflict between the two countries, considering the fact that it holds 20 percent of Azerbaijan's territory under its control. The Turkish Lobby in America is constantly persuading the Congressmen to argue lifting of section 907 which would facilitate much needed funds to this conflict-ridden impoverished state of the Caspian Basin. The US Congressman Lee Hamilton (D-Indiana) argued that Congress should lift the ban on Azerbaijan because a better relationship with Azerbaijan serves the US national interest, the interest of peace, and the long-term interests of Armenia as well.[57] An improvement in the status of Azerbaijan *vis-à-vis* Armenia will strengthen Turkey's position in the Caspian controversies.

The Caspian hydrocarbon deposits present the potential for tremendous economic benefits for all the five Caspian States. Turkey, which is not a Caspian State is likely to be doubly benefited by its affinity with Azerbaijan.

Turkey has acquired energy security and is likely to earn substantial revenues through Baku-Ceyhan oil pipeline when Kazakh oil is exported through this route. Ankara can offer technological assistance in the development of Azeri oil fields. However, Turkey will be able to enjoy these advantages only when peace in the region is ensured and all the parties related to Caspian oil are satisfied with the emerging arrangement of oil exportation.

The prolonged controversy over the legal status of Caspian Sea, Iran and Russia, sooner rather than later are going to realize that Azerbaijan which today owns the tremendous oil resources is to be given freedom to determine its own future. As a positive development, observes a Turkish scholar, Bulent Aras, Moscow began to give signals of compromise in this regard. But from the prospects of Azerbaijan, something near an equal distribution of Caspian's resources would mean "giving up the ambition of emerging as a major oil producer and a significant player in the world energy market". No doubt, the revenues from the Caspian oil are going to be huge, even to such large powers like Iran and

Russia, the ultimate decision on legal status of Caspian is not going to make much difference to their status as big powers in the Caspian region.[58] Hence, the likelihood of coming to a positive understanding acceptable to Azerbaijan, Iran and Russia is not less.

On the pipeline issue too, Turkey and Russia need to be realistic. With proper understanding about each other's interest, both can be host to pipelines to transport Azerbaijani oil. Russia will be required to review its policy on the role of the Russian private sector in addressing the deficiencies of the northern pipeline network. Russia alone cannot safely handle the huge volume of oil that increased exploitation of the Caspian will entail. It will have to update its pipelines and increase its carrying capacity in order to maintain its *numero uno* status in the oil exporting business.

Notwithstanding, selection of Baku-Ceyhan oil pipeline as the most viable route for exporting the Caspian oil via Turkey, a possibility of AIOC seeking other routes for the export of oil can not be ruled out. Turkish route may remain important but it may not be the only route for carrying oil from Baku to Europe.

The ambitions of all the Caspian Basin States may be accommodated if they work as partners and not as rivals outsmarting the other. Besides concentrating on the pipeline issue the Caspian States will have to pay attention to their internal rules and regulations and facilities which they can provide to foreign investors. From Turkey's perspective, it will be able to draw maximum advantages from its relations with Azerbaijan and involvement in the production and exportation of Caspian oil, if it can be helpful in resolving the Nagorno-Karabakh conflict and generate goodwill and spirit of co-operation and mutual dependence between Azerbaijan and Armenia. It is in Ankara's long-term interest that its north-eastern neighbours repose trust in it.

NOTES

1. Bulent Aras, *The New Geopolitics of Eurasia and Turkey's Position* (Frank Cass, London, 2002), p. 3.
2. According to authentic sources Turkey is expected to require roughly 22 million tons of crude oil annually (some sources put it at 55 million tons) by the year 2010. Tamel Iskit "Turkey: A New Actor in the Field of Energy Politics", *Perceptions,* 1, No. 1 (March-May 1996), p. 66.
3. Kenneth Mackenzie, "Azerbaijan and Neighbours", *World Today,* 48, No.1 (January 1992), p.2, and Philip Robins, "Between Sentiment and Self-Interests: Turkey's Policy Towards Azerbaijan and the Central Asian States", *Middle East Journal,* 47, No. 4 (Autumn 1993) p. 597.
4. Gareth M. Winrow, "Turkey's Role in Asian Pipeline Politics", *Jane's Intelligence Review,* 9, No. 2 (February 1997).
5. Temel Iksit, *op.cit.*
6. Bulent Aras, *op.cit.,* p. 8.
7. Don Morgan and David Ottaway, "Pipe Dreams: The Struggle for Caspian Oil", *Washington Post,* 4-6 October 1998.
8. *Indian Express,* May 1, 1997; also see Bruce R. Kuniholm, "Geopolitics of the Caspian Sea", *Middle East Journal,* (Fall 2000), p.549 and Huge Pope, "US Report says Caspian oil deposits might be twice as large as expected" *Wall Street Journal,* 30 April 1997, Rosemary Forstythe, "The Politics of oil in the Caucasus and Central Asia", *Adelphi Paper* 350, (London: 1996), p. 6.
9. "Armenia/Azerbaijan: Tensions Renewed in Nagorno-Karabakh", *Periscope Daily Defense News* Capsules, (26 June 1997).
10. Andrei Shoumikhin, "Economcs and Politics of Developing Caspian Oil Resources", *Perspectives on Central Asia* (November 1996), http/ www.cpss.org/casian w/novpers.html.
11. Bulent Aras, *op.cit.,* p. 9.
12. Andrei Shoumikhin, "New Developments Related to Caspian Oil", *Perspectives on Central Asia* (November 1996). Http:/www.epss.org/ casian w/canews.html.
13. Kenneth Weisbrode, *Central Eurasia: Prize or Quicksand? Adelphi Paper* 338 (International Institute for Strategic Studies (IISS): 2001), pp. 27-44.
14. Bulent Aras, *op.cit.,* p. 10.

15. *Turkey Daily News*, 16 February 1996.
16. Bulent Aras, *op.cit.*, p. 10.
17. *Voice of the Islamic Republic of Iran's First Program Network*, 28 December 1996 in Foreign Broadcast Information Service—Near East and South Asia (Hereafter FBIS-NES), pp. 96-251.
18. *Mayak Radio Network in Russian*, 4 January 1997 in Bulent Aras, *op.cit.*, p. 10.
19. ITAR—TASS, 28 December 1997 in FBIS—SOV, pp. 97-362, 1 January 1998.
20. ITAR-TASS, 30 January 1998, in FBIS-SOV, pp. 98-030, 4 February 1998.
21. *Anatolia*, 21 May 1999.
22. *Rossiyskaya Gazeta*, 22 June 1996 in FBIS-SOV, pp. 96-124, 27 June 1996.
23. *Interfax*, 19 May 1997, in FBIS-SOV, pp. 97-139, 22 June 1997.
24. "Pipeline Stakes", *Washington Post*, 390 October 1995, p. A-16.
25. "Great Game is Afoot Again as Rivals Crave Up Oil Bonanza", *Independent* (London), 21 May 1997. Also see Oumerserik Kasenov, "Russia, Transcaucasia and Central Asia: Oil, Pipelines, and Geopolitics" in Roald Z. Sagdeev and Susan Eisenhower (eds.), *Central Asia: Conflict Resolution and Change* (Chevy Chase: CPSS Press: 1997), p. 78.
26. Michael Rank, "Russia and Turkey clash over control of Bosphorus", *Reuters*, 25 July 1997.
27. "The Bosphorus: A Waterway at Risk", The Web Page of the Turkish Ministry of Foreign Affairs, http://www.mfa.gov.tr/grupf/Caspian 3.htm.
28. Temel Iskit, *op.cit.*, p. 70.
29. Georgy Dvali, "Tiblisi is pleased with Aliyev's visit to Ukraine", *The Current Digest of Post Soviet Press*, No.25 (1997), p. 49.
30. Ozlem Hersan, 'Taner'den Petrole Alternatif,' *Yeni Yuzyil*, 28 August 1997, p. 8.
31. Patricia Krauz, "Look What is Bubbling up in the Caspian", *Business Week*, 15 September 1997, p. 21.
32. Onmerserik Kasenov, "Russia, Transcaucasia and Central Asia, *op.cit.*, p. 71.
33. *Ibid*. On completion the BTC pipeline stretching from Azerbaijan to Turkey via Georgia is 1762 kilometer long and is supposed to transport one million barrels of oil a day.

34. Alexei Baliyev, "The Caspian Sea: Nobody Safe in the Eye of the Storm", *Rossiskaya Gazeta*, 18 July 1997 cited in the *Turkestan Newsletter*, No. 97, 28 July 1997 and Temel Iksit, Turkey: A New Actor, *op.cit.*, p. 65.
35. Ercan Ersoy, "Turkey to Lobby for Baku-Ceyhan Pipeline", *Reuters*, 21 August 1997.
36. Gulnara Achilova, "Crude Oil to Take Three Routes", *The Current Digest of the Post-Soviet Press*, No.19 (1997), p. 49.
37. *Reuters*, 14 July 1997.
38. *Inerfax*, 3 March 1998.
39. Onmerserik Kasenov, *op.cit.*, p. 68.
40. Shireen T. Hunter, *The Trans-Caucasus in Transition: Nation Building and Conflict* (Washington D.C., Centre for Strategy and International Studies, 1994).
41. "Iranian Leader Blames US for stoking Caspian Role", *Reuter World Service*, 12 April 1997.
42. *Ibid.*
43. Michael S. Lelyveld, "Give Us a Piece of the Action", *Journal of Commerce*, 8 August 1997, p. 3A.
44. Marshall Ingewerson, "The Next Great Game: Players Jostle to Pipe Home a Share of the Oil Prize", *Christian Science Monitor*, 25 August 1997, p. 10.
45. *Ibid.*
46. *Ibid.*
47. Bulent Aras, *op.cit.*, p. 17.
48. *Ibid.*
49. "Turkmenistan to Launch International Oil and Gas Tender Monday", *Agence France Presse*, 30 August 1997.
50. Bulent Aras, *op.cit.*, p. 19.
51. "Turkmen-Azeri Oil Field Disptue Remains Unresolved", *BBC Summary of World Broadcasts*, 8 August 1997.
52. Yuri Federov, "Russia's Policies Towards Caspian Region Oil: Neo Imperial or Pragmatic II?", *Perspective on Central Asia* (October 1996), http:/www.cpss.org/casian w/octpers.html.
53. Burent Aras, *op.cit.*, p. 19.
54. *Ibid.*, p. 20.
55. "US Wants Multiple Caspian Oil Pipeline Routes", Reuters, 23 July 1997.

56. Butent Aras, *op.cit.*, p. 21. The US assistance under this or any other act (other than assistance under title V of this Act) may not be provided to the Government of Azerbaijan until the President determines and so reports to the Congress, that the Government of Azerbaijan is taking demonstrable steps to cease all blockades and other offensive uses of force against Armenia and Nagorno-Karabakh. (Freedom Support Act) US Public Law 102-511, 102d Congress, 3rd Session, 24 October 1992.
57. Lee H. Hamilton, "Toward Peace in the Caucasus", *Christian Science Monitor*, 23 July 1997.
58. Bulent Aras, *op.cit.*, p. 23.

CHAPTER 4

Turkey in Post-Soviet Central Asia

The dissolution of the Soviet Union has drawn the attention of the world to the Turcophone republics. Turkey, till then had never thought of the Central Asian Republics (CARs) and about the existence of ethno-linguistic, cultural-religious commonalties with the people of Central Asia. Oil, of course, had always had been at the back of their mind but ever since Central Asia came under the domination of Russia and became an 'integral' part of the Soviet Union the Central Asian oil became Soviet oil to which Turkey being a staunch ally of the United States was not to have any access.

Now, suddenly the entire scenario has changed. The iron curtain was lifted and independent republics emerged in the southern Caucasian-Caspian sea region and Central Asia. Turkey suddenly realized that the new world belongs to Turks. The Turks of Central Asia are their ancestors who were left behind and remained subjugated to the mighty Soviet Union for several decades. The reaction was almost euphoric and to start with no doubt, nourished exaggerated hopes of Turkey's role in the newly independent states (NIS) of Central Asia.

During their first visit to the new republics, the Turkish leaders were able to note that they were not underdeveloped countries in need of elementary technical assistance. First impression of the metropolitan areas of Central Asia suggested that administratively and educationally they had attained high standards comparable to any of the developed states including Turkey.

The new states of Central Asia were very cautious while mixing up with the world outside. They were coveteously guarding their indepedence and maintaining a confident and self-respecting dignified profile.

Notwithstanding, their being fairly advanced states, they had still not come out of the communist mind set of the controlled economy. Despite having attained political freedom, economically they have been still under the control of Russia which had a firm grip on the entire economic system of the NIS. The gain was not one sided only. For the CARs, they did not have to immediately search buyers for their cotton, agricultural products and other exportable materials soon after the independence. It is easier for buyer than for producers to adapt to the changing markets. If Russia finds cheaper cotton, elsewhere Uzbekistan might face a long lasting crisis.

Notwithstanding economic interdependence continuing between the NIS and Russia, the west was busy propagating the Turkish model of economic development in Central Asia. Turkey was asked to sell its model to the CARs vigorously and try to draw them away from the Ruble zone as early as possible. When Suleyman Demirel, Prime Minister of Turkey visited Washington in February 1992, President Bush told him that "Turkey is a model for the countries of the region, and especially to newly independent republics of Central Asia".[1] Meanwhile, during a trip to several capitals in the region, US Secretary of State, James Baker urged the CARs to adopt the "Turkish model" of economic and political development. This rhetoric was supported by the British government and parts of western media.[2]

Turkey was encouraged in this endeavour by the warm response from the Central Asian leaders. President Islam Karimov during his visit to Turkey in December 1991 declared that he looked up to Turkey as an 'elder brother', while President Akaev of Kyrgyzstan compared Turkey with the 'morning star' guiding the Turkic people.[3] Demirel during his visit to all the Central Asian states except Tajikistan in April-May 1992 claimed among other things, that Turkey and Turkic republics "share the same blood, religion and language". This was seen as a "high point of the period of euphoria".[4]

Turkey's emphasis on linguistic and ethnic commonalty is debated by several scholars in the west and other parts of the world including the Turkish educated elite. "If ethnicity were defined in terms of language" argued William Hale, "then it was unclear how far the Turkish nation extended since many of its peoples to the east spoke languages akin to Turkish and sharply differentiated from the other main regional languages—Russian, Persian and Chinese".

Suleyman Demirel, Turkish Prime Minister spoke of 'Turkish world' in February 1992 supposedly "stretching from the Adriatic to the great wall of China".[5] Even if it implied cultural homogeneity over such a vast area it was a serious exaggeration.[6] In the linguistic sphere, the regional languages may be Turkic" but are not strictly Turkish (spoken by Turks of Turkey). The western Turkic (related to Turkish but not identical) languages like Azeri and Turkmen can be understood with great difficulty by speakers of Turkish language. However, the Turkic languages spoken in most of Central Asia—Uzbek, Kazakh, Kyrgyz and Uigur—are different, though related and the Turks of Turkey have to learn them as virtually foreign languages. When people from different Central Asian nations spoke to one another or to outsiders they normally do so in Russian, since there is no "standard" Turkic language, similar to mandarin Chinese or modern literary Arabic.[7]

Undeterred by such shortcomings Turkish leadership in 1991-92 constantly centered their policy toward the NIS "around fanciful notion of ethnic solidarity rather than mutual interest.[8] The political leaders who made frequent visits to Central Asia were Suleyman Damirel, Prime Minister of Turkey and leader of the Nationalist Action Party, Alparslan Turkes, whose ideology was based on pan-Turkism.[9] While giving assurances that Turkey harbours no pan-Turkic ambitions he maintained that "there is nothing wrong in Turks in Turkey declaring that Central Asia was the land of their forefathers and that their culture and history originated here".[10] He referred to Central Asia and Azerbaijan as a new community, "Eurasia" populated by Turks while Turkey could not administer this community of Turks it would "lead them to the world".

Alparslan Turkes was not the only leader who tried to build linkages on the basis of pan-Turkist ideology. President Turgut Ozal generated much more enphoric atmosphere than any of his associates. In his speech on 30-31 December 1992, he said that Turkey and Turkic republics should work together to make the 21st century a Turkish century".[11] Prof. Erol Manisali even proposed "formation of a community of Turkic Republics based on military, economic, political and cultural ground".[12] Turkes came out with another idea of setting up "a high council of Turkic Republics in which the Presidents, Prime Ministers and Foreign Ministers would meet under a revolving Presidency".[13]

However, these expressions were not well thought out declarations. They were emotional outbursts charged under the spirit of euphoria. When passions cooled down, Turkey realized that the Central Asian states have other supporters and well wishers besides Turkey. Iran and Russia have closer links with the CARs and their economic relations and security arrangement (CIS) are far more viable. Ankara will have to compete with them. Turkey will have to evolve its Central Asia policy spelling out its objectives, priorities, areas of interaction and mode of communicating in various walks of activity with the CARs. Ankara, however, was not prepared to give up its nationalist and ideological approach to Central Asia. Their nationalism was expressed more in Azerbaijan where Ankara supported Azerbaijan against Armenia in the Nagorno-Karabakh dispute between the two South Caucasian States. President Turgut Ozal during his visit to Central Asia even went to the extent of saying that "dropping a few shells on Armenia and sending a brigade of soldiers would be enough to stop Armenian aggression against Azerbaijan. It was an indication that the government was prepared to abandon the Ataturk's policy of neutrality, especially in the case of Azerbaijan.

However, by the end of 1992 it was clear that the so called euphoria was an outburst of excitement and sentimentalism generated by nostalgic "memories" of past. Ankara's overenthusiasm, pan-Turkish slogans, statements and programmes scared the CARs and they became lukewarm towards Turkey.

In the economic field too, in October 1992, Demirel prepared an ambitious agenda for the first "Turkic Summit" of the Heads of government of all Turkic States to be held in Ankara in the same month. Demirel also referred to the idea of a sort of "Turkic Commonwealth" or an "Association of independent Turkic states" not to be 'dominated' by Turkey. Other models suggested were that of Nordic Union of Scandinavian countries. The Summit was expected to produce an "Ankara Political Declaration" and an "Economic Declaration". President Ozal also hoped to create a "Turkic Common Market" with the gradual removal of all barriers of free trade and the development of new transport systems.[14]

However, once the leaders of the new republics had

assembled in Ankara, President Nazarbaev made it clear that he was against any grouping based on religious and ethnic criteria and that Kazakhstan could only participate in regional co-operation schemes on condition that they did not harm its commitments to other members of the CIS (Commonwealth of Independent States)—a clear sign that Russia should not be shut out. By the autumn of 1992, the Central Asian leders had evidently come round to a more realistic assessment of their connection with Turkey and the realization that adoption of any thing like a pan-Turkist programme create serious problems for them in their relations with Russia. Islam Karimov, President of Uzbekistan also supported this view. Thus, the Summit watered down the hopes of Turkey. The two Ankara declarations were also abandoned. The summit issued a simple joint communique on political and economic relations between the CARs and Turkey.

Once the idea of some sort of political and economic Union had been abandoned, Turkey concentrated its efforts on developing cultural and educational links with the region as well as in the field of trade and investment. On the first score, 10,000 scholarships were given each year to enable Central Asian students to attend Turkish High School and Universities. The Turkish International Co-operation Agency (TICA) affiliated to Foreign Ministry was established in 1992[15] to gear up technical assistance, training and cultural co-operation and the development of small industries in the region.

The ministry of Education also opened schools in Central Asia teaching the Turkish and English, besides the national languages, though they were outnumbered by privately owned Turkish schools. Religious brotherhood led by Fethullah Gulen also ran 73 schools in all the Central Asian states except Tajikistan, which is the only non-Turkic state in the region. While the Turkish state tried to represent itself as strictly secularist, it was apparent that part of attempted Islamic revival in Central Asia was also being sponsored from Turkey by private initiatives causing some embarrassment to Turkey's official representatives.

In official sphere the Turkish State Broadcasting Corporation TRT broadcast, TV programmes in Turkish *via* satellite on the special "Avrasya" channel. The regional states, however, were not happy about allowing a foreign broadcaster to have direct access to their citizens. The viewers also found the language difficult to understand. Turkey also supported the adoption of the Latin alphabet for writing the regional languages, as an alternative to the existing Cyrillic or the Arabic script suggested by Iran and other Muslim countries. In this campaign Turkey could derive some satisfaction as by 1996, Azerbaijan, Uzbekistan and Turkmenistan had officially adopted the Latin Alphabet although Cyrillic alphabets are also in use.[16]

In order to ameliorate the geographical disadvantage (no direct access to Central Asia), Turkey had sought to develop infrastructure projects not dependent on land links. First, Turkey has introduced regular flights to and from the leading capitals of the Central Asian States. During 1992, direct scheduled flights by the Turkish carrier, *Turk Hava Yo'lari* (THY) were established between Turkey, Uzbekistan and Kazakhstan. A year later it was extended to Ashkabat in Turkmenistan.[17]

Ankara's greatest success had undoubtedly come in the area of non-terrestrial infrastructure projects: telecommunication. Telecommunications has been referred to as the "industrial frontiersman" of Turkey's Central Asia policy.[18] In this area Turkey had a real comparative advantage over Central Asia's other neighbouring states, both in respect of manpower and technology. The PTT-Turkey's public sector telecommunication grant was quick off the mark in providing equipment, free of charge to the value of $ 25 million to the five republics. This enabled Turkey to create a dependent relationship at an early stage, which made the republics reliant upon Turkey for access to international lines. The Turkish private and joint venture communication companies, like *Netas* have consolidated this link by opening factories in Kazakhstan to manufacture the related materials.[19]

One of the most ambitious Turkish project in the region included the creation of the Black Sea Economic Co-operation (BSEC) scheme in June 1992. It included Black Sea countries—Albania, Armenia, Azerbaijan, Bulgaria, Georgia, Greece, Moldova, Romania, Russia, Turkey and Ukraine as members. The main goal of the BSEC was to strengthen economic co-operation among the member states based on free market principles. Turkey hoped to cultivate good will through this organization and brighten the prospect for an alternative to EU with which it is getting disillusioned (occasionally only). However, the internal and bilateral problems within and between member states constrained the successful implementation of the scheme.[20]

The main purpose of the formation of the BSEC was to draw the Black Sea states closer to Ankara and give the impression to Russia, Armenia, Greece, Bulgaria and Ukraine that Turkey wants their co-operation in charting out the possible routes for pipelines to carry Azeri oil from Azerbaijan to Europe. The Black Sea states can lend their support to these proposed projects.

Besides, Russia is one of major trade partners of Turkey. In 1995, Turkey's exports to Russia were 5.7% of its exports and 5.8% of its imports.[21] Moscow is the sole source of supply for the natural gas on which Ankara and Istanbul, with several other cities rely for pollution free heating. The importance of good relations with Russia is attested to by Turkey's lead in setting up the Black Sea Economic Co-operation Zone (BSECZ) which had been warmly welcomed by President Yeltsin.[22]

Turkey's sincerity was further confirmed by the fact that Turkey carefully abstained from supporting oppositional movements by Turkic ethnic minorities within Russia.[23]

ECONOMIC CO-OPERATION ORGANIZATION (ECO)

The Economic Co-operation Organization (ECO), a revised version of the earlier Regional Co-operation for Development (RCD) 1964 is another important regional grouping in Central Asia which was originally established in 1985 by Iran, Pakistan and Turkey the members of the dormant RCD. In November 1992, the organization was expanded to include seven new members, namely, Afghanistan, Azerbaijan, Kazakhstan, Kyrgyzstan, Tajikistan, Turkmenistan and Uzbekistan. Since the ECO's expansion, its long term perspective and sectoral priorities have been defined in the field of transport, communications, trade, investment and energy. However, in practice the ECO has largely remained inactive.

Finance Minister of Pakistan, Shaukat Aziz and Hidayat Amin Arsala, Vice-Chairman and Finance Minister of Interim Afghan government, both underscored the need for pursuing regional development strategies. Five possible linkages with the region were considered in the meeting held at Islamabad on 27 February 2002. The five possible linkages with the Central Asia via Afghanistan that were considered included oil and gas pipelines, electricity grid stations, road and rail links. Shaukat Aziz argued that a strong and stable Afghanistan would make these projects a reality although all the projects will be undertaken under the ECO umbrella. But Afghanistan is a nucleus for south and Central Asia.[24] However, stability continues to the evasive in this war-torn country.

The latest initiative to revive ECO was launched by Iran. Fearing a total exclusion from the region after increasing American presence in and around Afghanistan, Iran courted Pakistan for regional cooperation through ECO. Given the trade record of their bilateral cooperation, particularly in the context of Afghanistan, it may prove to be mere ambitious thinking. However, the external pressures and changing realities of the global political chessboard may bring them together to tap Central Asian markets with the co-operation of China on more broader terms.

India, China, Afghanistan and Pakistan are becoming more interested in operating in Central Asia through the ECO. Iran is desperate to lay its own pipelines network to Pakistan and India, has plans to build similar pipelines from the Central Asia to Iran. China also aims to construct pipelines from CARs to Xinjiang province via Afghanistan. Chinese stakes in the strategically Gwadar port could further boost its plans. Gwadar could serve as a regional hub for trade of goods and junction of oil and gas pipeline network in the region. However, the completion of such multi-billion dollar projects depends on American support. Since, US companies had long been aspiring to build an east-west energy corridor, they are eager to be the major players in such projects.

Turkey, at the moment, seems less involved in the ECO, perhaps the presence of Afghanistan and Pakistan and increasing interest of China in ECO inhibits Ankara from taking an active interest in this regional organization. It is also possible that Turkey is concentrating more on development of bilateral trade relation with the Central Asian states where a mutually satisfying framework can be evolved.

Turkey had initially undertaken massive economic responsibilities (US $ 3 billion). When faced with real situation it was discovered that Ankara would not be able to shoulder the burden alone. Still, the Turkish Exim Bank provided about US $ 1.1 billion in programme and investment credits to the new republics. Meanwhile, some private Turkish firms were reported to have invested over US $ 6 billion in the region and Turkish construction companies had important contracts for building hotels, airports, and industrial projects.[25]

While Turkey was hardly emerging as an economic giant in Central Asia, Turkish firms were particularly active in telecommunications, with small and medium sized Turkish businesses, often working with local partners, prominent in food processing and textiles.[26] However, the expectation that Central Asia would become a major focus for Turkey's total foreign trade proved wide of the mark. Although there was a substantial growth in Turkey's trade turnover with the five republics, from US $ 147 million in 1992 to US $ 939 million in1997, the simultaneous rise in Turkey's total foreign trade meant that the 1997 figure still represented only 1.3 percent of Turkey's total exports plus imports. By comparison, recorded trade with the whole of the rest of the CIS (excluding 'suitcase trade') came to almost US $ 6.2 billion, with Russia easily Turkey's biggest trade partner in the former Soviet Union.[27]

THE EU FACTOR

As discussed above, Turkey's early interest in Central Asia centred around its ethno-linguistic, cultural and historical ties with the region. This emphasis on ethno-linguistic dimension was largely motivated by Turkey's disillusionment with the EU which was keeping Turkey out on the ground of its belonging to a different religion, and culture. The emergence of newly independent states in its immediate neighbourhood belonging to Turkic races and speaking Turkic language (not exactly, only its very old version having just a few words from the modern Turkish) and looking towards Turkey with interests brightened Turkey's hopes. The sense of belonging to 'Turkic' states provided great solace to disenchanted Turks as 'Turkic identity' could provide a more welcome alternative to their search for 'European identity' although in reality Turkey would do any thing to acquire European identity by getting into the EU. In that case Turkic identity' would become a second ground for deriving psychological satisfaction. Turkey's option for Turkic identity might even soften the EU's intransigence and make it agreeable to Turkey's membership in the EU.

Ali Dinçer, the spokesman of the Republican Peoples Party (RPP) at the Turkish Grand National Assembly (GNA) argued that "Turkey has a very important potential in the Caucasus, the Middle East and Central Asia due to its close relations with these regions. Turkey should use this as a weapon against the EU and other economic and political powers".[28] For many Turks who were disappointed with Europe "the opportunity to assert a leadership role in a minor world region which was also the birth place of the Turkish nation seemed irresistible".[29]

The EU was a major determinant in Turkey's policy towards Central Asia in 1991-92 also, but Turkey acted more on its own notion. It cherished to have a region of influence which it could use to its advantage. On liberation of Central Asia, Ankara acted promptly by taking initiative in striking economic deals and cultural relations. As Yasmin Celik pointed out "Ankara was eager to define a new role for itself in the post-cold war period" by using its ethno-linguistic and cultural commonalties with the region.[30] The idea was reinforced by the European Union's rebuff for full membership in the Union. Psychologically, the emergence of the region provided Turkish people with a sense of pride in belonging to a wider ethno-cultural entity. Erdal Inonu, the Head of the Social Democratic People's Party (SDPP) argued that "these changes are ushering in a new period in which Turkey's role and political weight will be increased dramatically in the region and in the world".[31] The National Action Party was also active in promoting Turkey's ties to Central Asia.

Some of the Central Asian states, Iran and Russia understood the dynamics of Turkey's Central Asia policy and knew that behind its over enthusiasm is EU's indifference to Turkey. However, it may not be very correct to say that once the EU's membership is granted to Turkey, it will whole heartedly devote itself to the West and the European Union only. In reality, having membership in the EU, retaining hold over Central Asian republics, having share in the economy and natural resources of the Caspian Basin countries, getting pipeline routes passing through its territory will be enhancing its status in the EU and other western alliances. Thus, Ankara will be enjoying the benefits of both—East and the West.

Understanding Turkey's dilemma, the United States is already pushing Israel in Central Asia to make a place for itself in the community of liberal Muslim states, assist Turkey, and also pursue west's economic and political interest in the region.

Israel as a new entrant in southern Caucasus and Central Asia can deliver arms to Azerbaijan and tilt the balance in the Nagorno-Karabakh dispute in favour of Baku. The US could not do that owing to Congressional ban on arms supplies to Azerbaijan. Similarly, Israel can sell arms to Central Asian states independently or transfer armaments at the behest of United States. In these situations Israel might be blamed for arming the Central Asian States and thus creating instability in the region. It was not possible for Turkey to supply arms openly for fear of provoking Russia and Iran.

It appears that gradually United States would like to enter Central Asia and establish itself in Azerbaijan with the support of Turkey and Israel. US entry can end entire pipeline controversy at least seemingly. In reality, it would not be possible for the United States to construct and run the pipelines in disregard to geo-politics of the region and trans- frontier ethnic clashes between the republics which are going to provide route for pipeline through their territories.

In the context of balance of power in Central Asia, till date position is in favour of that grouping which has Russia as a member or a supporter. If Iran and Russia both are members in a grouping it would be most powerful. Turkey was faced with difficulty in this respect. In the Ankara supported geopolitical grouping besides Turkey rest of the countries—Azerbaijan, Georgia, Ukraine all are weaker in comparison to combined Russo-Iranian power. With Israel's arrival on the Central Asian stage and its independent interaction with the CARs as well as the South-Caucasian republics, Turkey's position is strengthened and its burden is lessened. The United States is gradually creating space for itself through its pro-American or somewhat committed allies in the region. America-Turkey-Israel will be a very strong alliance which might be able to outmaneuver Iran-Russia-Armenia configuration.

China, which is also a Central Asian state by virtue of sharing a 3700 kilometer long border with the three Central Asian states and its Xinjiang province inhabited by the Muslims of Central Asian origin besides others. As far as Russia is concerned, China did not have any problems so far. Beijing is not against the CIS, nor is it opposed to Russia's support to Iranian claims in the Caspian Sea and its participation in the politics of oil in the Caspian Basin especially in the pipeline controversy.

The Shanghai Co-operation Organization (SCO) formed in 1996 by five states—Russia, China and three Central Asian states—Kazakhstan, Kyrgyzstan and Tajikistan which together have a 3700 kilometer long border with China. In face of terrorist attacks from Afghanistan and Pak-Saudi sponsored *jihadi* onslaughts against Tajikistan during its civil war, Russia protected them. The Shanghai Organization aims at taking a collective action against the terrorist menace.

The SCO has also admitted Uzbekistan in 2001. Its focus is on combating terrorism and plans to establish a regional anti-terrorism headquarters in the Uzbek capital, Tashkent and also a secretariat by the end of the year 2002. This has since been setup in Beijing.

The Chinese Premier Wen Jiabao made three proposals to boost regional economic co-operation. The proposals are: (a) to promote the facilitation of trade and investment in a bid to realize the smooth circulation of goods within the framework of SCO as well as reduce and eliminate non-tariff barriers like those in customs services, quarantine standards and transportation; (b) to set certain large projects on economic and technological co-operation and give priority to those in transportation, energy, telecommunication, agriculture, home appliances light industry and textile; (c) to set a long term objective for regional economic cooperation and gradually set up a free trade zone within the SCO. These proposals suggest that China is not just watching the developments in Central Asia or keeping an eye on 'outsiders', 'intruders' and west's proxies. Beijing has elaborate plans to expand its presence in a meaningful manner which can be advantageous to all the states of Central Asia.

The presence of two comparatively well spelled out configurations—Turkey, Israel, US and Iran-Russia-China suggests that the region is going to remain an arena of rivalry between the two groups and local actors will continue fluctuating between one group or another. However, this is not what was expected to be the state of affairs in Central Asia at the end of a decade and half of their independence. The so-called "Great Game" which was going on for oil might target both oil and political power in the region. To minimize the possibility of China entering the arena of Central Asian politics, the US might not show its presence openly and continue to be present through proxy actors only.

TURKEY AND REGIONAL INTEGRATION IN CENTRAL ASIA

The Central Asian republics and their leaders have not developed a vision of future. They are following a policy of ad-hocism both in the foreign relations and domestic politics. The efforts in the direction of community formation or regional integration were left to those who in the interest of their own, like to keep the region divided—putting one country against the other by creating misunderstandings between them or fanning ethnic conflicts. On the domestic front too, there is no trace of democracy. Centralized power pattern of the days of former Soviet Union is still flourishing in the CARs.

Turkey could play the role of an integrator had it acted independently—free from Washington's prompting. It is in an advantageous position due to its ethno-linguistic, cultural, historical, religious affinities but after the phase of initial euphoria, in which it tried to establish its patronage over the region, Ankara concentrated primarily on Azerbaijan only. Energy became the chief occupation of Turkey. It started weighing each problem of the region through the prism of oil and gas exporting pipelines. Ankara tried to expand its trade and economic relations through institutional frameworks of ECO, TICA (Turkish International Cooperation Agency), BSEC (Black Sea Economic Co-operation), TURKSOY (Turkic Cultures and Arts Joint Administration) etc., but these could not lead to any community formation in Central Asia.

It is argued that Turkey's efforts have been half-hearted because its major concentration within the Central Asian region remained mainly on Azerbaijan and outside the region on the European Union. In fact the second target is more important than integrating the Central Asian republics into a community in which all constituents feel bound by a common policy, ideology, sense of commitment and identity of perceptions.

The western allies of Turkey, however, thought that it would be the 'core country' around which a "pro-western economic and security community" would evolve in Central Asia. The US overestimated Turkey's capabilities in this respect. The theories of international relations define a "community (security or non-security) as a group of people which have become 'integrated'. Integration means attainment within a region of a sense of 'community' and of institutions and practices strong enough and wide-spread enough to assume for a long time dependable expectations of 'peaceful change' among its population".[32] By sense of community, Karl W. Deutsch meant "a belief on the part of individuals in a group that they have come to an agreement on at least one point: that common social problems must and can be resolved by process of peaceful change".[33] Peaceful change means resolution of social problems normally by institutionalized procedure, without resort to large scale physical force".[34]

The pluralistic security communities are easier to be attained and maintained than formal unions provided their central aim is merely preservation of peace among the participants. This conclusion will not be true if socio-political aims other than peace predominate. Successful integration is attained, argues Ernst B. Hass, "when the subjective criterion of certain elite expectations is met: if the expectations of key elites in the region converge toward demands for peaceful change and other benefits thought to be obtainable only through the union, integration is underway".[35]

Besides, a successful integration is held to depend on the prevalence of mutually compatible self-images and images of the other actors participating in the process of unification. Further, successful integration takes place around a 'core area', a region possessing superior administrative skills, military power, economic resources, and techniques as well as capacity for receiving and assimilating the demands of the other regions so as to satisfy them.

Actors in the weaker areas look to the "core area" for leadership and help in the satisfaction of their demands, sympathetic response on the part of the elite active in the core area then begets progressive integration without in the least implying any "balance of power" among participating units.

However, a great deal of stress is placed on the "capacity" of the administrative system and the attitudes prevailing in the core area actively to respond to the needs expressed by others. In Karl Deutsch's terms, a successful integration equals the balance of load and capability in the network of social communication.[36]

As states move toward community, they no longer need to rely on the balance of power mechanisms to protect their security. Instead, observes E. Adler, states focus on "assurance, not deterrence".[37] Collective security, joint military planning and integration, unfortified borders, and free movement of people across borders and common definitions of both external and internal threats are all hallmarks of security communities. E. Adler calls security communities "inside-out-model" where states feel their interests as best served by being inside the community.[38]

Democracy is also considered most desirable pre-requisite of a pluralistic security community. Democracies normally do not wage war against each other. They promote compatible self images, values, principles, objectives and methods of resolving conflicts.

The above criteria, applied to Turkey's role as a leader of Central Asian states, expecting that the CARs will revolve around Ankara and seek its patronage does not lead to the conclusion that Turkey was the "core area/country" whose capabilities matched its responsibilities, that it was going to assume by virtue of accepting the leadership of Central Asian republics. In fact, this ambition was injected in the mind of Turks by the United States which was looking for a regionally strong state to save the Central Asian region from slipping back into the Russian arena or falling prey to Islamic fundamentalists active in the region at the behest of Iran, Afghanistan, Pakistan and Saudi Arabia. More than the Turkish government and its socio-political elite and intelligentsia, the American administration, political leadership and media projected Turkey as a 'key' country having capacity to bring all the NISs together in a Ankara-sponsored pro-West political grouping. Its ethnic, cultural, linguistic, historical and religious commonalties were considered valuable assets which Turkey can utilize in bringing the CARs together under its 'protective umbrella'.

However, in a couple of years' time it was proved that these assets are incapable of bringing the CARs together in the absence of a common agenda, policy, objectives, strategies and above all mutual trust and desire to forge regional unity. More than Turkey, it was the United States making more noises about Ankara's common ancestry with Central Asia's Turkic republics. If one goes by the theories of international relations given by scholars like Karl W. Deutsch, Lynn H. Miller, Gavin Boyd, Louis J. Cantori, Stevan L. Spiegel, Ronald Yelem and several others, suggest that regionalism as a phenomenon was encouraged by the superpowers, especially by the United States as a means of reducing the cost of containing the Soviet bloc.[39]

Louis J. Cantori and Steven L. Spiegel argue that ".... system consists of one state or two or more proximate and interacting states which have some common ethnic, linguistic, cultural, social and historical bonds and whose sense of identity is sometimes increased by actions and attitudes of states external to the system". This argument is relevant to analysing the role of Turkey in "promoting" Central Asian "community integration" on the basis of certain commonalties as discussed above.

However, by harping on pan-Turkism Ankara, instead of promoting regional integration tried to divide the Central Asian and Trans-Caucasian States into Turkic and non-Turkic groups and thus setting the one group against the other. Armenia, Georgia, Tajikistan are non-Turkic states. Pan-Turkism left no role for them in the 'emerging' Turkic configuration.

Turkey's claim to ancestral ties, common language, religious affinity are contested by several scholars on various grounds. It is widely argued that there have been no strong relations between the Turks and the Central Asian peoples since the Seljuq migration. Those Turkmen, who later established the Ottoman Empire paid little or no attention to the events in Central Asia and began to move further west, and concentrated on the affairs of their empire, composed by the Balkans and the Arab Middle East.[40]

In religious matters, as a Caliph, Ottoman Sultan acted as a protector of Sunni muslims. Ottoman Sultans kept a degree of ceremonial and diplomatic relations with the Turkic states in which religious feelings played a more significant role than the blood relations.[41] The Ottoman Empire, however, was unable to render any material assistance to these states in their wars against Iran and Russia. Russia's annexation of Central Asia terminated all relations between the Turks and the Central Asians and leaving only a vague memory of common ancestry.

On the linguistic plank, modern Turkish is different from the regional Turkic language, Kazakh, Uzbek, Kyrgyz and Turkmen. It is maintained that from the ninth to the thirteenth centuries there was a common Turkic language among the Turkic peoples, including the Turks. In the thirteenth century owing to demographic movements the Turkic language was divided into two main eastern and western branches.[42] The gap became further wider as a result of Soviet ethnic, linguistic policy toward Central Asia. Consequently, the Turkish dialects spoken in the Central Asian Turkic republics can not be easily understood by the Turks.[43]

The resurgence of pan-Turkish wave in the aftermath of dissolution of the Soviet Union generated an ambition for creation of a Ankara-led Turkic bloc in Central Asia. The pan-Turkist euphoria later subsided in face of reluctance of the CARs to base their relationship on ethnic grounds.

Had these ancestral, linguistic, religious and cultural factors been prominent, even then community formations or development of integrational tendencies would not have been possible. Having understood the inability of these factors in generating feeling of "regional unity", Turkey switched over to more practical, logical and viable avenues. The revival of ECO, establishment of BSEC and several other institutional arrangements holds more promise of interdependence between Turkey and the CARs. The widening of membership by including Greece, Bulgaria, Ukraine and other small states of the Trasncaucasian-Black Sea region may further enlarge the area of goodwill, co-operation and joint ventures in the field of regional developmental activities and programmes. In the long run such co-operation can lead to formation of non-security community among the Central Asian states.

Turkey's ability, will and resources are sufficient to make it a major power in the Central Asian region. However, its near obsession with the European identity through membership in the EU weakens its drive for leadership in the region. Ankara's multifarious commitments in NATO, OSCE, CSCE, its Kurdish problem, conflict with Syria over the water of the Euphrates-Tigris, of Baku-Ceyhan oil pipeline construction restricted its role as a key player in Central Asia.

There are several leaders in the domestic politics who suggest Ankara to simplify its role and reduce its various responsibilities emanating from its close connection with the US sponsored alliances and programmes. They often create contradictory commitments and confuse its performance. Commenting on frustration of the Government over the rejection of Turkey's membership in EU, former Foreign Minister of Turkey, Professor Mumtaz Soysal suggested that:

> This is the most opportune time to rid ourselves of the complex of being considered Europeans. We are Turks from Turkey. Turkey is a country with one bank in Europe and the other in Asia. The same thing can be said of our geography and culture. We must realize and accept this as such and we must turn this embarrassment into a sense of superiority.[44]

In reality it is obvious that Turkey's excessive slant in favour of West has led to severe imbalances in its foreign policy. Toward South Asia, South East and South West Asia, Middle East and Muslim Africa Turkey has absolutely no policy. They react when a situation concerning their interest arises or they rush to the countries of Asia when their expectations from the West are heavily watered down. Geographically Turkey is a meeting point between the East and the West but politically it could not became a bridge between them. Ian O. Lesser maintains that:

> The notion of a bridge suggests a country balanced between East and the West. In fact Turkish attitudes remain heavily weighed toward the western political and economic system, to the extent that "alternative" opportunities in the Middle East and around the Black Sea are often promoted as vehicles for increasing Turkey's value to Europe and the United States.[45]

Turkey is projected as a model of democratic-secular, republican state with Muslim ethos—most suitable for Central Asian Republics. When there was no possibility of having access to Central Asia, Turkey was seen in the western bloc as a liability which is to be kept along for serving the interest of the west vis-à-vis the Soviet Union in the cold war period. Kamal Karpat, a well known scholar and political analyst of Turkey has rightly put it:

> The features that make Turkey attractive as a role model were all adopted from the west. In other words, the west expected Turkey as a relay station to transfer those acquired values and modes of life to the newly emerging cluster of Islamic countries in the former USSR. Had thes Muslim countries of Central Asia been Christian as in the case of the Baltics—or had the West found another Muslim country to act as a better model—Turkey might have been promptly discarded.[46]

The West has put in the mind of Turkey that their role is of a bridge between West and the East and it cannot get away with its responsibility of playing this role. With such deep grounding in the West, how much of Turkey can be with the East—the Central Asia? Teoman Erel argued "Turkey will stick to Europe despite Europe's dislike for her".[47] In the same vein, a Turkish official spokesman for foreign affairs, Omer Akbel, said on one occasion that, "even in the worst of times, [Turkey was] the sick man of Europe, not Asia".[48]

David Barchard has very rightly argued that "Turkey first needs to make up its mind about whether or not it belongs to the West. Despite a very strong sense of national identity ... many Turks seem genuinely uncertain about this.[49] If Turkey considers itself a synthesis of west and east, it can take advantage of its synthesis of different cultures through "loose arrangements with several "clubs" or "regional arrangements",[50] which would be more conducive to its economic and political interests than obsessively committing itself to any one direction.[51]

NOTES

1. Philip Robins, "Turkey"s Ostpolitik: Relations with the Central Asian States" in David Menashri (ed.), *Central Asia Meets Middle East* (London, Cass, 1998), p. 135.
2. *Ibid.*, and Heinz Kramer, "Options.for Turkish Foreign Policy: Central Asia and Transcaucasus" quoted in William Hale, *Turkish Foreign Policy: 1774-2000*. (Frank Cass, London, 2000), p. 291.
3. Gareth M. Wintrow, *Turkey in Post-Soviet Central Asia* (London, RIIA, 1995), p. 133.
4. Philip Robins, *Turkey's Ost politik, op.cit.*, p. 133.
5. Gareth M. Window, *op.cit.*, p. 17.
6. William Hale, *op.cit.*, p. 288.
7. *Ibid.*, p. 288.
8. Nation, Craig R. "The Turkic and other Muslim Peoples of Central Asia, the Caucasus and the Balkans" in *Turkey Between East and West* (Bonlder: West View Press, 1996), p. 105.
9. Alparslan Turkes had become very popular in Azerbaijan and he, in fact, propagated ethnicity and linguistic affinity as a basis of solidarity between Azerbaijan and Turkey. See Yetkin Murat, *Ates Hattinda Aktif Politika*, p. 289.
10. Gareth Winrow, *op.cit.*, p. 18.
11. Quoted in Yucel Bozdaglioglu, *op.cit.*, p. 98.
12. Gareth Winrow, *op.cit.*, p. 18.
13. Gareth Winrow, "Regional Security and National Identity: The Role of Turkey in former Soviet Central Asia" in *Turkey: Political, Social and Economic Challenges in the 1990s*, ed. Cigdem Balim, et.al. (New York and Kol: E.J. Brill, 1995), pp. 22-50, p. 34.
14. Philip Robins, "Turkey's *Ost politik:* Relations with the Central Asian States" in David Menashri, ed. *Central Asia Meets the Middle East, op.cit.*, pp. 136-37 and Gareth M. Winrow, *Turkey in Post-Soviet Central Asia* (London, RIIA, 1995), p. 19.
15. Heinz Kramer, " Opposition for Turkish Foreign Policy: Central Asia and Trans-Caucasus", in William Hale, *Turkish Foreign Policy: 1774-2000, op.cit.*, p. 293.
16. Philip Robins, "Turkey's Ost Politik", *op.cit.*, p. 144; Gareth M. Winrow, *Turkey in the Post-Soviet Central Asia, op.cit.*,p. 47.
17. *Ibid.*, p. 144.
18. *Ibid.*

19. *Financial Time*, 4 December 1992.
20. Yucel Bozdaglioglu, *op.cit.*, p. 100.
21. Figures are for 1995, *Briefing* (Ankara), 22 April 1996, p. 19.
22. *The Independent*, 26 June 1992.
23. William Hale, "Turkey and Trans-Caucasia" in David Menashri, (ed.), *Central Asia Meets Middle East*, *op.cit.*, p. 153.
24. http://www.jang-group.com/thenews/Feb.2002–daily/27.2.2002/main/main3.htm.
25. William Hale, *Foreign Policy of Turkey: 1774-2000*, *op.cit.*, p. 294.
26. Gareth M. Winraow, Turkey in Post-Soviet Central Asia, *op.cit.*, pp. 32-33, and Heinz Kramer, *Options For Turkish Foreign Policy: Central Asia and Trans-Caucasus*, *op.cit.*, pp. 11-12.
27. Data for 1992 from Gareth M. Winrow, *Turkey in Post Soviet Central Asia*, *op.cit.*, p. 37; for 1997 from *Statistical Year Book of Turkey: 1998* (Ankara, State Institute of Statistics, 1999), pp. 515-516; See William Hale, *Turkish Foreign Policy: 1774-2000*, *op.cit.*, pp. 294-295.
28. TBMM (Turkish Grand National Assembly Minutes of Records (TBMM) 992, p. 377.
29. R. Craig Nation, 'The Turkic and other Muslim Peoples of Central Asia, the Caucasus and the Balkans" in *Turkey Between East and West*, ed. Vojtech Mastny and R. Craig Nation (Boulder, Westview Press, 1966), pp. 97-130, p. 105.
30. Yasmin Celik, *Contemporary Turkish Foreign Policy* (Westport, Conneticut, London, Praeger, 1999), p. 122.
31. TBMM, 1991, p. 562.
32. Karl W. Deutsch *et.al.*, *Political Community and the North Atlantic Area: International Organization in the Light of Historical Experience* (Princeton, NJ: Princeton University Press, 1957), p. 3.
33. *Ibid.*
34. *Ibid.*, p. 5
35. Ernst B. Hass, "The Challenge of Regionalism", in Stanley Hoffman (ed.), *Contemporary Theory in International Relations* (Prentice-Hall of India (Private) Ltd., New Delhi, 1964), pp. 224-225.
36. *Ibid.*
37. Fotios Moustakis, *The Greek-Turkish Relationship and NATO* (Frank Cass, London, Portland, OI: 2003), p. 98.
38. *Ibid.*
39. Gavin Boyd, "Regional Designing" in *Regionalism and Global Security*,

ed. Gavin Boyd (Lexingtonn, MA: D.C. Health & Co., 1984), pp. 175-177.

40. Mehmet Saray, "Political, Economic and Cultural Relations Between Turkey and Central Asian Republics", *Eurasian Studies*, 2 (Summer 1994), pp. 47-48.
41. Mehmet Saray, *op.cit.*, p. 49.
42. Fikret Turkmen, "The Issue of Common Turkish Script", *Eurasian Studies*, 1 (Spring 1994), p. 85.
43. *Ibid.*
44. David Kushner, "Self Perception and Identity in Contemporary Turkey", *Journal of Contemporary History*, 32 (1997): .219-233, p.232.
45. Ian O. Lesser, *Bridge or Barrier ? Turkey And The West After the Cold War* (Santamonica, CA: Rand; 1992), p. 5.
46. Patricia Carley, "Turkey's Place in the World", in *Reluctant Neighbour: Turkey's Role in the Middle East*, (Ed.), Henri Barkey (Washington DC: US Institute of Peace Press, 1996): 3-12, p. 10.
47. David Kushner, *Self Perception and Identity, op.cit.*, p. 232.
48. James Nathan, "Turkey on Edge", *International Relations* (13 August 1997) Z: 15-25, p. 19.
49. David Barchard, *Turkey and the West* (London: Boston and Henley: Routledge & Kegan Paul, 1985), p. 87.
50. Ziya Onis, "Turkey in the Post-Cold War Era: In Search of Identity", *Middle East Journal*, 49 (Winter 1995): 48-68, p. 54.
51. Yucel Bozdaglioglu, *op.cit.*, p. 109.

CHAPTER 5

Turkey and the Emerging Geo-political Constellations in Central Asia

The dissolution of the Soviet Union and termination of the cold war during 1989-1990, altered Turkey's international environment drastically. The security threat from the Soviet Union which had compelled Turkey to join the western alliances and become an integral part of the west's security network from Atlantic to the Pacific ocean had effectively ended but as the Soviet state had constitutionally dissolved, Russia had contracted territorially, and a series of smaller successor states emerged in the Black Sea region, Central Asia and Trans-Caucasia. Previously, it was surrounded on three sides by a single state although far more powerful than itself. Now Turkey is surrounded by smaller neighbours which are weaker than itself both militarily and economically.[1]

I
TURKEY AND THE EURO-AMERICAN CONFIGURATION: GAINS AND CONSTRAINTS

With the eclipse of cold war, the western alliances formed to protect Europe from the Soviet Union lost significance. The several members of the NATO and other US sponsored organizations started showing signs of independence and started drawing their own agenda of operating in the region liberated by the former Soviet Union. Turkey could also assert its independence and seek independent sphere of influence in the adjoining regions but owing to its total commitment to relationship with the west, in particular, with Europe and the US it could not think of reverting back to a neutral stance. Owing to its emotional inner urge to 'appear' European and part of the western community it stuck up to NATO and also continued efforts to attain full membership in the European Union (EU). A Turkish scholar has argued, "Turkey needed to stay in the alliance not because of NATO's important security guarantee, but also because this membership is a clear manifestation of her western vocation".[2] However, the changed political scenario in the Newly Independent States (NIS) of Trans-Caucasia-Central Asia, presence of 'enormous' deposits of natural gas (Turkmenistan) and oil (Kazakhstan) and Azerbaijan) motivated the West to plan a long-term stay in the region. Turkey being a Central Asian country sharing ethno-cultural affinity with the countries of the region and having geographical proximity and historical ties with the people of Azerbaijan, Turkmenistan, Kazakhstan, Georgia, Ukraine and Uzbekistan, was seen as a most useful vehicle to enter Central Asia. Turkey's democratic republican model along with its Islamic character also appeared a "welcome" feature for the CARs. This renewed utility of Turkey for the west facilitated its retention in the NATO and the west's security network.

The ideology of pan-Turkism which was safely lying hidden in the annals of history was also brought back to the lime light and made a focal basis of Turkey's relations with the people of Turkic republics of Central Asia. However, soon it was realized by the Turks that pan-Turkism as a basis of Turkey-Central Asia relations is no longer viable. Ankara dropped reference to pan-Turkism and tried to consolidate its relations on the basis of economic co-operation and partnership in the development and exportation of the Central Asian oil and gas to international markets via its own territory. The Baku-Ceyhan pipeline proposed by Turkey was welcomed by the oil exporting states of the Caspian Sea region even when it was not functional.

While Turkey was readily shouldering the responsibility of safeguarding west's oil interests in the Caspian Sea Basin States and the CARs by offering sumptuous financial, technological and material help to them despite its own economy facing severe decline. The Gulf War (1990-91) had made severe impact on its economic fortunes as it had to suspend export of Iraqi oil to the European markets through the Kirkuk-Yumurtalik pipeline traversing its territory and suffer the loss of huge revenues which it was earning by exporting Iraqi oil.

The Kurdish Peoples Party (PKK) was also threatening internal stability of the country at a time when the grip of the government, in face of the rising power of the Turkish Islamists was weakening on the polity and society. Turgut Ozal's party had lost election in 1991 and later his death in 1993 further aggravated the situation on the home front although on Turkey's Central Asia policy, there was no debate. In fact, people wanted Turkey to have pro-Central Asia policy and cultivate close relations with the countries of the Muslim world in West Asia, South and South-East Asia. Turks were disillusioned with EU's reluctance to give full membership to Turkey. The attitude of the US and the EU on the Cyprus issue had also frustrated the Turks.

Turkey adopted an independent attitude in its foreign policy related matters and kept its own national interest in mind. It established close relation with Azerbaijan, cultivated relations with Iran and Russia and started thinking in terms of having an economic partnership with Iran and Russia and also to co-operate in developing the economy of the NIS.

Several western scholars started thinking that Turkey would be drifting away from the west in view of new opportunities in Central Asia and West Asia. It might seek a "Middle Eastern" or "Turkic" identity rather than the European and thought that "it was in the interest of the West to regard Turkey an integral part of the western community which could maximise its relations with the Middle East and Central Asia".[3]

Zia Onis, a Turkish scholar also suggested that Turkey should look simultaneously to both the East and West and accept the fact that "Islam constitutes an important part of its cultural heritage".[4] In the western countries Turkey's importance was being realized afresh particularly in view of its role in the Gulf War (1990-91). The US Assistant Secretary of State, Richard Hollbrooke claimed that "Turkey is replacing Germany as the cutting edge of Europe", and described Turkey as United States' "New European front".[5]

Turkey's active support to the US-military venture in Afghanistan and later in Iraq and Ankara's tacit support to US attitude towards Syria (not Iran) have further proved the importance of Turkey for the West.

The increasing debate over Turkey's status in the western world symbolized the enhanced recognition to its importance for the west even in the changed international scenario. This enabled Turkey to move confidently and air its views freely on issues related to its own interests and interests of the west. The west's attitude on Cyprus issue and on the rise of Kurdish nationalism disheartened Ankara but somehow it could manage to get along with the United States and other allies in the NATO.

Turkey, US, NATO and the European Security

As a member of the post-world war II political, military and strategic configuration of the west in Europe, Turkey was positioned on the front line of Europe's defence against the

Warsaw Pact countries and the Soviet Union. As a member of the several US sponsored military pacts and alliances, as a member of the southern flank of NATO, and as a custodian of west's oil interests in the Middle East, Turkey had contributed a great deal to the strength of the western configuration in Europe and West Asia.

Notwithstanding its outstanding performance as an ally of the west and the United States, Turkey's status vis-à-vis the west came to be critically evaluated in the post-cold war period. In 1992, when Turkey's Defence and Economic Co-operation Agreement (DECA) with the United States came up for renewal, it was extended just for one year. It was pointed out that the US military presence in Turkey with which the DECA was mainly concerned, was drastically reduced. By the middle of the 1964, eight out of twelve US military bases earlier established in Turkey were closed down or handed over to the Turkish army. The vital NATO airbase at Incerlik, near Adana continued to be in operation. It was of crucial importance during the Gulf War and its aftermath. Consequently, US military aid to Turkey was also scaled down substantially—partly because of Congressional cognizance of its poor Human rights record and partly due to Ankara's declined relevance. The aid was discontinued altogether in 1999.[6]

Besides, the setbacks on Cyprus and Kurdish issue, and evasive attitude of the EU on Turkey's membership and discontinuation of the US military aid were seen as a severe blow to Turkey's status within the west' security edifice and also its position as an ally of the United States. Notwithstanding the declining significance of Turkey for the west, Ankara continued to play its conventional role as a member of the NATO and other security organizations. It supported the admission of new eastern European members to NATO (Poland, Hungary, and the Czech Republic in 1999) and that of the states of the former Soviet Union in the Organization for Security and Co-operation in Europe (OSCE), NATO's Partnership for Peace Programme (PFP) and the North Atlantic Co-operation Council.

The emerging difference between Turkey and the United States in their approach to Russia and Iran, however, could not disturb the general tenor of US-Turkey relations. The US government strongly supported the plan to build an "East-West Energy Corridor" linking the states of the Caspian basin to world market via Turkey, and avoiding Russian territory.[7]

Turkey participated in the actions taken by the UN, US and NATO in Bosnia-Herzegovina. However, it was not an easy decision for Ankara. On the one hand the domestic public opinion strongly favoured the Muslim side in the conflict in Bosnia and later in Kosovo although the Bosnian Muslims are not ethnically Turkic, but Turks saw them as the last ramnant of a once powerful Muslim presence in south-eastern Europe. During the 19th century, the Ottoman attention had been concentrated on the Balkans, as the primary zone of conflict between Islam and Christianity. However, Turkish government's spokespersons frequently emphasized that they regard the Bosnian conflict as a humanitarian issue, and not a battle between two religions. President Turgut Ozal said that Bosnians will not be allowed to become a second Andalusia—a reference to the massacres and expulsions of the Muslims and Jews of Spain in the 15th century. The Islamist forces in Turkey compelled the government to intervene independently in Bosnia to save the lives of the Muslims. On the other hand, Turkey had to restrain itself and refuse to step too far out of line with the policies of the western allies, primarily the United States.[8]

In case of the Gulf War too, Turkey participated in the war to fulfill its commitment to be on the side of the west as an ally in NATO. In view of Turkey's relations with Iraq (Iraqi oil pipeline passing through Turkey and their economic co-operation in other fields too) it would have adhered to its traditional policy of staying away from Middle Eastern Conflict,[9] but it was not possible to reconcile this policy with the need to maintain relationship with the United States, the UN and the western powers in general. Saddam Hussain's refusal to vacate Kuwait led to embargo against Iraq. Turkey had to suspend oil transport from Iraq to Europe *via* the pipelines passing through its territory from Kirkuk to Yumurtalik. Turkey could not stay away from the United States' decisions regarding the "war against terror" in Afghanistan and again during the US attack on Iraq, which with the passage of time, turned into a full-fledged war.

During the Erbakan-Tansu Ciller (1996-97) coalition government, the Islamic forces became extremely powerful in Turkey. Necmettin Erbakan visited a number of Muslim countries including Iran and Libya, which were blacklisted by the United States. The Erbakan-Ciller government was ousted in June 1997. However, Islamist and their role in politics of Turkey is showing an upward trend. The recent Presidential election in Turkey in which an Islamist candidate could win the election despite Army's lack of trust in him and its open disapproval to his candidature suggests that Islamist forces are gaining strength in Turkey's politics although they do not appear to be going against the basic principles of Kemalism.

Kurdish Issue

The problem of the Kurds is peculiar. It is an international problem because the Kurds are inhabited not only in Iran, Iraq and Turkey (large population of Kurds is in these three countries) but they are in Syria, Lebanon, Germany, France and in small numbers in several other countries including Caucasian republics. For most Westerners, the Kurdish problem is like the liberation process of national minority, comparable to countless similar problems around the earth.

The West Asian Kurdish populated countries have kept their Kurds isolated from the main population, backward, uneducated and deprived of civil and political rights. They are not organized and owing to clan-related conflicts they further remain disunited.

The Iraqi Kurds are organized in three political parties besides in several tribal-clanist groupings. The traditional forces are represented by Masoud Barzani, son of Mullah Mustafa Barzani who played a leading role in creating political awakening among the Kurds of Northern Iraq. His party—the Kurdish Democratic Party (KDP) prefers autonomy within the framework of Iraqi State.

The modernizing phalanx is led by Jalal Talabani and his party PUK (Patriotic Union of Kurdistan) is supported by those who have come out of the clan based Kurdish society. They are educated and want to have an independent state of their own. The PKK is inspired by Marxist—Leninist ideology and favours armed revolutions. Abdullah Ocalan is a leader of the PKK (Turkish Branch). Jalal Talabani and Hizbollah find support in Iran—Barzani's stronghold lies in the north-west around Dahok while Talabani has influence in Erbil, Kirkuk and Sulamaniye.

Ankara enjoys good relations with the Barzani faction as it wants autonomy within the state but it is not comfortable with the PKK (which had supporters in the former Soviet Union and leftist countries—Syria, Iraq, Central Asian republics etc.) and the PUK which are separatists and believe in armed struggle for independence. However, whatever happens with the Kurds in Iraq it has repercussions on Turkey immediately.

In March 1991, a brief Kurdish rebellion against Saddam Hussain broke out in Iraq. Turgut Ozal, Prime Minister of Turkey permitted the PKK leader, Jalal Talabani and KDP's Mohsin Dizai to make a secret visit to Turkey as these two

Kurdish factions were keen to come in touch with European and American leaders through the good offices of Turkey. During and after the Gulf War, the Iraqi Kurds were being looked after/by the United Nations.

The embargo imposed against Iraq during the war was lifted in 1996 when Saddam Hussain accepted to abide by the Security Council Resolution 986 of April 1995, which allowed Iraq to export oil to the value of US $ 2 billion in each six-month period. This "oil for food" programme was beneficial to Turkey as Iraq's major oil exports were *via* Kirkuk-Yamurtalik pipeline traversing Turkish territory, which was partially re-opened. This new arrangement was estimated to bring in about US $ 500 million per year to Turkey which was in a way compensating for the cost of the embargo.

Maintaining diplomatic poise Turkey while toeing the official line taken by the US on Iraq was helping Saddam Hussain in many ways. Ankara continued to press for the removal of all sanctions against Iraq and later in 1998, the Turkish Foreign Minister Ismail Cem visited Baghdad. He submitted concrete proposals to end sanctions and restore Iraq's sovereignty over the Kurdish regions.

The Kurdish problem suddenly took an ugly turn in 1996. The Palestinian Organization leader, Yasser Araft having visited Turkey in 1995, opposed strong Arab criticism of Turkey and refused to support the PKK (leftist Kurdish organziation). Abdullah Ocalan, the leader of the PKK with the outside support (from West Asia mainly) created problems for Turkey. Ocalan was operating from Syria. When international support in favour of Turkey strengthened Syria expelled Ocalan in October 1998. He went to Germany, Italy, Greece and other countries but no body granted asylum to Ocalan. However, on 16 February 1999 he was arrested at the Nairobi airport.

The Ocalan saga ended but Turkey's Human Rights record came into prominence. In order to suppress insurgency, and secessionist movements generated by external political elements from various Kurdish parties, Turkey had to take stern measures against the Kurds. The Human Rights watch groups, other NGOs, Human Rights Commission of Europe and the United Nations turned against Turkey. Ankara's case for EU membership was almost ripe in 1989 but the Kurdish problem, Human Rights issue, and the Greece-Turkey conflict over Cyprus ruined it. Ankara's membership issue was deferred by the EU once again. The disappointment caused by EU's attitude, led Turkey to turn to Central Asian republics and seek accommodation also with its immediate rivals—Iran and Russia.

The CFE Revision of Conventional Arms Limitation Clauses

By the later 1990s, the EU was determined to develop its defence institutions. At the meeting of the European Council in Cologne in June 1999, the EU leaders agreed to take final decision on this by the end of the year 2000 under the Maastricht Treaty of 1991, the EU countries had undertaken to develop their "defence vocation" as an integral part of the development of the Union.[10]

The vehicle for this was to be the West European Union WEU founded in 1954 and lying defunct for all these years. Its role in the new circumstances would be to strengthen the European pillar of the Atlantic Alliance (AA) and formulate a common defence policy.[11] Within this, France and Germany proposed the creation of a European Security and Defence Identity (ESDI) to be developed outside the NATO.[12] In 1962. Turkey along with Norway and Iceland had joined the WEU as all the three were members of the NATO but not of the EU. In fact, the critical defence issues were still settled by the NATO Council in which Turkey fully participated. In practice the WEU was not more than a talking shop. Nonetheless, the idea that Turkey might be excluded from future defence structures under the aegis of the EU was disturbing Ankara. The main cause of Turkish resentment was psychological, that is to say, that in the case of EU, the West Europeans were treating Turkey as no more than a distant relative allowed into the European garden but not into the house.

Turkey's main worry was that since it is not a full member of the EU and all those new arrangements for European Security are to be outside the NATO, Turkey may not find a seat in this organization.

The former Turkish Foreign Minister, Kamran Inan, in great anguish asked in June 1996: Why should Turkey contribute to the defence of Europe if there is no guarantee that the WEU would contribute to the Security of Turkey"?[13]

At a NATO Council meeting at Berlin in June 1996, the alliance adopted the concept of Combined Joint Task Force (CJTF) as multinational formations under which forces assigned to NATO could be used for operations led jointly or entirely by the WEU. The WEU Ministerial Declaration issued at Erfurt in November 1997, made it clear that "Turkey would have the right to a full role of participation and decision making in any WEU sponsored operations using NATO assets and capabilities. However, the WEU was an organization without teeth. As Manfred Worner, the Secretary General of NATO in 1991, suggested that we must be realistic and realize that neither the emerging European Political Union (EPU) nor the WEU will have for the foreseeable future an operational defence capability able to be deployed[14] without the US/ NATO assistance. It turned out to be true. In Yugoslavia in 1990, the operations were conducted under the auspices of NATO or the UN and not the WEU. Heinz Kramer has rightly put that "most of the NATO assets which could be made available for WEU-led operations are in fact US assets, making the WEU's ability to act on its own very limited.[15]

Later at the Helsinki meeting of the European Council in December 1999 a plan to set up a Rapid Reaction Force (RRP) of up to 60,000 soldiers to conduct the EU-led military operations was adopted. If this occurred Turkey could be locked out of the new defence structure of the EU unless or until it was accepted into the EU as a full member. This stand of the EU was strongly criticized since Turkey's geographical situation between the Balkans, the Middle East and Trans-Caucasia placed it at the heart of the zone where challenges to European security were most likely to arise. Gulnur Aybet argued "a European Security architecture cannot be envisaged without Turkey".[16] Robin Cook, the British Foreign Secretary had conceded this point in December 1998, in the meeting of the North Atlantic Council that "as we take this project forward, we do not just seek the tolerance of our colleagues who are not members of the EU, we want their enthusiastic support for the enterprise in which we are engaged and also their participation wherever it is appropriate".[17]

Among other issues, the application of the CFE treaty limiting conventional forces in Europe signed in 1990 had some important implications for Turkey. The treaty had set limit on conventional weapons in the new states in Trans-Caucasia-Central Asia and the Black Sea region. However, in 1993, Russia sought relaxation in the limit on the ground that it needs to deploy more forces in the Caucasus for "peace keeping operations". This proposal was strongly opposed by Turkey and other members of NATO. The CFE was revised in 1999 to provide formal national ceilings in five categories of conventional weapons with sub-limits on separate flanks. Since Russia was already violating the limit during its campaign in Chechnya, Turkey along with other signatories of the CFE's revised draft decided to hold it back until Russia fulfilled its part of the bargain.

Turkey and Greece however were benefited by the limits

set on various categories of weapon in the CFE treaty as it was much higher than their existing inventories. Moreover, the treaty did not prevent qualitative improvements providing the numerical ceilings were adhered to (like replacement of absolute material with the new one). In the process of "cascading", the NATO members could transfer modern hardware which was disallowed by the treaty in the Central European front to Greece and Turkey. As a result Turkey received over 1000 modern tanks and 600 armoured cars from Germany and other NATO countries and ended up with a 25% bigger and modernized arsenal than what it had at the beginning of the CFE process.

The balance sheet of Turkey's gains and constraints as a member of the western alliances suggests that Turkey had gained much more than what it has contributed to the western security. The geo-strategic location of Turkey qualified it to get financial aid under the Marshall Plan (1947). In view of Soviet threats to Turkey, although they have been more vocal and less real, enabled it to be covered under the Truman Doctrine (1947) and its security (along with Greece) was considered vital to the security of the West European States as well as of the United States.

Turkey, owing to its basic obsession with the Westernization-Europeanization made every effort to get into the North Atlantic Treaty in 1952. It was a difficult task for the initiators of the Treaty as Turkey was the only Muslim country admitted in the community of Christian states. The Scandinavian and Benelux countries had opposed its entry into the NATO but in view of the valuable services rendered by the Turkish armed forces in the Korean war and its willingness to sacrifice its people, resources and interests to safeguard the interests of the West made it "highly qualified" to get a seat in the NATO.

NATO fortified Turkey's security and ensured its prolonged association with the West. Its role in organizing Middle East Defence Organization (MEDO) with Egypt as a "key country" in 1950-52 and later in the formation of the Northern Tier Alliance (the Baghdad Pact, 1955), strong criticism of the Bandung Conference, and its support to Britain and France during the Suez Crisis (1956), etc., are examples of Turkey's commitment to the western bloc. Interesting point is that Turkey was never made to show its real military prowess since the Korean war (1950-52). It became a part of West's collective security network which was once described by Charles B. Marshall in a tongue-in check observation that "collective security is a generalized notion of Nations banding together in undertaking a vague obligation to perform unspecified actions in response to hypothetical events brought on by some unidentifiable state".[18]

Turkey received sophisticated weapons, air-crafts, tanks, armoured cars and what not for 'fighting' the enemy (Soviet Union). It had ceased to be an enemy after 1947. Anakra was never faced by the Soviet menace –all its fears were imaginary. It is true that the presence of a powerful Soviet Union in its immediate neighbourhood and its iron curtain on Central Asia-Transcaucasia along with Eastern Europe kept Turkey locked out of the region and it was "forbidden" to have any contact with the Muslim republics of the former Soviet Union.

With the desovietization of the region, freedom has dawned on Central Asia—Transcaucasia and Turkey is feeling free to have access to the people of Turkic origin and to their resources—oil and gas and other minerals. Initially, Turkey moved in with its "pan-Turkist" ideology at the proddings of the west and tried to cultivate relations with the countries of this region on that basis. After suffering a few rebuffs from the Turkic states, it came down to business—having economic relations, collaboration in exploration, extraction and export of oil and gas from Central Asia to Europe. Here too, it was looking after interests of the western-American oil concerns besides seeking exit points for the Caspian oil *via* Turkey so that it could earn oil revenues by exporting oil through pipelines traversing Turkish territory.

Turkey feels constrained by the US obsession with Iran and Russia and its intransigence on the non-involvement of these two states in the oil affairs of the Caspian region. The US is opposed to the use of their existing pipelines besides the construction of new pipelines that would pass through the Iranian or the Russian territory. Turkey resents this stand. Ankara, conversant with the geopolitics of oil and importance of Russia in keeping the trans-frontier ethnic problems of the region in check wants the participation of Russia in the oil exports to Europe from Azerbaijan and Kazakhstan.

Iran's geographical proximity and its common border with the Central Asian and Caspian Sea States facilitates a shortest possible route for carrying the Central Asian oil *via* its territory to Europe but owing to the US opposition to Iran's inclusion in the pipeline projects Turkey feels compelled to keep Iran out against its own wish.

Turkey is having fairly developed trade relations with Tehran and Moscow. It is importing gas from both—Iran and Russia. The Baku-Ceyhan pipeline to carry Azeri oil to Europe *via* Turkey, bypassing Russia and Iran had been proposed by Turkey to find a wayout to *impasse* caused by the US stand.

Ankara is asserting its independence in having agreements with Azerbaijan, Turkmenistan, Kazakhstan and trying to find a solution to the Nagorno-Karabakh problem to mitigate tensions between Armenia and Azerbaijan. Turkey wants the Russian help in solving this ethnic problem. In fact, Russia owes help in this matter. At the time of formation of independent states of Azerbaijan and Armenia, it had placed the Azeri populated Nachicheven under the Armenian sovereignty and Nagorno-Karabakh which is populated by Armenian people under the sovereign jurisdiction of Azerbaijan. These are constant irritants to peace and stability in the region. Why not these two states exchange the territories which belong to them but separated by an arbitrary arrangement imposed by the former USSR. Turkey and Russia together can sort out this problem by holding direct talks between Armenia, Azerbaijan, Turkey and Russia. It would be a great contribution to peace, integrity, stability and well being of the region.

Turkey's relations with Azerbaijan and presence of a huge Azeri population in Iran can bring positive results in terms of inculcating better understanding between Turkey, Iran and Azerbaijan which would mitigate imaginary fears and feelings of distrust between them and facilitate easy transport of Azeri oil *via* Iran to Turkey and then to Europe. The improvement in the relations between the local players in the oil game and their combined assertion of control over the oil and gas resources of the region would also minimize the heat in the politics of pipelines in the southern Caucasus. Such symptoms are getting visible more and more. Today, the United States, Britain and Europe are not confronting Russia directly. They have reposed trust in Turkey and Israel which is the latest entrant in Central Asia along with Greece. These two countries want to gain spheres of influence with the help and support of Turkey which has more or less 'stabilized' in the region. Turkey's growing interest in the activities of Israel and Greece is enhanced by its emboldened profile in Transcaucasia.

The so called "Great Game" made too 'great' by the regional and external contenders for power and influence in the oil-rich region of Central Asia by constantly harping on the same theme has now come into the arena of Turkey, Iran, Russia and the outside non-Turkic, non-Central Asian entrants—Israel and Greece which might get further minimized when actual volume of oil resources of the Caspian will be authentically established.

Turkey and Israel have been coming closer since the 1973 Arab-Israeli war and Turkey's frustration over the Cyprus issue which was not supported by any country in the world. However, during this period, owing to disillusionments with the west over Cyprus issue Islamic forces had become powerful in the domestic politics of Turkey. Under their influence Turkey had drifted away from the west and supported the Arab countries' stand on the Palestinian issue. Turkey demanded from Israel the return of the territories occupied through use of force during the 1967 and 1973 war with the Arabs. In the UN General Assembly in 1975, Turkey voted in favour of anti-Israel resolutions which called "Zionism—a kind of recism".[19]

The relations with Israel started improving after the mid-eighties when both states exchanged diplomats at the Ambassadorial level in 1986. Turgut Ozal, the Turkish Prime Minister regarded relations with Israel as a "window on future events" and claimed that "for Turkey to play a role in solving the problems of the Middle East this window must remain open".[20] However, a real breakthrough came after the termination of cold war and collapse of the Soviet Union.

Greece, another new entrant in Central Asia, is a traditional "enemy" of Turkey. The major issue of conflict is Cyprus—an small island in the eastern mediterranean with just half a million population (82% Greek Cypriots and 18% Turkish Cypriots). Turkey has forcibly taken 37% of Cyprus' territory and is occupying it since 1974. The Turkey-occupied part has been named by Anakra as Turkish Republic of Northern Cyprus (TRNC). Turkey was trying to seek recognition to TRNC by the southern Caucasian states especially Azerbaijan. Greece has also come to seek support of the Caucasian countries (Armenia, Azerbaijan, Ukraine, Iran) in its favour.

What is interesting is that the two adversaries striving for opposite aims are pretending to be fellow travellers in Central Asia and hoping that they will be helpful to each other in attaining their desired objectives in the region—share in the oil pipelines carrying Caspian oil to Europe.

Turkey has come to realize that it can not have a monopoly over Caspian oil as the Soviet Union did. It can not be a replacement of Russia. Its rivalry with Iran is neither advantageous to Turkey nor to its Caucasian friends as the decision on the status of the Caspian Sea (sea or lake) depended equally on Iran and Russia both. By antagonizing Iran, Turkey may only ruin the prospects of its Caspian Sea Basin friends—Turkmenistan, Kazakhstan and Azerbaijan. Ankara has come down to accept that a wider grouping of aspirants in Central Asia may be more viable than a smaller one. This is likely to encourage formation of regional geo-political and economic configurations of the countries of the Trans-Caucasian-Central Asian region.

II
RUSSIA—TURKEY—IRAN TRIANGLE

Despite the new actors having emerged in Eurasia in the post-cold war era, the major actors in the North-South axis are Russia, Turkey and Iran which form a strategic triangle. The dissolution of former USSR reduced the size of the territory under Moscow's control, but Russia still occupies a vast portion of Eurasia. Despite several economic difficulties and political crises, Russia remains an important actor. Its territory is contiguous with Georgia, Azerbaijan and Kazakhstan, making it strategically important for the transport of Caspian oil and gas. Russia can offer transport up to Novorossisk, but this Black Sea port is not operationable in winter and transporting vast quantities of oil by tanker through the Bosphorus, a difficult channel to navigate, poses grave environmental risks to Istanbul. Other pipeline projects passing through Russia are opposed by Turkey.[21]

Russia has ceased to be militarily a superpower although it is still a nuclear power with tremendous capabilities and resources to develop it further. However, within its borders, the ethnic conflicts keep taxing its military power. Kenneth Waltz maintained that "Russia is now limited to its own territory for military action, and cannot easily project military force into the territories of its neighbours".[22] The war in Chechnya demonstrated the qualitative deterioration in the Russian armed forces. True, Russia is impermeable to direct territorial challenges from outside because its nuclear arsenal constitutes a powerful deterrent. But this nuclear umbrella does not cover the grey zones to the south of Russia's borders, including Central Asia and the Caucasus, which are open to rivalries concerning territorial influence and control.[23]

Turkey and Iran share several geo-political commonalties but differ markedly in state ideologies and alliance partnerships. Turkey is a secular country, a NATO ally and an important member of the West's security community. Iran is an isolated Islamic state. Both control strategic waterways such as Bosphorus and the strait of Hormuz and tend to act as a counter-weight to Russia in the Caucasus and the Caspian Sea Basin region.

Iran, since the *Shia* revolution staged by Ayatollah Khomeini in December 1979, has been treated as an outcast by the western community of states in particular by the United States and some of its allies and associates. The European countries, regardless of American opposition, maintain good workable relations with Iran. In the post cold war world when equations between the superpower, America and its rival in Eurasia—mainly Russia have changed and a great game for establishing control over the natural resources—oil and gas of the Caspian sea Basin states has commenced, Iran also wants to utilize the post-cold war developments to its advantage. Iran is one of the five Caspian Basin states (Russia, Azerbaijan, Turkmenistan and Kazakhstan) and has a direct access to the Indian ocean. It controls major part of the global energy resources. Iran is already a market for Turkmenistan's gas and commands useful pipelines to carry it to external markets as well. Iran acts as a barrier to Russia's entry in the Gulf region, where there are important US interests. As a Turkish Foreign Minitry Official, Ozdem Sanberk has observed: "the new global political fault line in the post cold war period is not along the East-West divide but along the north-South divide. Being situated on the fault line, life for Turkey, Iran and southern Caucasian states is full of challenges as well as opportunities.[24]

A study of interests of Turkey, Russia and Iran, individually and convergence and divergence in their interests in Southern Caucasus and Central Asia will be helpful in understanding the nature and viability of emerging power constellations in the region.

Russia's Interests in the Southern Caucasus

During the cold war era, Russia's south meant Turkey, Iran, Afghanistan. In the post-Soviet period, south meant southern Caucasus and Central Asia which have been an integral part of the USSR. In the post-Soviet era, the area covering south Caucasus, Central Asia, Middle East, the Gulf region and eastern Mediterranean has come to be seen by several scholars as a single unit—"greater" or "expanded" Middle East. However, neither the nature nor the intensity of the interactions among the countries of these regions since 1991 permit the conclusion that a greater or extended Middle East has emerged as a political entity with its own boundaries and patterns of regular interaction. The NIS in Central Asia and the southern Caucasus have chosen to diversify their relations, looking very much in western direction, while at the same time struggling to contain the influence of Islam.

Russia is extremely interested in the developments along its southern periphery for national security and geopolitical reasons. For Russia, the southern Caucasus presents an especially imminent security threat not only because instability has dominated the region but also because it is viewed as a potential transition belt that would relay security challenges, such as the "Islamic extremism" aggravating in the expanded Middle East to Russia's south.[25]

A study of Russian history suggests that both Czarist-Russia and the Soviet Union were intensely sensitive to challenges from the southern periphery. First, the British Empire posed the greatest threat to Russian rule in Central Asia in the 19th century. It has come to be known as the "Great Game". In the Caucasus, the Ottoman and Persian Empires, the former rulers, seemed poised to challenge Moscow's rule.

During the cold war era appeared a new global actor as a source of threat from the south—the United States. The US-led military alliances were formed to "contain communism" and "encircle the USSR", but the USSR managed to leapfrog this encirclement and formed friendship and military alliances with Egypt (until 1973), Syria, Iraq, the Palestinian Liberation Organization (PLO), Yemen, Libya and Algeria. Soviet Union enjoyed enormous power and influence in many parts of South-West Asia until the late 1980s when it staged a strategic withdrawal.[26]

Four situations guided Russian policies towards the 'south' in the 1990s: (a) ethnic separatism in the Caucasus; (b) the rise of Islamic fundamentalism; (c) regional and extra-regional encroachments into Russia's "sphere of influence"; and (d) Russian "neo imperial impulses" concerning the Commonwealth of Independent States (CIS).

Anatoliy Chekhoyev, Deputy Chairman of the Committee for CIS Affairs argued in 1997: "The Trans-Caucasian region remains an area of vital interest for Russia, a fact which is defined by the importance of the region's geopolitical position for Russia's security and for the prospects of its economic development.[27] Anatoliy's views reflect a broad consensus that the most serious external challenges to Russia's security interests lie in the southern Caucasus, which is adjacent to the northern Caucasus—the most problematic and troubled region in the Russian Federation.

The greatest security concern of Russia is that the countries of the southern Caucasus have been gripped by the large number of conflicts of ethnic-secessionist nature.[28] Armenia and Azerbaijan have fought over Nagorno-Karabakh and Georgia has fought Akhazians and the south Ossetian separatists. Ceasefires have been held in both cases for several years now. Russia has acted as a regional peacemaker and played a dominant third party role in the regional and international efforts at crisis management and conflict resolution.[29] Moscow's approach in general is to keep the conflicts or problems, primarily if not exclusively, a Russian or the CIS responsibility. In February 1993, President Yeltsin had asked the UN and the CSCE for some kind of a mandate for Russia to act freely in the former Soviet territory:

> The moment has come when responsible international institutions including the United Nations, should grant Russia special powers as a guarantor of peace and stability in the region of the former Soviet Union.[30]

The demand was popularly labelled as the "Russian Monroe Doctrine" and hence, was never conceded. However, this did not dissuade Russia from its responsibility and it used force whenever required to maintain peace and stability in the region.

Russia's role as a "peace maker" and "regional stabilizer" has been somewhat controversial. Some scholars maintain that in several cases the ethnic uprisings in the South Caucasian States were instigated by Russia as was the case with Abkhazia and South Ossetian separatists. It was alleged that Russian and north Caucasian volunteers made the bulk of the Abkhaz forces which routed the Georgian forces in 1993.[31] In the autumn of 1993, Azerbaijan and Georgia were pressurized into joining the CIS and signing the 1992 Tashkent Treaty on collective security in return for Russia's pledge to uphold their territorial integrity. Between 1993 and 1995, the Soviet Defence Minister, Pavel Grachev secured agreements for two military bases in Armenia and three in Georgia and for Russian patrol troops on the borders of these countries with their negibhours—Iran and Turkey.[32]

Russia's security concerns and its policy of keeping a tight hold over the NIS in Trans-Caucasia and Central Asia emanate from some real and some imaginary fears.

In the first place Russia worries about the destabilizing effect of the ethnic conflicts which might involve neighbouring states owing to their ethno-cultural and religious commonalties. The prolonged Chechen crisis and alleged involvement of external forces—Turkey and Armenia confirmed its worst fears.

Owing to the apprehensions related to ethno-cultural conflicts' threat, Russia demanded changes in the Treaty on Conventional Armed Forces in Europe (CFE) 1990 in order to revamp its military presence in the region. At the First Review Conference in Vienna in May 1996, Russia was allowed to keep almost three times more weapons than the old flank limits permitted and to shrink the size of the area where flank ceilings applied.[33]

Islamic Militancy

The rise of militant Islam in Central Asia which entered from Afghanistan and Iran to Tajikistan during the civil war in 1991 (onwards) is also seen as a threat to security and stability of the Central Asian region by Moscow. In Russia's vicinity about 20 million citizens profess Islam.[34]

Chechnya's embrace of Islam as part of its national identity, signs of the spread of Wahabism—an Islamic sect in Saudi Arabia—in the northern Caucasus,[35] the unresolved struggle in Tajikistan and the "near complete victory of Taliban in Afghanistan (1994-95), taken together, seem to have brought the fundamentalist threat to Russia's door steps in the south.[36]

Pan-Turkism

Russia has been apprehensive about Turkey's presumed pan-Turkic aspirations in the Caucasus and Central Asia and openly accused Turkey of collusion with the Chechen separatists. In 1998, Yegor Stroyev, Chairman of the Federal Council (Upper House of Russian Parliament) categorically opposed the idea of establishment of a Confederation of Trans-Caucasian Peoples including Turkey, Chechnya and other republics of the North Caucasus.[37]

Turkey tried to make it clear that although it is an active player in the southern Caucasus and Central Asia, its basic motive is to help the NIS consolidate their independence and deepen economic relations rather than to promote pan-Turkic or pan-Caucasian projects.[38] Pan-Turkism was only a marginal force in Turkish Society and is largely confined to pockets of intellectual and political circles. Turkey in general was seen as an anti-Russian country. Sergey Karaganov, a prominent member of the Russian Political elite had summarised Russian view of Turkey's interest in Southern Caucasus in an interview in 1996: "These places (Caucasian-Central Asian States) are

Russia's backyard. Nobody can play in these fields without Russia's consent".[39]

As a counter allegation Turkey also alleged Russian support to Abdullah Ocalan, the Kurdish leader and giving him asylum in Russia. Primakov's public renunciation of co-operation with terrorists in general and with Ocalan in particular seemed to restore confidence in the Turkish-Russian relations.

US Military Activities in South-Caucasus and NATO's Expansion

The growing military influence of the US and the NATO in its south at a time when its own military power is at the lowest, disturbed Russia greatly. Several developments provoked such reactions—the US led joint military exercises such as those of the Central Asian Battalion (Centrasbat) in 1997 and 1998 in Central Asia,[40] the deepening of military co-operation between NATO and the southern NIS under the PFP programme, the vocal allusions to NATO as an agent of peace and stability in the Southern Caucasus by Haider Aliev of Azerbaijan and Eduard Shevardnadze of Georgia and intimations that NATO forces could be an alternative to Russian peace-keepers in the southern Caucasus.[41] The visits of NATO's secretary General, Javier Solana to Tiblisi and Baku in 1997 and 1998 respectively aroused such apprehensions.[42]

NATO's expansion in southern Caucasus further alarmed Russia. Shevardnadze and Aliev were keen to join NATO but would they settle for NATO peace keeping in regional conflicts and NATO's protection to the prospective oil pipeline that would transport the "main oil" from the Caspian Sea was beyond Russia's tolerance. Russia has not really come to terms with NATOs eastern expansion and would react to expansion in the southern Caucasus.

Caspian Oil and Pipeline Projects

Caspian Sea fossil fuel has also aggravated the competition between regional and extra-regional aspirants for having larger control over the oil resources of the south Caucasian-Caspian Basin states.

The Russian foreign ministry has tried to preserve Russia's political hold over the Caspian Basin's oil wealth by manipulating the economic dependence of the NIS on Russia for energy resources such as in case of Ukraine, and for pipeline for outlets to the world markets as in the case of Azerbaijan, Kazakhstan and Turkmenistan.[43]

On the question of new pipelines to transport Azerbaijani oil to world market Russia is following a zero-sum strategy, rejecting the multiple pipelines' proposal advocated by the United States. The Baku-Tiblisi-Ceyhan pipeline proposed by Turkey to carry the Azeri oil has also been opposed by Russia on economic and geo-political ground. The Russian alternative was the Baku-Novorossisk pipeline through which oil has been flowing since the autumn of 1997.

However, the private energy company of Russia-Lukoil has taken a liberal view and joined the international consortia for the development and export of non-Russian Caspian oil, thus securing for Russia a substantial decision making role on issues critical to Russian national interests in the region. Another leading interest group, *Gazprom* has concluded multi-billion dollar energy deals with Turkey.

Russia attaches great importance to the CIS as a Security Umbrella for the NIS of the south Caucasus and Central Asia. According to a Russian foreign policy analyst, "the new key political guideline was to assume the role of 'security guarantor' in the CIS and to turn 'near abroad' into Russia's sphere of influence."[44] The new orientation to the 'near abroad' and the policies to support it have given rise to a general suspicion in the west and in some of the CIS countries that Russia may have become a neo-imperialist.

Notwithstanding, the generally negative reception in the west of the new assertiveness of Russia towards the NIS and the CIS, the west did not react effectively, first because driven by a "Russia first" policy, it did not wish to undermine Yeltsin's power, and, second, because it was not willing to shoulder the costly responsibilities of managing transfrontier ethnic conflicts in the former Soviet space?[45] In 1994, some analysts went further, suggesting that the west had no important interest in these regions—a view that stands in sharp contrast to the views of the US Government that had evolved in 1997. Implicitly, perhaps the west was content to have "Russia volunteer to act as the single regional stabilizer", argues Gennady Chufrin.[46]

Turkey has emerged as a formidable rival of Russia in the southern Caucasus and to a lesser extent in Central Asia. Turkey has a strong economy as it has been developing dynamically at the beginning of the 1990s and over the past decade has made such a powerful economic break through that the world seriously started talking about the "Turkish miracle" and the "Turkish model". Turkey became the first NATO member to purchase Russian arms, helicopters and armoured personnel carriers. In February 1996, Oleg Davydov, Russian Minister for Foreign Economic Relations and First Deputy Chairman of the Coordinating Council for Russia's Military Technical Policy, announced that the value of Russian exports to Turkey totaled $ 25.7 million in 1993, $ 15.4 million in 1994 and $ 70 million in 1995.[47]

The Turkish diplomacy also made good strides by setting their foot in every corner of the Near East as mediators and peace-makers (Balkans).[48] Their construction firms are numerous and effective. They have been able to establish business in Arab Emirates and other Muslim countries at profitable terms. Yet, their strength is much larger in Russia. At the end of 1997, work carried out by Turkish construction firms in Russia amounted to over $ 12.3 billion. In contrast to the amount of contracted work undertaken by Turkish companies in the Turkic republics totaled only $ 6.5 billion.[49]

It is interesting to note that while the republics (CARs) are attracted by the secular path of development in Turkey, the Turks themselves base their hopes on identity of language and culture. The west has readily made economic help available in a hope that Turkey would act as a barrier to the spread of Islamic fundamentalism of Iran. Turkey's free market economy developed in the 1990s and its success in the agriculture sector have made it attractive to Turkic Muslims in the immediate years of their freedom. During the visit of Turgut Ozal to Muslim republics of Central Asia Islam Karimov, the President of Uzbekistan declared publicly that: "I announce to the world that my country will forward by the Turkish route", and Nursultan Nazarbaiev, President of Kazakhstan announced: "We want to implement a free market economy and the only model we have is Turkey,[50] however, despite these enthusiastic utterances and display of preference for Turkey, the CARs are aware of the importance of Russia in their security, economic development and internal stability in face of ethnic problems. Turkey can not do much in these matters. Hence, Russia also just watches Turkey's overtures in Central Asia unperturbed.

What disturbs Russia is Turkey's endeavours in the oil sector where it wants to outmaneuver Russia by negotiating oil deals and pipeline routes with the Caspian Basin states individually. The main point of discord is the transport of Caspian oil to European markets. Russia offered a "northern route" through Russian territory (including Chechnya) up to the Black Sea port of Novorossisk and on by Sea through the Bosphorus and Dardanelles. In response to this suggestion,

Turkey tried to reject the idea of transporting oil through the Black Sea straits referring to the ecological dangers which this route would inevitably involve.[51]

Turkey insisted on a route through Azerbaijan and Georgia to the port of Poti from there by tankers to the Turkish coast, then by pipelines through Turkey to the port of Ceyhan and further again by tankers to its ultimate destination—the consumers. It succeeded in obtaining support of all the concerned parties including the United States for Baku-Tiblisi-Ceyhan oil pipeline.

Russia tried to impress upon the concerned parties by suggesting another most viable route—a pipeline from the Bulgarian port of Burgas to the Greek port of Alexandopoulis which could take the oil round the straits and remove ecological dangers. Turkey owing to its anti-Greece mindset remained averse to this proposal too.

The politics of pipelines is extremely complicated although the single obvious reason behind the intricate moves of Turkey, Iran and Russia is to acquire export routes for the Caspian oil *via* their own territory and earn revenues. Russia wants to retain the control over regional countries, the natural resources of the region, and is opposed to the participation of external partners in the Caspian oil deals and export arrangements. Whereas, Turkey wants to keep Iran and Russia excluded from the oil exporting pipeline routes to please the United States which is opposed to Tehran's participation in the Caspian oil deals particularly when the US or the American companies are participating in it.

Russia is also concerned about its own status in the Caspian region's oil resources. Prior to the dissolution of the Soviet Union, Moscow had a total monopoly over the production and export of oil from the Caspian-Central Asian region. The construction of new pipelines, bypassing its territory would mean an end to its access to the Caspian oil affairs. Hence, it opposed the Turkish proposals.

The bickerings caused by constant demonstration of distrust and rivalry in the Trans-Caucasian oil pipelines are having their spill over effect on the nature of overall relations of these two prominent States of the region.

Russia alleged Turkey's hand in encouraging the Chechen rebels by offering them arms and material assistance. Turkey categorically denies this charge. Russia fears that behind Turkey's role in Chechen affairs is America which might be pressurizing Turkey to create instability in the Russian federation during the immediate years of collapse of the Soviet Union.

Now, it is being felt that the increasing power of Chechen rebels and secessionists aided by the fundamentalist militants from the West Asian Arab countries, Afghanistan and Pakistan has become a threat not only to stability and territorial integrity of Russia, but it will be a threat to the entire Central Asian-south Caucasian region.

With this realization the attitude of Turkey and also of the United States and its allies is softening towards Moscow. Thus, the geopolitical configuration comprising Russia, Turkey and Iran which appeared difficult to be formed, does not look that remote now. If Turkey and Iran like Russia are interested in the peace, stability and affluence of the people of southern Caucasus (the area of Turkey's major interest) and Central Asia, sooner or later they may come round to forming this most viable and mutually advantageous grouping in the post-Soviet Central Asia.

Russia and Iran

Of the three constituents of the proposed triangle Russia feels much closer to Iran than to Turkey. Ankara's staunch pro-Americanism, its obsession with "European identity" of

Turkey and its desire to emerge as a major power (if possible sole custodian of Caspian oil) in Central Asia discourages Moscow from going closer to Turkey. Ankara is aware of Russian inhibition and often tries to mitigate it but it is not possible for it to come out of the western "cocoon" in which it had willingly got arrested in the post World War II period.

Iran, isolated by the USA's "dual containment" policy, has emerged as Russia's primary partner in West Asia and also now in Central Asia. Influential circles in Russia had already seen in Iran a potential ally in maintaining regional stability in Central Asia and the Caucasus, above all by the containment of Islamic fundamentalism, and in checking Turkish influence in these lands.[52] Russian-Iranian co-operation for the completion of the nuclear plant in Bushehr and Russia's sale of dual use missile technology have been sustained despite strenuous US objections.

Russian-Iranian nuclear and missile co-operation and the question it raises about the role of Russia in Iran's presumed nuclear weapon programme are taken very seriously in the region, not only in Tel Aviv but Ankara and other capitals too. Russia maintains that its assistance to Iran's peaceful nuclear programme does not violate the 1968 Non-proliferation Treaty (NPT). For its part it urges Israel to join the NPT. Turkey is especially sensitive to Russia's arms exports to the region given that their ultimate deployment would raise potential threats to Turkish security.[53]

Iran's strategic position as a link between the Caspian Sea and the Persian Gulf, between the Caucásus and Central Asia, and between the Middle East and South Asia, huge manpower and enormous oil and gas resources besides other minerals make it a most desirable and outstandingly important member of any configuration that emerges in Southern Caucasus and Central Asia.

Iran shares the Caspian Sea with Russia, Kazakhstan, Turkmenistan and Azerbaijan and on the legal status of Caspian Sea, Tehran is in favour of the stand taken by Russia—Caspian is a lake and its resources should be divided equally. However, some changes are appearing in the attitude of Moscow and also of the other Caspian states which suggest that an amicable solution to the identity of Caspian will be found soon. Iran is well placed to be a route for the transport of oil and gas from the region to international markets. However, the pipelines are not complete and are not in a position to be in operation due to some gaps. For example, there are no pipelines to bring the oil from the north of Iran to Iranian terminals on the Persian Gulf. However, the new railway from Mashad to northern Iran to the Iranian port Bandar Abbas on the Persian Gulf is to cut the distance from Central Asia to the Persian Gulf by 900 km.

Iran has tremendous economic potential, which at the moment is constrained by American sanctions imposed in the aftermath of Shia Revolution in Iran in 1979. The US depicts Iran as a menace to international peace and order and includes it in the lists of states supporting international terrorism. Hence, Russia-Iran relations are developing against the background of US pressures on Iran. The US accuses Iran of amassing the weapons of mass destruction, its support to terrorism, its opposition to Arab-Israeli peace although Iran has contradicted all these allegations and expressed willingness to have good relations with the United States, especially in the southern Caucasus and Central Asia. Iran argues that it is not interested in making weapons of mass destruction but wants to develop its nuclear programme. It is likely to run out of fuel reserves in 10-15 years, even though at present it owns ten percent of the world's oil and 20 percent of its natural gas.[54] Russia had undertaken to construct a power plant at Bushehr, a port on the Persian Gulf. However, the Gulf war between Iraq and Iran caused serious damage to it and delayed its completion. Russia maintains that its assistance to Iran's nuclear programme does not violate international conventions on non-proliferation of nuclear weapons and argues that it resembles the one supplied to North Korea by the United States.[55]

The Russian-Iranian relations are greatly marred by a US threat in early 1999 to restrict Russia's access to the international satellite launch market which is worth hundreds of millions of dollors a year to Russia. For allegedly leaking nuclear technology to Iran without having any substantial evidence to prove its allegations the US administration placed sanctions on 12 Russian institutions including three in January 1999. The Russian Foreign Ministry was quick in commenting on sanctions on 25 February 1999: "We categorically will not accept attempts to talk to Russia in the language of sanctions and pressures".

Iran's anti-Americanism has cost it dearly and it has to remain under the shadow of US pressures all the time. But, precisely, Iran's strong commitment to its ideology and firm determination to stick to it notwithstanding the pressures is appreciated by Moscow. Russia has shown tremendous courage by retaining relations with Iran despite American opposition.

Initially at the beginning of the post-cold war years, Iran proposed to form the Economic Co-operation Organization (ECO) which included other countries besides the six former republics of the Soviet Union. Russia had formed Commonwealth of Independent States (CIS) to provide security and economic assistance to the NIS of Central Asia. Moscow believed that the two organizations will be in conflict as they are mutually exclusive. Russia discouraged the CIS states from joining the ECO. However, when passions cooled down, it was realized that the ECO was a complementary institution that could undo the ill effects of years of lack of contacts in the whole region and it was also understood that without developing roads, communication networks, expanding transport facilities, improving trade and monetary transactions and establishing necessary infrastructure it was impossible to boost economic co-operation in the region as a whole[56] and these developmetnal projects would benefit Russia as well.

In order to strengthen economic relations and all round communication with the people of Central Asia, Iran has undertaken to complete roads connecting the north of Iran to the south. With their completion exceptional facilities will be created for transportation and trade exchanges between the CARs and Russia. Iran is interested in playing an active role as a corridor in the Gulf for the transit of Russian and Central Asian goods to other parts of the world, like to South East Asia, China, Japan and Australia. The Volga-Don waterway is another route for the transit of Iranian goods to Europe.[57] Iran and Russia are, in fact, working as complementary partners to make up for each others' shortage of essential linking routes. Iranian territory offers the best and most suitable passage for oil and gas pipelines. At present there is competition over different routes for pipelines. This competition can simply be turned into collaboration. Russia and Iran can work as partners here. Turkey, owing to its geo-strategic location and historical linkages with the people of Central Asia can play the role of a "harmonizer" and "stabilizer" in the region and help in bringing the warring ethnicities together on a negotiation table and resolve their conflicts.

The Russia, Turkey, Iran triangle is feasible and can be most advantageous geo-political grouping in the Central Asian region. Of the three to be constituents, two—Russia and Iran share each others perceptions and agree over the plans, programmes and strategies commonly drawn about the region but Turkey's commitment to the West, especially the US and

NATO and its near obsession with the membership in the European Union make it shaky and uncertain about its future moves—in case it is admitted to the EU.

However, the possibility of formation of this configuration is much more stronger than that of other proposed groupings of interested partners in the region. There are several factors which make it more viable: Russia, Turkey and Iran are powers close to Central Asian states and have stakes in the territorial integrity, stability, security and development of the region. Russia and Iran are firmly committed to keep the natural resources of the Caspian Sea region under the control of the Caspian states only and do not agree to external patronage over the countries of Central Asia.

It will not be fair to cast aspersions on Turkey's stand on the proposed triangle because of its commitment to the West. These commitments were undertaken when the world was bi-polarized and in the cold war Turkey had preferred to join the western bloc.

However, in the post Soviet period, Turkey is becoming aware of the constraints on its capacity to act freely and is trying to assert its independence in several matters related to its foreign policy. Anakra has voiced its disagreement over the US policy of keeping Iran and Russia outside the Caspian Sea basin oil and the pipelines proposed to be constructed to carry Azeri oil to Europe *via* Iran.

Ankara had taken the risk of inviting US displeasure by showing opposition to US economic sanctions against Iran under the Iran-Libya Sanctions Act (ILSA), signed by the President in August 1996 imposing penalties on any foreign corporation investing more than US $ 20 million in the Iranian oil and gas sector.[58] Ankara does not agree with the US obsession with Iran-sponsored fundamentalism and believes that it is an ideology Iran adheres to but it has nothing to do with the fundamentalist activities in Central Asia. On the

Chechnya issue too, Turkey considers it an issue of Russia's domestic affairs. These are positive signs of possibility of change in Turkey's stand on Central Asian issues. Still, the EU decision on Turkey's membership would be a decisive factor.

There are several supportive structures that, if employed, can promote regional co-operation and provide strength and viability to the emerging geo-political and economic configurations of the states of Central Asia and adjoining regions that are coming up. For example, the organization of Black Sea Economic Co-operation (OBSEC), the Economic Co-operation Organization (ECO), The Turkish-Russian Businessmen's Association (TRBA), the Organization of Co-operation of the Caspian countries (OCCC) and so on.

Emerging Equations between Russia, Iran and Turkey

The Russia, Turkey, Iran Configuration, as examined above, notwithstanding several discrepancies in the perceptions and objectives of the three key countries, represent a desire for forming a grouping of the region's core countries which can collectively safeguard the interests of the south Caucasian-Central Asian countries and their resources.

The discrepancies are the result of their earlier notions about each other, which in some cases have taken the form of obsessions. In Russia the fear of *Cordon Sanitaire* is still in the minds of people, especially those who lived in the era of "containment of communism" and "encirclement of the USSR". They find Turkey's excessive slant towards the United States, its almost "perpetual" subordination to the "will" and "interests" of Washington as reasons for the lack of trust between Russia and Turkey. On its part Turkey having gone through the era of "Iron Curtain" feels that Moscow will act as a "rival" and establish its monopoly once agains over the resources of the Caspian region.

Russia is able to trust Iran more easily despite the fact that Tehran had been the most dependable ally of the West until 1979. The *Shia* revolution under Ayatollah Khomeini followed by the "hostages crisis" (5 November 1979) and later the Iran-Iraq war created a climate of distrust between Turkey and Iran. For Turkey, besides the Soviet Union, a new powerful enemy had emerged in its immediate neighbourhood although Iran did not display any kind of enmity towards Ankara. Iran tried to be helpful during the Iran-Iraq war. The Iranian charge d' affaires in Ankara, Ahmad Mossavi Zade while trying to dissuade Turkey from joining the US-sponsored embargo against Iran, said that during the Shah's regime Turkey had received from Iran "not a single drop of oil" but Khomeini's Iran had made strenuous efforts to aid Turkey, providing it with 2.4 million tons of oil a year.[59] The Iranian President Bani Sadr in an interview told *Cumhuriyet* on 10 May 1980 that "the two Nations' 'common destiny' is a good enough reason for them to collaborate against western hegemony".[60]

Iran kept shipping crude oil and distillates without demanding cash payments. Turkey's oil debt to Iran, which stood at $ 77 million in February 1980, rose to $ 277 million by July of the same year. At that time Turkey had already exhausted the $ 300 million credit line opened for it by Iran.[61]

Turkey, however, was careful to the policy guidelines it had set for itself when the crisis began. Ankara, refrained from engaging in any anti-Iranian act on the bilateral level, but supported as a matter of principle the US position on the hostages affair. Turkey, in fact, was walking a narrow path between the constraints imposed by its relationship with Iran on the one hand and its wish not to alienate Washington on the other.[62] What bothers Russia is Turkey's two-edged policy. It wants to cultivate relations with the major player in Central Asia but does not want to deviate from the policy line set by the United States. Yet, in view of its earlier record, it is hoped that Ankara would maintain its commitment towards the southern Caucasian states in the same way it is keeping towards the United States.

In case of Iran, Russia does not have problems. Ideologically it is anti-West and anti-America. It is strict follower of the Islamic ideology but does not make it a basis of relationship in all cases. The ideological dimension differs from country to country. Hence, Russia trusts Iran.

Russia and Iran on Identity of the Caspian Sea

On the issue of determining the identity of the Caspian Sea Iran is constantly supporting the Russian line. Moscow have been advocating the Caspian's characterization as *lake* as determined by the treaties of 1921 and 1940 concluded between Russia and Iran. According to these treaties the resources of the *lake* (Caspian Sea) were to be divided communally.[63] Russia is now softening its stand. At a regional conference in November 1996, its Foreign Minister, Yevgeny Primakov, made an offer that would allow each littoral state exclusive economic rights within 72 kilometers (45 miles) of its shore as well as in those hydrocarbon fields beyond this limit where extraction has already begun.[64]

Notwithstanding Azerbaijan's opposition to this 72 kilometer limit on 28 April 1998, the Russian and Kazakh Presidents announced in Moscow their agreement to a pact for the division of the resources underneath the Caspian Seabed. The agreement was signed on 6 July 1998 is applicable to all Caspian States. Iran is not agreeable to this decision and has registered its protest to it. Iran is not able to digest how Moscow could change its stand unilaterally without taking Iran into confidence when it was always supporting Moscow's line on the Caspian Sea.

Iran's major problem with Russia arises only in the matter of pipelines. Iran wants new pipelines (as many as possible) to traverse its territory so that it earns revenues; retains influence in the southern Caucasus; maintains parity with Russia; and acquires an equal status in Central Asia *vis-à-vis* Moscow, which is not an unreasonable expectation. Nonetheless, Russia and Iran are tied together in an unbreakable bond which can be disturbed only by the United States.

In addition to Russia-Turkey-Iran triangle, some other configurations like Turkey, Azerbaijan, Georgia (with US-Israel backing), Russia, Iran, Armenia or the bigger constellations like Russia, Iran, Syria, Greece, Armenia and the Republic of Cyprus on the one hand, and Turkey, Azerbaijan, Georgia, Israel, on the other, are also being figured out.

In view of the background of these new aspirants for partnership in the emerging constellations in Central Asia, their objectives, national interest and international behaviour suggests that they need not to be taken seriously because they are showing willingness to join these configuration for fear of being left out. Such configurations are neither effective nor viable.

International alliances are formed by the countries having identical self image, perceptions and objectives to attain through joining in the pact or treaty or whatever is the form of configuration. Besides, it develops around a "core country" or "key actor" which has superior administrative and managerial skills and "capacity" to respond to the needs of the various constituent units to their satisfaction. A proper balance between load (responsibility) and capability is the key to success of any alliance.

From this point of view the configuration like the one having Russia, Iran, Syria (only to end its isolation and boost its morale in face of US-threats and Israeli pressures), Greece (to strengthen its position vis-à-vis Turkey on Cyprus issue), Armenia (which holds a grudge against Turkey) and the

Republic of Cyprus (it needs friends who can pressurize Turkey and discourage it from its aggressive attitude towards the Greek Cypriots) is an amalgam of states like the defunct CENTO of the Cold War era, with contradictory aims and objectives which if admitted to the grouping will constantly be vying to draw it in their favour and thus defeat the very objective of protecting the Caspian region from the external encroachments.

Same applies to another grouping having Turkey, Azerbaijan, Georgia, Israel and possibly Ukraine as well. With the exception of Turkey and Azerbaijan none have common policies, perceptions, objectives and means to attain them. They will be depending on Turkey. It is difficult to say that without the US support Turkey has sufficient resources and capabilities to shoulder the new responsibilities that would entail out of this configuration.

As far as Russia is concerned it has practically good relations with both Turkey and Iran although secretly it holds a grudge against Turkey for monopolizing Azerbaijan on the basis of its historical ties and both belonging to the same ethno-linguistic (Turkic) stock. Turkey's opposition to those pipeline routes which are to traverse Russian territory and Moscow's objection to pipelines carrying Azeri oil passing through Turkish territory suggests lack of proper communication between the two states. Both are rivals, both are ambitious and both understand the geo-political and geo-strategic compulsions that determine their attitude towards each other. For a successful alliance identity of interests and common perceptions on how to serve those interests is necessary. Any external interference can be damaging to the integrity of alliance. Prime Minister, Victor Chernomyrdin declared during his visit to Turkey in December 1997 that "others should not be allowed to decide how the Turkish-Russian relations evolve. We may expect genuine Russo-Turkish co-operation or rapproachment only if perceptions of insidious Russo-Turkish rivalry in the Caucasus and Central Asia ceases and if Russian perceptions of Turkey as an extension of US hostility toward Russia can be overcome".[65]

Russia openly prefers Iran to Turkey because it cannot allow a US ally to gain power in its neighbourhood. The preference for Iran is clear in its nuclear technology policy. Moscow believes that Tehran is more manageable than Ankara because of latters commitment toward the Western alliance.

Turkey is upset by Moscow's weapon transfers to Iran and offering help in strengthening its nuclear programme. Turkey thinks that political Islamists in Turkey, who are known to envy Tehran regime might get in touch with the Iranian Islamist forces to enhance their status in the eyes of international fundamentalist forces. However, the results of 1999 elections in Turkey had proved such fears baseless. The Virtue Party, which favours political Islam had lost voter support. However, since then Islamist forces have gained strength and showed that power by putting politicians with Islamic bent of mind in the office of Prime-minister and President recently.

However, the ideological gap between the two important players in the southern Caucasus—Turkey and Iran, despite their being closest neighbours, does not allow them to be strategic partners in Central Asia. Their normal relations in economic and trade affairs continue to flourish. In August 1996 Turkey signed an agreement to purchase Iranian gas in the next twenty three years, making Iran largest supplier of gas to Turkey after Russia. A pipeline to carry gas from Iran to Turkey is there and a new pipeline to connect Iran with Turkmenistan is going to be constructed. The construction of pipeline between Iran and Turkey and Turkmenistan and Iran may turn out to be advantageous to all the three states. However, it is not necessary that it would turnout to be disadvantageous to Russia.

Lately, it has been noticed that Russia's stand on the status of Caspian Sea is undergoing change. Moscow is adopting a softer attitude on this issue. At a regional conference in November 1996, Russian Foreign Minister Yevgeny Primakov made an offer that would have allowed each littoral state exclusive economic rights within 72 kilometers (45 miles) of its shore as well as in those hydrocarbon fields beyond this limit where extraction had already begun. Azerbaijan is not agreeable to 45 miles of exclusive ownership which is a far cry from the roughly 212 miles contemplated by the UN Convention. Notwithstanding the Azerbaijan's objection to the above proposal, Russian and Kazakh presidents announced in Moscow their agreement to a pact for the division of the resources underneath the Caspian Seabed. According to this agreement signed on 6 July 1998, the Caspian Seabed will be shared by all the Littoral States.

The 1998 Russian policy shift, however, was not well received in Tehran. A spokesperson of Iran's Foreign Ministry referring to the agreement between Russia and Kazakhstan said that "any bilateral agreement which is incompatible with the existing legal regime of the Caspian Sea is not valid and not recognized officially by the Islamic Republic of Iran.

Iran adjoins an area of the Caspian with relatively meager mineral deposits and not surprisingly its position traditionally has been very close to that of Russia. Tehran held the view that "all issues related to the Caspian's exploitation should be settled by the five states that touch its shores". This view was shared by Moscow as well.

Turkmenistan also has not been consistent on this issue. Initially it agreed to its characterization as Sea, but at the end of 1996, it began to move toward the Russian-Iranian camp. Early in 1989, however, Turkmenistan returned to its original position when Saparmurad Niyazov came forward with the assertion that two oil fields previously claimed by Azerbaijan, both among the richest deposits in the Caspian lie in the Turkmen sector.

The countries involved in the Caspian controversy are all convinced that the anticipated revenues from the exploitation of the Caspian's mineral reserves will provide a significant boost to their economies and bring in much needed foreign currency. The recent shift in the Russian stand on Caspian has turned Iran and Turkmenistan closer to each other.

Politics of Pipelines

The two assistant professors of Bilkent University, Ankara have constructed a thesis around the geopolitics (also politics) of the pipelines' controversies. They maintain that the intensity of interactions inside the Russia-Turkey-Iran triangle was increased in the late 1990s but the recession in oil prices in 1998-1999 devalued many political interests. Another negative aspect is the possibility that Caspian oil and gas reserves may have been exaggerated. Oil and gas deals underline triangular rivalries today, and the competition for influence over the NIS of Central Asia and Caucasia is conducted through pipeline projects where investor firm's calculations of benefits do not necessarily match governmental interests.[66]

The United States sides with Turkey in the Caspian pipelines' controversy, because Turkey is entering into direct confrontation with Russia and isolating Iran. The US support to Baku-Tiblisi-Ceyhan pipeline is an indication of Turkey's power in the region.[67] This project was to cost $ 4 billion which is more than the Tengiz-Novorossisk pipeline ($ 3 billion) and far more than Baku-Supsa pipeline or the Baku-Novorossisk one which crosses the territory of Chechnya.[68] It is difficult to justify the construction of such an expensive pipeline, in spite of the US support to it. However, it has provided great solace to Ankara although it is transporting only Azeri oil so far.

Another possible alternative is a pipeline from the Caspian to the Gulf through Iran which could impair Turkey's strategic importance. Although, the US support to this route will not be forthcoming owing to Iran-Libya Sanctions Act 1996 which prevents support to countries accused of supporting international terrorism. However, the US in May 1998 declared that it has no objection to Russian, French, Malaysian investments in developing the Iranian gas fields. The US attitude is gradually softening as the US oil companies view Iran from different angle, some like AMOCO, do not wish to be involved while others like Mobil are willing to explore the advantages of cheap transportation for Caspian energy.[69] A proof of this trend is the $ 400 million oil swap deal by which oil companies would pump Caspian oil to northern Iran for domestic use and an equal amount would be released in the South from Iranian ports on the Gulf. The European countries have already expressed interest in deeper economic co-operation in Iran. They are more concerned about immediate economic returns rather than going into politico-religious character of the Iranian State. This trend suggests that market forces would compel the US to end sanctions against Iran.[70]

However, the competition for oil would be almost worthless if recent energy estimates prove exaggerated. The prospect of a "no big deal" in Caspian oil and gas could also weaken the triangular rivalry between Russia, Turkey and Iran. Then the other local issues would tip the balance, such as filling the power vacuum left by the eclipse of the Soviet power.

The Turkish scholars argue that at the moment, the US is setting a barrier against Iran and Russia to prevent them from having a larger share in the Caspian oil. Turkey is the trump card of this project. A secular Turkey could set a precedent for the Central Asian states and Azerbaijan to follow. But, in contrast, the prospect of "no big deal" would lead the USA to de-emphasize the fact of Turkey as a secular regime and not to count on Turkish assets such as historical and cultural ties across the region. Were oil not an issue, Russian weakness would also not seem so important to the United States. The Russian threat to counter NATO enlargement with southward expansion are hardly serious.[71] In that case, instead of favouring secular Turkey, the US might prefer a combined Turkey-Iran Muslim thrust in dealing with Asian Russia and its backyard.[72]

A Four Dimensional Alliance and Regional Power Balance

The EU is constantly evasive on the issue of Turkey's entry as a full member. This situation is likely to continue unless some fresh crisis crops up to revive Ankara's importance in the Western security system afresh. The threat perceptions related to Turkey—such as terrorism, Islamic fundamentalism, Greek-Turkish disputes, the Armenian issue and even the water dispute with Syria continue to be problems in the way of Turkey's membership in the EU.

Russia's case is also more or less the same. The rejectionist EU policy with respect to Russia and Turkey has warmed up the two towards each other. Like the current EU policy towards Russia and Turkey—the US-Iran rapproachment too could make Turkey and Russia more aware of their common interest. It is argued that US insistence that the EU should admit Turkey would be understandable only in a context where the US attempted to revive normal relations with Iran.

The triangle can be made viable by other means as well. Russia and Turkey may contemplate co-operation with Kazakhstan over a pipeline connecting China to the Caspian reserves.[73] Russo-Turkish Co-operation along these lines would form a powerful attraction force from which Iran could not easily be able to isolate itself.[74] The EU stand on Turkey and the American policy towards Iran may ultimately lead to formation of a large Eurasian bloc having Russia, Turkey, Iran and China. Then inclusion of China in the Russia, Turkey, Iran triangle would transform it into a powerful worldwide bloc, although such a constellation of forces would be subject to a multiple constraints.

The Russian, Turkish, Iranian, Chinese co-operation would mean the emergence of an amalgam of forces over a portion of Eurasia far more vaster than the "Heartland" that Mackinder so many years ago assumed to be the key to world domination.[75] It would necessitate a total revision of the US military doctrine.[76] The progress or reversal of such a project is still in the hands of Euro-American bloc. If the US ends Iran's isolation; EU gives up resistance to Turkey and Russia; the Caspian reserve do not turn out to be as enormous as propagated; the entire politics over pipelines is turned futile or energy loses priority as a strategic issue, then the momentum built in favour of the proposed geo-political configuration would subside automatically.

However, at the moment, the EU's stand on Turkey's membership and policy of the United States towards Iran are likely to strengthen Russia, Iran, Turkey triangle. China practically is already present in Central Asia and Trans-Caucasia. It is not necessary for Beijing to have a military alliance with the countries of the region. The Shanghai Cooperation Organization is a sufficient arrangement for the security of Central Asia. China can add to the viability of Russia-Iran-Turkey triangle more by staying out than joining it.

Notes

1. William Hale, *Turkish Foreign Policy—1774-2000* (Frank Cass, London: 2000), p.191.
2. Omur Orhun, "The Uncertainties and Challenges Ahead: A Southern Perspective", *Perceptions* (Ankara), Vol.4, No.1 (1999), p.30.
3. Paul B. Henze, "Turkey Towards the 21st Century", in Fuller and

Lesser (eds.), *Turkey's New Geo-Politics: From the Balkans to Western China* (Boulder Co., West View, 1993), p.2.

4. Zia Onis, "Turkey in the Post-Cold War Era: In Search of Identity", *Middle East Journal,* Vol.49 (1955), pp.48-49.
5. Bruce R. Kuniholm, "Turkey and the West", *Foreign Affairs,* Vol.70 (1991), p.34, and also quoted in Meltem Mufluler-Bac, "Turkey's Predicament in the Post-Cold War Era", *Futures,* Vol.28 (1996), p.257.
6. Mahmut Bali Aykan, "Turkish Perspectives on Turkish-US Relations concerning Persian Gulf Security in the Post-Cold War Era: 1989-1995", *Middle East Journal,* Vol.50 (1996), pp.345-346; also Kemal Kirisci, "Turkey and the United States: Ambivalent Allies" in B. Rubin and Keaney (eds.), *US Allies in a Changing World* (London, Cass: 2000).
7. Kemal Kirisci, Turkey and the United States, *op.cit.,* and also Gulnur Aybet, "NATO's New Missions", *Perceptions* (Ankara),Vol.4, No.1 (1999), p.73.
8. William Hale, *Turkish Foreign Policy: 1774-2000* (Frank Cass: London: 2000), pp.260-263.
9. Meltem Muftuler-Bac, "Turkey's Predicament in the Post Cold War Era", *Futures,* Vol.28 (1996), p.259.
10. Quoted in John Roper, "The West and Turkey: Varying Roles, Common Interests", *International Spectator* (Rome), Vol.34 (1999), p.92.
11. Quoted in Anthony Hartly, Maasthricht's Problematic Future", *World Today,* Vol.48 (1992), p.181.
12. Gulnur Aybet, *NATO's Developing Role in Collective Security* (Ankara, Ministry of Foreign Affairs, Centre for Strategic Research, 1999), p.46.
13. Quoted in Kemal Krisci, "Post-Cold War Turkish Security and the Middle East", MERIA Journal (published on Internet), No.2 (1997).
14. Quoted in Anthony Hartley, "Masstricht's Problematical Future", *World Today,* Vol.48 (1992), p.181.
15. Heinz Kramer, "Turkey's Place and Role in the Emerging European Security Architecture", quoted in William Hale, *Turkish Foreign Policy, op.cit.,* p.233.
16. Gulner Aybet, "Turkey and European Institutions", *International Spectator* (Rome), Vol.34 (1999), p.109.
17. Stephen J. Gommershall, "NATO and European Defence", *Perceptions* (Ankara), Vol.4, No.1 (1999), p.77.

18. In Ernest W. Lefever (ed.), *Ethics and United States Foreign Policy* (Cleveland: Meridian Books, 1957), pp.38-39.
19. Ismail Soysal, "The Middle East Peace Process and Turkey", *Turkish Review of Middle East Studies*, 8 (1995/1995): 69-98, p.69.
20. Yucel Bozdaglioglu, *op.cit.*, p.149; Meltem Muftuler, "Turkey: New Player in the Middle East Politics", *Mediterranean Quarterly*, 6 (Fall, 1995), 110-120, p.116.
21. Nur-Bilge Criss and Serdar Guner, "Geopolitical Configurations: The Russia, Turkey, Iran Triangle", *Security Dialogue*, Vol.30, No.3 (September 1999), p.366.
22. Kenneth N. Waltz, "The Emerging Structure of International Politics", *International Security*, Vol.18, No.2, 1993, pp.44-79 and p.52.
23. Nur Bilge Criss and Serdar Guner, *op.cit.*, p.366.
24. *Turkish Daily News*, 31 May 1995.
25. Gennady Chufrin (ed.), *Russia and Asia: The Emerging Security Agenda* (Sipri, Oxford University Press, 1999), pp.209-210.
26. Kanet, R.E. and Alexander, J.T., "The End of the cold war and the 'new World Order': Implications for the Developing World" and Kremenyuk, V.A. , "Russia's a New Thinking" and the Third World, (ed.) Mesbahi M., *Russia and the Third World in the Post Soviet Era* (University Press of Florida Gainsville, Fla, 1994), pp.192-225 and 125-126 respectively.
27. Foreign Broadcast Information Service, Daily Report—Central Eurasia (FBIS-SOV), FBIS-SOV-97-120, 30 April 1997.
28. Naumkin, V.V., *Ethnic Conflict in the Former Soviet Union* (Russian Centre for Strategic Research and International Studies: Moscow; 1997).
29. For Russia's role in Nagorno-Karabakh Conflict see Kazimirov, V. (Russian Ambassador at the Negotiations), "A History of the Karabakh Conflict" *International Affairs* (Moscow), vol.42, no.3 (1996), pp.182-185.
30. *Financial Times*, 1 March 1993, , p.1. On Russian peace keeping see Allison, R., *Peace Keeping in the Soviet Successor States*, Chaillot Papers (Western European Union Institute for Security Studies: Paris, 1994); Jonson L. and Archer, C. (eds.), *Peace Keeping and the Role of Russia in Eurasia* (WestviewPress: Boulder, Colo, 1996).
31. Nichol, J., "Trans-Caucasus' Newly Independent States: Political Development and Implications for US Interests", CRS Issue Brief for Congress, Library of Congressional Research Service (CRS), 20

December 1996, URL<http://www.fas.org/man/crs/95-024.htm.

32. Gennady Chufrin, *op.cit.*, p.211.
33. "Russia allowed time to fulfil CFE Treaty", *Moscow Times*, 4 June 1996, p.3. Also Lachowski, Z., "Conventional Arms Control", SIPRI Year Book", 1997; *Armament, Disarmament and International Security* (Oxford University Press, Oxford, 1997), pp.476-484. Turkey was opposed to Vienna-based negotiations on the modernization of the CFE Treaty. The two countries reached a compromise in bilateral negotiations in January 1999, paving the way for the endorsement of the modernization Treaty at the OCSE Summit meeting to be held in Istanbul in November 1999.
34. Official Russia distinguishes between Islamic Fundamentalism and Extremism. See. Sevastianov, I., "Islamic Fundamentalism and Extremism are not the same", *International Affairs* (Moscow), Vol.42, No.3 (1996), pp.171-181.
35. An official attempts to fight Wahabism see "Conference in Russian Caucasus discusses separatism", *Moscow Radio*, Rossii Network, 31 July 1998, FBIS-SOV-98-210, 7 August 1998.
36. Titorenki, V.Y., Islamism and Interests of Russia in FBIS-SOV-95-056-S, 23 March 1995, pp.11-16.
37. Yermakova, L., "Russia Federation Council delegation to visit Caucasus" in *Reuters*, 20 January 1998, URL <http"//www.briefing, reuters.com/cgi-bin.>. For role of Turkey in Chechen crisis see Baluev, D., "Moderation in the National Idea", *International Affairs* (Moscow), vol.42, no.5/6 (1996), p.107 and Kortunov, S., "Russia in Search of Allies", *International Affairs* (Moscow), vol.42, no.3 (1996), p.162.
38. Gennady Chufrin, *op.cit.*,p.213.
39. Sezer, D.B., "From Hegemony to Pluralism: The Changing Politics of the Black Sea", *SAIS Review* (John Hopkins University, School of Advanced International Studies), vol.17, no.1 (Winter/Spring 1997), p.18.
40. Gennady Chufrin, *op.cit.*, p.215 and also pp.214-216.
41. Saradzhyan, S., "Georgia seeks UN not Russian Peace Keepers", *Moscow Times*, 5 August 1998 in *Reuters*, 5 August 1998.
42. For views on NATO's interests' in the southern Caucasus see de Witte P., "Fostering Stability and Security in the Southern Caucasus", *NATO Review*, vol.47, no.1 (Spring 1999), pp.14-16.
43. Blank, S.J., "Energy, Economics and Security in Central Asia: Russia

and its Rivals (US Army War College: Carlisle Barracks, Pa., 10th May 1995) in Gennady Chufrin, *op.cit.*, p.216.

44. Blum, D.W., "Domestic Politics and Russia's Caspian Policy", *Post Soviet Affairs*, vol.14, no.2, (April-June 1998), pp.145-149.
45. Arbatov, A.G., "Russian National Interests", (eds.) R.D. Blackwill and S.A. Karagonov, *Damage Limitation or Crisis: Russia and the Outside World*, CSIA Studies in International Security, no.5, Brasscy's: Washington, D.C., 1994), pp.54-67. And also Kortunov, A., " Russia, the 'near abroad and the West', (ed.) G.W. Lapidus, "*The New Russia" Troubled Transformation* (Westview Press: Boulder, Colo., 1995), pp.143-192; Covington, S., "Moscow's Insecurity and Eurasian Instability", *Eurasian Security*, vol.4, no.3 (autumn 1996), p.451.
46. Gennady Chufrin, *op.cit.*, p.218.
47. *Monitor* (James Town Foundation), 2, 31 (February 14, 1996).
48. "Retsepty Stabilnosti", *Izvestia*, 9 March 1991, p.5.
49. *Turkish Economy in Figures*, DEIK (Foreign Economic Relations Board Bulletin, Turkey), February 1998.
50. Sullivan, S. and Kohen S., "The Turkish Model is on Display", *News Week*, 2 February 1992, p.23.
51. *Ibid.*
52. A.G. Arbatov, "Russian National Interest" (eds.) R.D. Blackwill and S.A. Karaganov, *Damage Limitations or Crisis: Russia and the Outside World*, CSIA Studies in International Security, no.5 (Brasscy's: Washington D.C. 1994), p.71.
53. Gennedy Chufrin, *op.cit.*, p.221.
54. *The Economist*, 14 March 1998, p.50.
55. *Ibid.* Besides Bushehr, Iran has several other civil nuclear plants with small reactors, including an experimental one at Tehran University provided by the United States before the Islamic Revolution.
56. *Financial Times*, 26 February 1999, p.2.
57. Abbas Maleki, "Iran and Russia: Neighbours without Borders" in Gennady Chufrin (ed.), *Russia in Asia: The Emerging Security Agenda* (Sipri, Oxford Press: 1999), p.191.
58. William Hale, *Turkish Foreign Policy: 1974-2000, op.cit.*, p.313.
59. Hurriyet, 23 April 1980.
60. *Cumhuriyet*, 10 May 1980, quoted in Alon Liel, (translated by Emanuel Lottem), *Turkey in the Middle East: Oil, Islam and Politics* (Lynne Rienner Publishers, Inc., Boulder, London, 2001), p.171.

61. *Ibid.*, p.171.
62. *Ibid.*, p.177.
63. Yuri Federov, "Russia's Policies Toward Caspian Region oil: Neo-Imperial or Pragmatic"? *Perspective on Central Asia* (September 1996) at https//www.cpass.org/casian w/setpers.html.
64. Mikbail Peresvezbin, "Ashkabad 'Trio' Remedy to Become Quintet", *Russian Press Digest*, 14 November 1996, p.3.
65. Nur Bilge Criss and Serdar Guner, *op.cit.*, p. 373.
66. Nur Bilge Criss and Serdar Guner, *op.cit.*, p. 372.
67. Dan Morgan and David Ottaway, "US-Russian Rivalry Flares over Kazakh Oil", *International Herald Tribune*, 7 October 1998.
68. David Kramer, "A Pipeline Fixation Distorts US Policy on Caspian Affairs", *International Herald Tribune*, 4 December 1998.
69. Morgan and Ottaway, note 65.
70 Nur Bilge, Criss and Serdar Guner, *op.cit.*, p. 372.
71. Ali L. Karaosmanoglu, "NATO Enlargement and then South: A Turkish Perspective", *Security Dialogue*, vol. 30, no.2 (June 1999), pp.213-224.
72. Nur Bilge Criss, *op.cit.*, p.373.
73. China already has a plan for an oil pipeline stretching from Kazakhstan-Russia Frontier at Aktyubinsk and Uzen to its territory. Jan Kalicki, "US policy in the Caspian Pipelines, Partnership and Prosperity" *Middle East Policy*, Vol. 6, No. 2 (October 1998), pp. 145-149.
74. Nur Bilge Criss, *op.cit.*, p. 374.
75. Halford Mackinder, *Democratic Ideals and Reality* (New York: Henry Holt, 1999).
76. Michael Klare, "New American Military Strategy", *Le Monde Diplomatique* (November 1997), quoted in Nur Bilge Criss, *op.cit.*, p. 375.

CHAPTER 6

Turkey, Israel and Greece in Trans-Caucasia and Central Asia

Since the disintegration of the Soviet Union perhaps Turkey was the first country which was frantically seeking political space for itself in the adjoining region of Trans-Caucasia and access to the natural resources of the Caspian states. Besides ensuring its own energy security, Turkey was interested in constructing pipeline to carry Azeri oil to Europe *via* Turkish territory. In the politics of the pipelines and competition for establishing spheres of interest in the newly independent states of the Central Asia—Trans-Caucasia Iran and Russia were seen as formidable rivals. Hence Turkey supported the west's line of approach and succeeded in getting the Baku-Tiblisi-Ceyhan (BTC) pipeline which is now carrying the Azeri oil to European markets via Turkish territory.

The competition for oil and gas-carrying pipelines and struggle for establishing sphere of influence in Central Asia has now lost heat and consequently Turkey's rivalry with Iran and Russia is also on the verge of getting subsided.

Recently, the new entrants have emerged as Ankara's competitors in Central Asia-Trans-Caucasia which Turkey had come to treat as its exclusive domain. Notwithstanding the reference to Jews having a happy and safe life during the Ottoman period and having enjoyed good relations with the republic of Turkey, the contemporary history suggests that Turkey initially was opposed to the creation of the state of

Israel. It voted against the partition resolution and supported the Arab states on the entire Palestinian issue. However, later as part of its pro-west policy, Turkey like other members of the western alliance endorsed the US policy towards Israel. Ankara extended diplomatic recognition to Israel and opened its embassy in Tel Aviv. Turkey tried to maintain a balance in its relations with the west including Israel and the East—the Arab-Muslim world. After the formation of the Baghdad Pact 1955, Turkey openly supported Israel during the Suez Crisis (1956) and after the revolution in Iraq (1958) shifted the Baghdad Pact from Baghdad to Ankara.

Anakra's attitude towards the west and Israel underwent a drastic change after the Cyprus crisis in 1964. Turkey reduced its diplomatic representation in Israel to the minimum level and drifted its loyalty towards the Arab world. There was a minor shift in its stand in early seventies but after the Arab-Israel war of 1973, Turkey further cemented its ties with the Arabs. The 1974 Cyprus episode and attitude of western allies of Ankara frustrated it again and it decided to remain with the Muslim states of West Asia. Turkey revived its relations with Israel in late 1980s.

In the post Soviet period Israel's own initiative in cultivating relations with the Central Asian countries is motivated by its national interest and oil needs. Its developed economy, especially armament industry needs outlet and Central Asian regimes appear to be a favourable market. However, in addition to these, the Israel's initiative in Central Asia appears to be at the behest of America.

Same applies to the other entrant, Greece which has suddenly become interested in Central Asian—Caspian politics and seeking economic and political ties with the countries of this region. It is maintained by the analysts of Central Asian affairs that Greece wants to counter the Turkish strategy of seeking Central Asian support in its favour on Cyprus issue—recognition to the TRNC. However, this argument does not hold much strength because the TRNC came into existence in

1974 and since then not a single country has agreed to recognize it. Another argument, that Greece wants oil pipelines to pass through its territory holds grounds. Yet another argument that, Greece is, at the moment, President of the European Union, it can utilize this position in making Turkey agreeable to its stand on various outstanding issues between the two countries also appears convincing.

However, to understand the strategy of Israel and Greece in Central Asia it is necessary to look into the two cases independently.

TURKEY AND ISRAEL : NEW ALLIES IN SOUTHERN CAUCASUS AND CENTRAL ASIA

Turkey and Israel are the two democratic and committed pro-American states in the entire West Asia. Both are highly militarized, equipped with sophisticated weapons and supporting a strong economy have potential to emerge as powerful regional leaders in their own right. The situation around them facilitates their emergence as regional powers. Turkey and Israel owing to the pro-western orientation of their polity, society and foreign policy, and association with west's global security system have been close friends. Yet, the graph of their relationship has not been straight and smooth. There have been ups and downs in their relations but the two mature nations have steered clear through difficult phases in their history, caused by the international circumstances. In the desovietized Central Asia and West Asia they foresee a great future in staying together and charting a common course which may benefit both equally.

The collapse of the Soviet Union in 1990 and emergence of independent sovereign republics in Trans-Caucasia and Central Asia having vast oil and natural gas resources and mineral wealth have made the region centre of international attraction. A large number of regional and external powers are vying with each other for seeking spheres of influence and control over the natural resources of the Caspian Sea Basin states.

Turkey is a Central Asian country and enjoys ethno-linguistic, religious and cultural ties with the people of Azerbaijan, Turkmenistan, Kazakhstan, Ukraine and with people of Turkic stock inhabiting the other countries of Central Asia as well. Owing to its geo-political and strategic location, commanding the important waterways, the Turkish straits—Bosphorus and Dardanelles, access to the Mediterranean and the Black Sea linking Europe to Asia, particularly West Asia and Central Asia, Turkey is in a more advantageous position than any other regional contender for power and influence in Central Asia.

Iran and Turkey are the two most formidable rivals in the region. But Turkey having early historical linkages with the Turkic republics, having common ancestry and cultural and linguistic commonalties is in a stronger position because it enjoys easy acceptability in Central Asia. Its international status as a member of NATO, close strategic linkages with the Untied States and Europe, membership in several west-sponsored military and non-military organizations make it a more welcome partner to the countries of Trans-Caucasia-Central Asia. Yet, Iran's influence and its capability to stall Turkey's ambitious plans for establishing firm control over the resources of the Caspian Sea states is not insignificant.

Russia being a "parent state" having ruled over the entire region for a long time is still a towering power, which despite their separation enjoys the confidence of the newly independent states (NIS) of Central Asia—Trans-Caucasia. However, the NIS are cautious in dealing with Russia as they fear its power and influence in the region. The Central Asian Republics are covetously guarding their freedom, sovereignty, territorial integrity and natural resources.

Of the three major regional contestants for power and influence in Central Asia—Turkey, Iran and Russia—Turkey is in a much better position than Iran and has succeeded in generating a favourable climate for itself in the region. As compared to these, Israel—the new entrant in the contest for power and influence in the region is not only new but a total outsider whose acceptability would depend on its utility for the countries of the region. Israel has registered its presence in the region in the 1990s only.

However, this is not Israel's first attempt to create a sphere of influence in the Greater Middle East region (Central Asia). In the 1950s the Israeli leader David Ben Gurion sought to generate a non-Arab Middle Eastern Alliance which would have consisted of Turkey, Ethiopia, Iran and Israel. This attempt, called a "periphery strategy" ultimately failed. The fall of the Shah of Iran in 1979 sealed the project for quite sometime.[1]

After the failure of the "periphery strategy", Israel was seeking to develop ties with any 'moderate' Muslim state willing to assist Tel Aviv in the effort to undercut its anti-Muslim image or the perception that all Muslim countries are aligned against it. Israel is moving with a more comprehensive vision as part of its new strategy to gain greater influence in the region, with special emphasis on the new republics of Central Asia.[2]

The rapidly shifting balance of the 1990s and the new developments stemming from the acceleration of globalization have forced Israel to re-evaluate and re-orient its foreign policy strategy. Bulent Aras has listed them as: (1) to solve its border conflicts and to form a security belt within the peace process; (2) to conclude the process of integration and recognition as a legitimate equal state in the region in this security belt; (3) to gain diplomatic flexibility in manipulating the inter-state conflicts of the Middle Eastern countries; (4) to exploit the resources of the region and introduce multi-state projects with the support of international Jewish organizations; (5) after gaining legitimacy in the region, to open up to Asia and then to develop its diplomatic and economic relations with more and more southern countries; (6) to use the opportunities created by the complex web of relations mentioned above to reach an influential position in the formation of global strategies and to escape from the conflicts of the Middle East to establish a greater global presence.[3]

Israel relates its earlier attempts for developing a sphere of influence in Central Asia to justify its new strategy in the region. The Israeli administration appears keen on proving that its interest in the region is not new. Central Asia appeared on its agenda even before the CARs had won their independence from the USSR.

Some scholars of Israeli policy in Central Asia argue that one of the objectives of these early attempts has been to set a barrier against the expansion of Arab and Iranian influence in the new republics. It wanted to counter the efforts of the Arab countries to draw Central Asian republics into the Arab-Israeli conflict and pre-empt the threat of Islamic fundamentalism.[4] Martha Brill Olcott, the well known specialist on Central Asian Republics and politics of the region contests this view and argues that Central Asian states remained hostile to Israel for the sake of obtaining assistance from the Arab countries.[5] It is also argued that what dissuaded the Central Asians from approaching the West Asian states for assistance was the fear of getting entangled with the various problems of that region especially the opposite stand taken by the countries of West Asia on the Palestinian issue.

Yasser Arafat's visit to Kazakhstan in early 1992 to mobilize the Central Asian Republics' support for the Palestinian cause perhaps alarmed Israel. Kazakhstan's recognition to the Palestinian State was seen as if the Palestinians are drawing the Central Asian republics in the Arab-Israeli conflict. The intensity of Israel's concern prompted it to write letters to the American Congressmen urging them to use their influence to persuade Kazakhstan to reduce its interaction with the Palestinians. Tel Aviv also approached American Secretary of State, James A. Baker III to ask Kazakhstan to reconsider its newly established relations with the PLO.[6] However, the high profile Israeli intervention made any impact neither on the PLO nor on the Central Asian Republics. Arafat was invited by Uzbekistan in February 1992 and Tajiksitan also established diplomatic relations with the Palestinian state.[7]

The relations of Central Asia with the Arab countries continued to grow. In April 1992, an Uzbek delegation went to Saudi Arabia and participated in a conference convened to seek recognition to the legitimate rights of the Palestinian people and a just solution to the Palestinian problem. The heightened tensions among the Central Asian Muslims on the Palestinian issue forced Israel to cancel the Dagestan-Israel Friendship Society's conference.[8]

Israel is an outsider in Central Asia but some of its strong points are admired by the Central Asians. It is a powerful state, politically and economically strong and a democratic, secular state with tremendous diplomatic skill and fortitude to face the challenges and coming out unscathed. The Central Asian leaders are strong but their hold on the people is not by consent but by force. They are not able to introduce genuine democracy despite continuous proddings by the United States. Owing to Israel's close relationship with the United States it is seen by some Central Asian states as a "gateway to the west" and to the US in particular.[9]

On its part Israel finds Central Asia as a lucrative trading partner and a good market for Israeli goods. Its access to the oil of Azerbaijan and Kazakhstan will enhance its energy security and reduce its dependence on western oil companies. In its maneuvers Israel is having the US backing. Tel Aviv is seen as an additional proxy to safeguard the American interests in the Caspian oil, besides Turkey.

Israel is moving systematically, arranging its interests in an order of priority. It agrees to "power vaccum" thesis but realizes that one cannot fill the vaccum just by being present in Central Asia. Israel wants to help the CARs in introducing democracy step by step and to the western style governance in the region.[10] Israel has chosen to enter Central Asia through an alliance with Turkey which is rooted in the region. There is a convergence of interests and policies between the two countries in Central Asia. Turkey is also motivated by the desire to sell the Turkish model: parliamentary democracy, free market economy, secularism while retaining Islam in the socio-political life of the country. The resurgence of the Turkic world afresh has enhanced geo-strategic significance of Turkey. Since the Israeli model has same contours there will be no competition.

Ankara's own gain is not less significant in befriending Israel. Tel Aviv enjoys the support of the strongest pressure group "the Jewish Lobby" in the American politics. The friendship with Israel may expand the pro-Turkey environment in the western capitals. Turkey can have access to Israeli armaments produced in Israel and may even set up "joint ventures" in the field of armament production. In view of Iran's developing nuclear programme and its capacity to develop further, friendship with Israel which posses advanced nuclear technology and armaments provides great solace to Ankara.

Turkey realized that Israel was better positioned in Washington and hoped that Israel's influence and particularly its lobby could be harnessed to further Turkish interest, such as arms transfers.

In the 1990s, Israel made concerted efforts to instruct the American Jewry on the strategic significances of Turkey. Several American—Jewish organizations due to their interests in the Jews of Central Asia welcomed the improving relationship between Turkey and Israel and initiated regular interaction with the Turkish authorities visiting United States. In July 1999, Barry

Jacobs, an American Jewish Committee official said ". . . we will be Turkeys friends officially in Congress". Israeli lobby has helped in toning down the criticism of Turkey in Congress over the human rights issues and in attempts to revoke the 1992 Congressional restrictions on US and Turkey's ally Azerbaijan (Section 907 of the Support Freedom Act). The Jewish lobby also supported Turkey's claim for Baku-Ceyhan oil pipeline.

From Israel's point of view, cooperation with Turkey may neutralize some of the basic hurdles in its attempt to penetrate into the Central Asian markets. Turkey can also counter the Iranian threat to Israel. The Turkish Prime Minister Tansu Ciller, during her visit to Israel in the Autumn of 1994 had discussed the joint investments in Central Asia. Moscow Radio in its broadcast said that Turkey and Israel are aiming at joint investments in the former Soviet republics ranging from agriculture to environmental protection".[11] In December 1996, a joint delegation of the representatives of the business concerns of both Turkey and Israel (100 Turkish firms and 30 Israeli firms) visited Central Asia and negotiated joint projects.[12]

The Turkish-Israeli alliance seems viable because even the conservative Islamists are favouring joint ventures and joint investments with Israel in Central Asia. In 1996 and early 1997 a series of agreements were signed and many were related to military cooperation. Turkish military admires Israel's fighting prowess and wants to shape their armed forces on the same pattern. The Turkish General staff Cevik Bir argued that "Turkey and Israel are two great democracies of this region and we must show that democracies can work together in every sphere of activity".[13]

Israel's entry into Central Asia has proved beneficial to Turkey in one more respect. Earlier Turkey was moving alone and facing the Iranian and Russian opposition single handedly. With Israel's arrival now a tripartite group 'Turkey, Israel and United States" has emerged which is collectively executing the assistance programme in Central Asia.[14] Israel clearly aims to retain American support while planning to diversify its own foreign policy prerogatives at a time when the Arab Nations are preoccupied with peace negotiations with Israel.

TURKEY-ISRAEL CO-OPERATION IN CENTRAL ASIA

The background for Israel's entry in Central Asia was prepared when close relationship between Israel and Turkey commenced in 1992 and several Turkish and Israeli minister visited each others country and tried to expand their existing relationship on strategic, political and economic levels and evolve convergence of interests between the two countries.

The bilateral trade between Israel and Turkey grew from $ 54 million in 1987 to $ 850 million in 1998. Fostering military trade (which is usually excluded from the official statistics) as well as revenue from tourism was estimated by Turkish Ambassador to Israel Barlas Ozener at $ 1.5 billion in 1998.[15] In 2000, Israel's exports to Turkey were $ 430 million and imports from Turkey were $ 586.6 million which is more than expected.

Economic relations were complemented by the intensification of cultural ties. Israeli tourism to Turkey stock rocketed from 7000 travellers in 1986 to 160,000 in 1992 and 350,000 in 1994 (around 18% of total tourists of Israel). Academic exchanges increased and new programmes in the field of history, culture, politics, language and literature were introduced in each other's Universities. Tel Aviv saw great potential in Turkish-Israeli ties.

The enhanced political and economic status in Central Asia and newly acquired significance of Turkey in the foreign policy and security considerations of Central Asia attracted Israel towards the CARs. Tel Aviv found Turkey too willing to "introduce" the new "entrant" to the CARs.

In the field of strategic partnership Ankara was happy to see Israel's willingness to co-operate with Turkey and evolve a common strategic platform to operate from in Central Asia and adjoining countries in West Asia like Syria,[16] Jordan, Lebanon and possibly Iraq after the warlike situation subsides and the elected government gets stabilized there.

Ankara and Tel Aviv both are opposed to radical Islam in the region. Turkey faces serious problems at home because of emerging Islamist forces under the banner of Welfare Party which has appeared under various names at different times. Ankara always feared Iran and Saudi Arabia which could enhance the influence of Islamic groups active in Turkey. Co-operation with Israel offers Turkey support in its strategic backyard.[17]

Another meeting point between Turkey and Israel is to contain spread of weapons of mass destruction—a favourite engagement of the United States too. As far as Turkey is concerned it was never faced with the threat of WMDS. It was well protected by the US-NATO security umbrella but Israel always lived under the shadow of danger from the neighbouring countries suspected for having the WMDS. The nuclear programme of Iran and Iraq and possibility of Syria having obtained the WMDS heightened the Tel Aviv's concern for the presence of the WMDS and need to destroy them or force the countries having nuclear capabilities to dismantle the entire nuclear programme and surrender or destroy the WMDS which are under their possession. In this context, both Turkey and Israel invariably encourage US involvement in the region.

Israel produces weapons and is in the business of weapons' sale internationally. Turkey hopes to be benefited by Israel's skills in this field. Joint exercises, training to military personnel, and above all export of arms to Turkey figure on the agenda for co-operation in military affairs. Moreover, Israels arms sales policy allows transfer of military technology to Turkey's defence industries.

In December 1996, a deal worth $ 630m million was negotiated which requires upgrading of the Turkish fleet of fifty four Phantoms. The first 26 jet fighters to be upgraded at Israeli air craft industries (IAI) arrived for retrofitting at Lahav plant in March 1997 and the remaining twenty-eight to be upgraded at the Airforce Repair and Maintenance Plant (ARMP) at Eskishehr, Turkey. The F-4 deal represented the biggest foreign contract for IAI.[18]

This Turkey, Israel, US strategic co-operation group holds advantages for all the three. Turkey was boldly holding the fort for the United States in the Caspian region and Central Asia and was trying to minimize the Russian influence and obstruct anti-Turkey and anti-American alliance formations. Since, Russia is deeply involved in the Central Asian region and closest to the Caspian region, Turkey always found itself weak *vis a vis* Russia, Iran, Armenia grouping. With the arrival of Israel as a supporter of Turkey and a country serving the interests of America Ankara's status has got enhanced and it feels more confident in dealing with the Central Asian republics and the Caspian Basin states.

Turks are going to gain much more from their military links with Israel in their relations with Syria and Cyprus. Moreover, the option to buy arms from Israel has added flexibility in the international market, which in any case is the buyers' market. For Israel, Turkish opening is going to be extremely beneficial. It has given a huge market to Israel for trading in Central Asia. Its association with the Turkic masses of Central Asia would remove the "anti Muslim" stigma attached to it for its attitude towards the Arab states of West Asia and atrocities committed on the Palestinians. For massive mass support Central Asia and South Caucasia hold great promise.

ISRAEL AND THE CENTRAL ASIAN REPUBLICS

By the end of 1992, Israel had given official recognition to Azerbaijan, Kazakhstan, Kyrgyzstan and Tajikistan. With Turkmenistan it established diplomatic relations in 1993.

Initially Israeli administration gave priority to trade and diplomacy over Jewish connections as these countries have substantial Jewish population. In each one of the Central Asian republics the Jewish Friendship Societies are existing from the pre-independence period. The relations between Israel and the Central Asian Jews have been strengthened after the 1990s. They have become stronger after the collapse of the Soviet Union. For example, in March 1992, the Jewish Agency organized a conference on the Israeli economic experience in Tashkent. In June, an Azerbaijan-Israel Friendship Society convened a meeting in Haifa and called for support to the Azerbaijani administration in its struggle against Armenia. It later organized activities during the Jewish religious festivals. A summer camp for children from Kazakhstan and Kyrgyzstan was also organized in September of the same year. Israel has also raised its diplomatic representation in these republics to the Ambassadorial level.

In Central Asia Turkey's main concentration is on Turkmenistan and Kazakhstan. Azerbaijan with its enormous oil wealth, geographical proximity and clsoe ethnic-linguistic and religious linkages is closest to Turkey. However, Israel is keen to have relations with all the breakaway republics although its priority is also Azerbaijan, Turkmenistan and Kazakhstan as besides oil and natural gas the presence of a large Jewish population in these republics is an added attraction.[19]

Azerbaijan

Israel established diplomatic relations with Azerbaijan a little later after its attaining independence. The Iranian media opposed the entry of the "anti-Muslims' Jewish State in Azerbaijan which is the next door neighbour of Iran.[20] In the Nagorno Karabakh dispute between Azerbaijan and Armenia like Turkey, Israel was also supporting Azerbaijan and it supplied arms to Baku during the prolonged armed conflict with Armenia in 1988-1994.[21]

The *Analytical Review* of Turan News Agency has argued that Azerbaijan considers Israel as a potential strategic partner and at times they express bewilderment over the slow growth of their relations.[22] Another analyst of Azerbaijani affairs Sule Kut argues that according to Azerbaijani officials Israel as a secular, democratic and militarily powerful western country may be a threat to the Middle Eastern countries but it is an asset to Azerbaijan. The Jewish community residing in Azerbaijan enjoys good relations and special privileges in many respects.

The communication between the people of Azerbaijan and Israel has increased due to initiation of charter flights regularly commuting between the two countries since 1992. Israeli Embassy in Baku, opened in February 1993 gives priority to enhancing political, economic, cultural and military cooperation with Azerbaijan.

Owing to Iran's opposition to Israel's increasing presence in Azerbaijan, Tel Aviv's officials have to constantly counter the allegations and clarify the purpose of their presence "which certainly is not to harm Iran". The IRNA (Iranian News Agency) commented on a visit by Israeli Intelligence Delegation in August 1995 that it was there (Baku) to train Azerbaijan's intelligence officials and secret agents to spy over the neighbouring state. Lowell Bezanis once agreeing to Iran's charges against Israel said that "Azerbaijan's interests in Israel and *vice versa* stem from their mutual fear of Iran and its fundamentalist policies. By cultivating close and mutually beneficial relations with Azerbaijan, Israel wants to win plaudits from United States. The Israeli and Azerbaijani officials admit that their cooperation aims at weakening the Russian hold over the region and counter its pressure on Azerbaijan and Georgia. Iran's close relations with Armenia and its support to the latter on Nagorno Karabakh issue is also seen as "dangerous" and needs to be countered. The first Israeli Ambassador to Azerbaijan, commenting on flourishing

Azerbaijan-Israel relations said that "he has brought them from zero to .... a high level". In the first four months of 1996, the Israeli export to Azerbaijan amounted to roughly $ 3.5 million.[23]

The Prime Minister of Israel, Binyamin Netanyahu, on his way back to Israel from his visit to Japan and South Korea stopped at Baku to meet President Haider Aliev on 29 August 1997. Highlighting the nature and value of relationship between Israel and Baku he said:

> We are two ancient peoples who have achieved independence in the last decades and now the task for us as independent nations is to continue to develop our countries. . . . I also find great hope in that fact that we have relationship as we do have with Turkey, with Jordan, with Egypt, between the Jewish state and predominantly Muslim states. . . . This gives us hope that all the children of Abraham can find peace and friendship under the same sun that rises over the Caspian Sea and sets over Mediterranean.[24]

Netanyahu while promising to transfer technological know-how to Azerbaijan expressed concern over the possible sale of nuclear technology by Russia to Iran which shares a long land, air and sea border with Azerbaijan. Expressing satisfaction over Baku's emergence as a major oil supplier to Israel, Netanyahu said that "a pipeline project that would carry Azeri oil across neighbouring Georgia and Turkey to the north-eastern corner of the Mediterranean sea and a prospective under water extension to Israel". We are involved in this project . . . it will enable us to buy oil at a much lower price".[25]

Israel is always emphasizing upon the "three sided co-operation between Israel, Turkey and Azerbaijan in curbing the tide of Islamic fundamentalism emanating from Iran. The Tehran Radio blasted Azerbaijan for hosting the Israeli Prime Minister saying:

> Baku has been playing a dangerous game by receiving this Zionist regime's expansionist Prime Minister. By doing this it has destabilized its own ties with the Islamic states in the region and the world.[26]

Armenia also joined Iran in condemning Israel and Azerbaijan's growing ties in the region. The Armenian Foreign Minister Alexander Arzumanyan also viewed the close co-operation between Turkey and Tel Aviv to be extremely dangerous for the region, saying that it was even more dangerous for Azerbaijan to join them.[27] He underlined the importance of Tehran-Yerevan ties at a time when regional co-operation was rapidly expanding.

Shimon Stein, the Deputy Director of the Israeli Foreign Ministry Department for the CIS and Central Europe during his visit to Baku in January 1999 said that: "the potential exists for developing economic ties between Azerbaijan and Israel". He noted that Israel supports the Baku-Ceyhan oil pipeline as it is going to be advantageous to the entire Southern Caucasus region from both economic and strategic angles. It will put an end to Baku's dependence on other countries (Russia). President Haider Aliev has invited the Israeli aircraft industry to modernize his Topolov presidential aircraft at the Bet Shemesh plant, near Tel Aviv, and invited Turkish and Israeli security experts to train his private guards units.[28] Israel's pragmatic approach to its relations with Turkey and thrust in South Caucasus is leading to stronger ties between the three countries—Israel, Turkey and Azerbaijan. The US blessing to this tripartite friendly grouping in Central Asia further ensures its prospects of emerging as a most viable three-power alliance in Caspian Basin region.

Tajikistan

Tajikistan's plentiful human resources and rich minerals attracted attention of Israel. Tel Aviv was prepared to invest in Tajik economy but the prolonged civil war, increasing role and power of Islamist forces over the political leadership of Tajikistan, its ethno-linguistic cultural linkages with Iran and Tehran's political and diplomatic influence over Dushanbe discouraged Tel Aviv from getting further in.

The Tajik government and Islamic forces impressed upon Israel that there exists absolutely no danger to Israeli investors, businessmen and industrial ventures in Tajikistan.[29] The Islamic parties also assured Tel Aviv that no harm will come to Israelis in Tajikistan from the Islamic forces active in the country.[30] However, the anti-Israel and anti-US attitude among the Tajik people and Tajikistan's political, linguistic, cultural and above all emotional closeness with Iran works as serious constraint which Tel Aviv could not overcome. However, after the war in Afghanistan the political climate in Tajikistan is not anti America, although their sympathy for Iran remains intact. In today's Tajikistan Israel may not find the environment hostile to it.

The diplomatic relations between Israel and Tajikistan are at the ambassadorial level and some private business concerns are engaged in Tajikistan but at the official level Israel is still maintaining a low profile in Tajikistan.

Uzbekistan

Uzbekistan is one of the republics of Central Asia which are close to the United States. The US wanted to groom Uzbekistan as a future leader of Central Asia. Its huge manpower (23 million), developed agriculture, higher level of education, rich cultural and historical heritage as Centre of learning, fabulous monuments, museums, libraries and archaeological assets make it a most favoured destination for tourists from the world over.

It is a multi-ethnic state which has people of Turkic and Persian stock besides the original Uzbeks. The languages spoken are Turkic, Persian, Russian and Uzbek, which has developed enough to be an official language of the country.

Israel has had a more substantial relationship with Uzbekistan, the dissemination of irrigation technology forming its core. Israel's *Beta Shita* Company signed an agreement in September 1992, for the construction of a high technology irrigation scheme in the Andejan region.[31] Another significant and upcoming project is Akkurgan Demonstration Farm. It is one of the agricultural demonstration activities established under the special co-operation programme developed in the Central Asian Republics by MASHAV, the Centre for International Co-operation of Israel Ministry of Foreign Affairs, in co-operation with the US Agency for International Development (USAID).[32]

The MASHAV-USAID programme aims to address key agricultural issues and promote economic endeavours as well as international co-operation. It reflects Israel's commitment to share appropriate technologies, know-how, human resource training and practical experience again in agriculture and rural development with the Central Asian republics. Several training programmes and educational courses are also being conducted by the Israelis both in Uzbekistan and Israel.[33]

Uzbekistan is a major cotton producing country. This mono-culture farming was introduced by the Soviets in Uzbekistan. Israel is taking interest in improving the cotton production both qualitatively and quantitatively. According to a *Financial Times* report in May 1992, the Israeli projects in Uzbekistan have shown a 30% increase in the cotton output while reducing the consumption of water by two-thirds of the normal use—prior to introducing the Israeli techniques.[34] Sadik Safayev, the Foreign Trade Relation Minister of Uzbekistan has said that Israel attaches great importance to economic relations with Uzbekistan and that four Israeli companies are regularly dealing with Uzbekistan.[35]

Turkmenistan

Israel-Turkmenistan relations commenced little later than other republics of Central Asia. Despite the delay in recognition economic relations between the two states commenced in 1992. Israel offered agricultural technology and number of projects for rural development.[36] Since the cost of irrigation and desalination were expected to cost $ 10 billion, they had to be shelved as Turkmenistan was not in a position to raise that much of amount.

Since the official recognition to Turkmenistan in 1993, economic co-operation has increased. In 1994, Turkmenistan's Deputy Prime Minister visited Jerusalem and Shimon Peres of Israel also visited Ashgabat. A number of bilateral accords were signed. The US Israeli joint project on education and technology transfer in agriculture is an outstanding sign of co-operation for development.[37] The volume of trade between Turkmenistan and Israel exceeded to $ 40 million in 1995.[38] In addition to this, in March 1995, Turkmenistan and Israel concluded an agreement on co-operation in health care, under which Israel provided assistance to Turkmenistan in child and maternity care, medical insurance, organization of ambulance services and supply of medical equipments.[39] The Israeli firm Ben Shannar Associates, extended financial services in Turkmenistan and also in Uzbekistan and Kazakhstan.[40]

In the field of Turkmen gas Israel is providing valuable services to Turkmenistan. The Turkmen President Turkmanbashi Saparmurad Niyazov visited Israel on 25 May 1995 to meet his Israeli counterpart Ezer Weizmann as well as Prime Minister Yitzhak Rabin and the Foreign Minister Shimon Peres for talks focussing on bilateral economic relations. Israel is involved in a $ 100 million irrigation project and a scheme to build a gas pipeline to Turkey from Turkmenistan, which has world's largest gas reserves.[41] The executives of *Merhav*, an Israeli Company which has invested in Turkmenistan, is of the opinion that it is possible for the pipeline to be extended to Israel.[42]

The *Merhav* has also signed a $ 500 million contract to upgrade the Turkmenbashi refinery in Turkmenistan in August 1996. The project is aimed at improving two units, a Continuous Catalytic Reforming and Fluid Catalytic Cracker and financing a third new unit for processing lubricating oil.[43] The representative of *Merhav* Yosej A. Maiman appeared on Turkmen television with Turkmenbashi and the Turkmen media paid special attention to the Maiman company and its officials as they are the key figure in the settlement of these deals.

Israel seems all set to establish a firm hold over the economy of Turkmenistan as well as other republics of Central Asia. As compared to Turkey, it has more potential in financing and supervising the execution of projects in Central Asia. Yet at present it is not a competitor of Turkey. It is an ally, a partner—who is seeking Ankara's help in making a place for itself in Central Asian-Caspian Sea Basin states. Tel Aviv has very carefully avoided entering those regions which are plagued with chronic trans-frontier ethnic conflicts. Only in Azerbaijan, it is following the footsteps of Turkey and supporting Baku against Armenia. It would have been better had Israel remained neutral. At least one of the two (Turkey and Israel) could have a chance to mediate in the Karabakh dispute.

Kazakhstan

Israel has developed close relations with Kazakhstan in spite of its early hesitation owing to the presence of one million people of German origin and about 40% of Russian origin in Kazakhstan. Tel Aviv, however, has overcome the inhibition and providing assistance in agriculture-related projects and technological co-operation in Kazakhstan. The outstanding Israeli companies—*Beta Shita, Netafim,* and *Merhav*—are handling important projects in Kazakhstan. In February 1992, four different projects targetting tomato and cotton production were signed between the two states, since then the output of tomato and cotton had multiplied six-fold within three years of introduction of Israeli techniques.[44]

In October 1992, several other agreements were signed between the two countries, following which Israel's Lachist firm has made significant investments in Kazakhstan.[45] Its Dairy Foundation project is the largest known initiative in agriculture and animal husbandry to date. In a short period this project has increased milk production by 60% while reducing the expenditure considerably.[46]

The Palestinian issue concerns the Kazakh population although its intensity is not so much that can derail the relations with Israel. The initiation of the peace process between Israel and Palestinians is welcomed by Kazakhstan. The Kazakh Foreign Ministry promptly issued a statement that: "positive changes in the Middle East leading to peaceful settlement of the Arab-Israeli conflict should become irreversible in the interest of establishing mutual confidence, developing broad economic co-operation in the region and creating an integral security system in Asia".[47]

Kazakhstan's telecommunication network is also being built by Israel. In the entire Middle East, Israel is in an advantageous position in the production of telecommunication equipment. Another project included technology transfer in telephone, telex and telegraph. Israel has also established direct satellite and telegraph connections to Uzbekistan. Since the visit of the Kazakh Prime Minister Terescenko to Israel, direct flights between Israel and Kazakhstan have also commenced.

Israel is moving patiently in Kazakhstan. With the presence of one million people of German origin and about 40% Russians, Israel is cautious not to provoke the sentiments of the either of the two or both. Kazakhstan, however, finds Israel useful and a dependable ally which is being given due recognition.

Kyrgyzstan

Kyrgyzstan established diplomatic relations with Israel in January 1993. Notwithstanding the opposition from Muslim countries, Asker Akaev opened Kyrgyz embassy in Jerusalem. The two governments agreed to co-operate on a wide range of subjects including media, science, technology, cultural activities and joint venture investments. Additionally, Israel has also supplied an important part of the debt requirement of the public and private sector in Kyrgyzstan.[48]

Israel has emerged as a more effective foreign power in Central Asia which has established a firm foothold in a short span of time. It is genuinely interested in developing its own sphere of influence and in order to expand its trade relations is interested in increasing the economic potential of the Central Asian republics. Tel Aviv is contributing a great deal in improving the infra-structural facilities in Azerbaijan, Turkmenistan, Kazakhstan and Uzbekistan. Israeli help has brought about a tremendous improvement in the agricultural activities in the region and the output in important commodities has also increased. Israel, despite an enthusiastic and welcoming response from the regional countries, is maintaining a low key profile for fear of provoking Iran and Russia, the other two legitimate rivals for power and influence in Central Asia-Trans-Caucasia.

Initially, Israel used to be critical of Iran and its Islamic doctrine and often made allegations publicly. However, in the course of time it has shown great moderation in its declarations towards Iran and Islam especially after 1995 elections. Israeli Prime Minister Netanyahu in some of his speeches said that Israel had no dispute with Islam. Netanyahu since then relaxed political pressure on Iran and in 1996 he used Germany's Chancellor Helmut Kohl as a conduit to Iran to ask President Rafsanjani to prevent terrorist attacks on Israel.[49]

Turkey and Israel together may help in relaxing tensions

in Central Asia and generate a climate of mutual trust between Turkey, Iran, Azerbaijan, Israel. They can play an exemplary role in co-operating to improve democracy and economic performance in the enlarged Middle East, provided the US does not disturb their applecart by its hostile and warlike stance towards Tehran.

Tel Aviv has acquired a foothold in the economy of Central Asia as in almost every republic Israeli agricultural experts, technocrats, telecommunication experts and executives of big business companies are present and helping their indigenous counterparts.

However, Israel is yet not relaxed. The existence of nuclear weapons and technology in Iran disturbs Tel Aviv. According to a report prepared in France, the Mossad and the CIA are keeping a close eye on the nuclear energy experts' activities in Central Asian States.[50] Moscow's readiness to sell two nuclear reactors to Iran and the possibility of the installation of Russian S-300 surface to air missiles in the Republic of Cyprus (Greek Cyprus) has alarmed Israel. The S-300 surface to air missiles could endanger not only Turkey but also Israel's freedom of action in the eastern Mediterranean.[51] The worsening security scenario forces Turkey and Israel to develop new security initiatives. Neither country should ignore the possibility that any hand overplayed by Turkey and Israel, together with the US, could encourage Moscow to attempt to revive its fortunes as a great power by again playing the role of a patron to the more radical regimes of the region.[52]

In nutshell, the convergence of interests between Turkey and Israel in Central Asian-Caspian region has helped Ankara in gaining a reliable friend. It is obvious that soon the trio-Turkey, Israel and the US would forge a strategic alliance with Azerbaijan as a key country and try to monopolize its natural resources. The presence of several fault lines might come handy to them in their endeavours in Central Asia.

TURKEY AND GREECE IN TRANS CAUCASUS: STRANGE 'BED-FELLOWS'

Turkey and Greece, notwithstanding their long association during the Ottoman Empire, have not enjoyed a comfortable relationship. More than Turkey, Greece is still haunted by the trauma caused by some of the disturbing events,[53] which took place in the mid-fifteenth century, during the First World war and again in1974 when Turkey invaded Cyprus and captured 37% of the territory of the island state in order to 'secure the future' of the 18% Turkish Cypriot population of Cyprus.

Turks on their part dislike the Greeks for their role during the First World War. After the defeat of the Ottoman Empire in the war, the allied powers started pressing for the implementation of the four secret agreements,[54] which proposed the division of the Ottoman Empire among the victorious powers.

After the October (1917) Revolution the Bolsheviks renounced all claims on Turkish territory. Hence, out of contest for territories of the defeated powers. In early 1919, the Greek Prime Minister, Venizelos presented at the Paris Peace Conference a formal claim to the possession of Smyrna (Izmir). According to St. Jean de Maurienne Agreement it was assigned to Italy but for want of Russian ratification it lapsed. Lloyed George and Clemenceau supported the Greek claim. The British in particular encouraged Greece to occupy Smyrna as they thought the Greeks will be more amenable to the British policy in the Mediterranean. On May 15, 1919, under the protection of Allied naval support, Greek troops landed at Smyrna. The invasion was declared by the allies to be in accordance with Article 7 of the Armistice Agreement. The Greek occupation of Smyrna had a powerful impact on the war weary Turks who could not countenance the thought of being ruled by a minority element which were considered as second class citizens of the Ottoman Empire.[55] The forces of

Mustafa Kamal Ataturk repulsed the attack and liberated Turkey from the occupation forces within no time but the "scars" of the humiliation suffered have not healed as yet. The occupation of northern Cyprus, perhaps has given great satisfaction to Turkey as it could settle the scores with the Greeks. The Turkish military action in Cyprus and forcible occupation of northern Cyprus has generated great aversion and distrust for Turkey in Greece.

Commenting on the obsession of Greece' with Turkey, Nachmani has observed that: "The conflict with Turkey interests the Greeks more than any other foreign policy issue". A study of the Greek press found that this topic was covered more thoroughly than any other question, while in the Turkish press it ranked only sixteenth. Indeed, the Greek press devoted six times more space to Turkey than did its counterparts.[56]

MAJOR POINTS OF DISCORD BETWEEN GREECE AND TURKEY

The termination of cold war and eclipse of the Soviet power which put the entire Third World into disarray at least for sometime, heightened the Turkish threat in the perception of Greece. Athens felt that with the declining significance of the NATO in the post-Cold War world, the US might not feel interested in restraining Turkey. According to Greece, the vacuum created in the Balkans with the collapse of communism and the Soviet Union beckons Turkey. Ankara is endeavouring to penetrate Bosnia, Macedonia, Bulgaria, Kosovo and Albania and "let us not forget Cyprus" warned George Papandreou, former Greek Minister of Education (Foreign Minister since 1999).

Greek fears are not baseless. Turkey has threatened war if Greece expands territorial waters around its islands from 6 miles to 12 miles. In 1996, Prime Minister Tansu Ciller claimed 3000 Aegean islands and islets as Turkish and warned that a

Greek attempt to take these territories would be considered by Ankara as *casus belli*.[57] The other issues of conflict between Greece and Turkey are Muslim Turkish ethnic minority group in western Thrace, ownership of minerals on the Aegean continental shelf and control of air plane flights over the Aegean. Turkish forces and fortifications opposite the Greek Aegean island are kept on high alert.[58]

CYPRUS ISSUE

The most outstandingly crucial issue is Cyprus. Turkey exercised its superior military power with determination to achieve its goal—partition of the Island state of Cyprus. The forcible occupation of any region, area or territory of a state is against the norms of international behaviour in the post World War II world. Besides, Israel (which occupied large territories on the West Bank, Gaza, Sinai and Golan Heights during the Arab-Israeli war of 1967), Turkey is the only country which has snatched a huge part of the territory of Cyprus and is unlawfully retaining it despite severe criticism made by the world community.

Cyprus is a small island in the eastern Mediterranean which is 600 miles away from Greece and just 60 miles away from Turkey. Of its half a million population 18% were Turkish Cypriots (now they are inhabiting the Northern Republic of Cyprus, the occupied part of Cyprus) and 80% Greek Cypriots living in the Republic of Cyprus. The Turkish invasion of Cyprus in 1974 and forcible seizure of its territory (37% of the total area) has compelled Greece to increase its defence expenditure which is highest among the NATO members' defence budget. Greece has developed its army, navy and air force and stationed troops in Cyprus so that Turkish attack on the Republic of Cyprus would immediately bring the Greek soldiers into action.[59]

The verbal warfare and psychological intimidation between the two has kept the political climate in the region charged with hostile emotions.[60]

However, the atmosphere in the Aegean has changed dramatically after the August 1999 earthquake in western Turkey and the September 1999 earthquake in Athens. The Greek and Turkish rescue missions rushed to help each other. Donation were collected in each country for the other's benefit. These sincere gestures strengthened the gap between the allegedly tough and stubborn governments and the two friendly peoples. The people love to explain that the conflict is between the governments and not between citizens. The Greek and Turkish media picked up the momentum and contributed to building up a new understanding between the two countries.

SHARING THE AEGEAN SEA RESOURCES: PROBLEM OF TERRITORIAL WATERS AND CONTINENTAL SHELF

There exist, no doubt, some serious and outstanding problems between Turkey and Greece, especially in the Aegean Sea and its resources in the continental shelf which are claimed by both the countries. The 1982 Convention on the Law of Sea has stipulated the extension of territorial sea and the contiguous zone to 24 sea miles. Besides, the economic zone of 200 sea miles is also permitted to all littoral states. However, this applies to open seas. If the sea is small like Black Sea, Caspian, Aegean, Baltic etc., and it is shared by more than one country then the demarcation of territorial sea, maritime belt, contiguous zone and economic zone etc., will have to be determined with mutual consent of all concerned parties.

Greece has periodically expressed its wish to expand the territorial waters around its islands (numbering 2000) from 6 to 12 sea miles. Turkey's position is that if each one of Greece's more than 2000 islands are allowed to have 12 miles of territorial waters, the entire Aegean would become a Greek Sea. In fact, 64% of the Aegean will go under Greek control and leave only 24% as international waters. Each Turkish ship leaving Turkey's Aegean ports on way to the Mediterranean would have to go through the Greek waters. Turkey itself is keeping 6 mile territorial waters around its Aegean islands while holding 12 miles territorial waters in the Mediterranean and the Black Sea.[61]

Problems of Greece emanate from its perceptions of Turkish policy in the region. At times, particularly in the times of tension between the two states, Turkey has behaved erratically like violating the airspace of the Greek islands in the Aegean and not abiding by flight information region (FIR) and Athens' aerial control in the Aegean Sea. The Aegean FIR was determined in 1952 by the International Civil Aviation Organization (ICAO) and Turkey has to abide by it. Greece is apprehensive that Turkey might seize the islands by military means as it has placed the finest units of its Aegean Sea Army in the region.[62] Greece claims that Turkey is deliberately provoking crisis in the Aegean Sea. In fact, these are not very serious issues. They have been made serious by the mutual distrust and irrational attitude of both towards each other. The matter can be resolved through negotiations or a direct talk across the table.

The another issue related to exploitation of the resources, particularly oil of the continental shelf of the Aegean Sea which is being used by Greece only. The Laussane Treaty of 1923 has allotted the entire Aegean Sea, apart from the Turkish coast, to Greece. The Aegean contains the only one Greek oilfield and that too is running out. In 1980s it produced 1 million tons of oil annually, which has come down to 600,000 tons in the 1990s.

Greece is disturbed by the information given in the text books of the Turkish Military Academy published in May

1997. which states that the Aegean islands are a direct continuation of Anatolia's continental shelf and thus have no continental shelf of their own. The Turkish declaration that the Aegean Sea and its islands belonged to those who owned Anatolia, meaning that now they belong to Turkey. Tansu Ciller's statement that the 3000 islands of the Aegean Sea belong to Turkey. Such declarations and statements questioning the existing situation and ownership on the Aegean islands provoke counter reactions from the Greeks.

TURKISH MINORITY IN GREECE

The presence of Turkish minority groups in Greece further aggravates the situation. Athens calls these group "Muslim minority groups" and Turkey calls them "Turkish minority" in Greece and criticises Athens for suppressing them, thus preparing a background to intervene on their behalf.

As a counter allegation Greece complains of the repression of Greek orthodox Christians in Istanbul, who numbered 100,000 in 1923, and were down to 5,000 in 1988.

Greece also charged that the Turkish involvement with the Muslim minorities in Macedonia, Albania, Kosova and Bulgaria was based on the same justification that Turkey put forward in the context of its military intervention in Northern Cyprus. Some outrageous publications like *"Turkish Minority of Western Thrace* and *Macedonian Minority in Greece: A Human Tragedy within the Boundaries of the European Union"* brought out by the Turkish Ministry of Foreign Affairs also keep the political environment charged with high tension.

Athens' own share in adding to these tensions is no less either. It declared April 24, a memorial day to commemorate Armenians killed by Turks during the World War I. Greece had given shelter and support to Turkey's Kurdish rebel, Abdullah Ocalan.

However, the best way to end such bickerings and eliminating all misunderstandings is to initiate a dialogue. The European Union and the United States want that both Greece and Turkey resolve their problems peacefully through dialogue and understand the need for co-operation instead of harping on historical and other conventional issues that had cropped up between them several centuries ago.

The European Union has tried to calm down the temperatures in both the countries by insisting on a proper, prompt and comprehensive dialogue between Greece and Turkey as both are important members of NATO.

THE EU FACTOR

Greece is a member of the EU and Turkey is an applicant for its full membership which is still under consideration. Earlier Turkey had threatened that if Cyprus is admitted to EU, Turkey will use veto on NATO's admission of new members. Athens also threatened that if the EC members initiate talks with the Turkish Republic of Northern Cyprus (TRNC), it will block Turkey's entry into the European Union.

A change is witnessed in the attitude of both Greece and Turkey, after the 1999 calamity—earthquake in both countries. This facilitated agreement on the Helsinki decision (December 1999) which suggested inclusion of Turkey in the group of candidates for membership. Athens attached its own stipulations on the decision: that solution of the Cyprus problem may not be a precondition to Turkey's membership in the EU, its territorial disputes with Turkey be referred to the International Court of Justice at the Hague within a specific time and same conditions apply to Turkey as to the eleven other states seeking membership, the need for an enhanced dialogue on human right.[63]

THE US AS A FACTOR IN TURKEY-GREECE RELATIONS

Some kind of a "bilateral détente" has been initiated in the Turkey-Greece relations with the help and support of the EU members but Greece harbours several grievances against Washington too. Athens feels that the US regarded Turkey as a strong cold war ally and more of an asset for US interests than Greece. To enlist Turkey's support during the Gulf War (1991), the US government continued to hold back from effective action against Turkey on its occupation of Cyprus. Greece draws a parallel between Iraq's occupation of Kuwait and Turkey's occupation of Cyprus but President Bush declared explicitly that his campaign for the solution of the Middle East Conflict would not include Cyprus. The latter dispute has to be decided by the Untied Nations, and thus deferred its settlement for an indefinite period.

The people in Athens are dismayed by the fact that the US gives preference to Turkey and willingly gives aid and transfers modern weaponary to Ankara whereas Greece has to request even for the enhancement of economic and military aid. In disgust, also compelled by its own foreign policy considerations, Greece opposed the US and the NATO policy during the Kosovo crisis and refused to act against the Serbs out of affinity with the orthodox Church. Again, contrary to the US stand, Greece did not show sympathy for the Bosnian Muslims. Turkey not only endorsed the US policy and actions but occupied a central position in solving the Balkan crisis. Turkey enjoys the support of the Jewish lobby in the United States and is having excellent relations with Israel despite its early (1974 onwards) deviations when Turkey under the impact of Islamic forces in it domestic politics adopted a pro-Arab-Islamic policy and supported the Palestinians against Israel. The shift in favour of Israel has come lately, after 1999.

THE POST-SOVIET DEVELOPMENTS

The developments of far-reaching significance which took place in the regions around Turkey have benefited Ankara greatly. With the collapse of the Soviet Union and emergence of independent sovereign Muslim-Turkic republics have suddenly enhanced its prospects of becoming a major power in the region. Along with the USSR, Saddam Hussain, Syria and the Kurdish threats have vanished. Without exercising any force, it could persuade Syria and Greece to refuse shelter to Abdullah Ocalan, the Kurdish rebel leader. Notwithstanding, enormous criticism by the world community and opposition put up by Greece and the European community, Turkey has succeeded in retaining the occupied part of the Island Republic of Cyprus.

Turkey has made successful inroads in Trans-Caucasus and Central Asia. With Azerbaijan, Georgia and Ukraine, Ankara has established cordial relations and could obtain approval to construct the BTC—a pipeline to carry the Azerbaijani oil via Turkey to Europe through the territory of Georgia. The Baku-Tiblisi-Ceyhan (BTC) oil pipeline has been constructed and is made operational in 2005.

ANKARA SEARCHING NEW FRIENDS AND IMPROVING RELATIONS WITH THE ADVERSARIES

Turkey's enhanced co-operation with Israel has emboldened its security perceptions. Having realized the consequences of Turkey's new found strength and access to energy resources of the Caspian Sea Basin States, Greece has dropped its hostility towards Turkey and is trying to seek accommodation in Central Asia.

Greece like other players in the Caspian oil deals, is also interested in attaining energy security and seeking oil pipelines route from Azerbaijan to Europe via Greek ports. With the favourable wind blowing from Aegean to Ankara, Greece may hope to seek Turkey's support in getting such a favour from Azerbaijan.

The Turkey-Greek rapproachment commenced in the later part of 1999 and the bilateral relations between the two improved. The talks were initiated between Turkey and Greece on energy, cultural matters, security and earthquake precautions etc., between the Mayors of Athens and Istanbul, Demitris Avramopoulos and Ali Mufit Gurtuna visited each other and concluded agreements covering culture, trade, tourism and technical support.

The two most important statements made by Turkey and Greece generated a favourable climate for better relations between the two. First, the Turkish Defence Minister, Sabahattin Cakmakoglu announced that Turkey would decrease the number of its military exercises in the Aegean. Second, Dimitris Apostolakis, the Greek Deputy National Defence Minister declared that Athens saw no threat in the Turkish-Israeli military co-operation. "Assurances exist that there is no intention of creating an axis to threaten another country in any way whatsoever .... I hope nothing like this will cross any one's mind".

In January 2000, bilateral agreements were concluded on illegal immigration, fighting terrorism, cross border crime and fraud, organized crime, money laundering, double taxation, co-operation in shipping, energy, scientific, technological cooperation and environment protection. "On many fronts this could be the period of most intense diplomatic activity among Greece, Cyprus, Turkey and the Untied States .... in years", writes John Sitilides.[64]

The revelation of secret Greek support to the PKK leader Ocalan could deteriorate the relations between Greece and Turkey but Greece made amends in time before a damage could be done to their relations.

The Kosovo crisis also played some role in bringing normalcy in Turco-Greek relations. When flared up it affected both Turkey and Greece as they were involved ethnically, politically, militarily and religiously. However, the chemistry between Greek and Turkish foreign ministers, Papandreou and Ismail Cem prompted the countries to prefer cooperation to confrontation. Bulent Ecavit, the Turkish Prime-Minister, who had ordered the military intervention in Cyprus in 1974 offered compromise with the Greeks. This certainly was a gracious gesture, most unexpected one.

GREECE IN TRANS-CAUCASIA

The interest of Greece in Caucasus began in 1994 when the politics of oil pipelines in the Caspian region became intricate. Each one of the active players—Turkey, Iran, Russia—were suggesting new routes for the construction of oil pipelines to carry Azeri and Kazakh oil to European markets and they all wanted the oil pipelines to traverse through their territory. Greece also developed an ambition to become one of the players in the oil game.

The Greek policy makers have been displomatically active at building ties with the three Caspian Sea states of the region—Armenia, Georgia, Azerbaijan. It established bi-lateral relations in diverse fields of activities but the geo-political developments of the region had been the force that drew Athens close to the Transcaucasian states.

Bulent Aras argues that "Athens' primary aim has been to develop allies against its main international rival Turkey".[65] He, however, maintains that "because of the lack of geographic proximity with the region Greece will not be able to emerge as a formidable competitor of Turkey".[66]

GREECE AND ARMENIA

The Greek Foreign Minister and officials visited Armenia in 1994 to explore the meeting points on which a beginning can be made. Greece offered to help Armenia in the context of the EU whenever situation would arise. It also offered its good offices for bringing about peace in Karabakh by participating in the peace keeping force being raised by the Organization of the Security and Cooperation in Europe (OSCE). In 1995 even the Greek Cypriot Government of the Republic of Cyprus expressed desire to send its troops to the peace keeping force in Nagorno-Karabakh.[67]

Military co-operation between Greece and Armenia was put on the top of the agenda during the visit of Armenia's President Ter-Petrosyan to Athens in July 1995.[68] Armenia's Major General Arutyunyan said that military cooperation with Greece aims to strengthen the defence capacity of the two countries.[69] The Greek Defence Minister Arsenis is quoted to have said that Greece wants, Yerevan to be drawn into Athens' regional policy—which seeks military cooperation with Russia, Armenia, Bulgaria, Iran, Iraq and Syria against Turkey.[70]

The Armenian President Ter Petrosyan invited the Greek President Stefanopoulos to Armenia for an official visit. Stefanopoulos expressed his feeling by saying:

> Bilateral relations are excellent and there are absolutely no problems shadowing them. Everyone is well aware of the Greek people's feelings towards the Armenian people. We have a history of friendly relations which goes back 2000 years. During all periods of our history we were very close to each other. Now, we want to develop our excellent relations further.[71]

Commenting on the above statement a Turkish analyst and scholar of Turkish politics and foreign policy has observed that "if one sets aside the actual yield of relations between the two countries, the Greek President's words seem sincere and include very basic principles of mutual trust and peaceful relations. A pre-requisite of such good neighbourly relations is to assure other countries that any step taken will also increase regional well being and does not constitute a threat to other countries of the region.[72] Perhaps this comment is prompted by an 'unpleasant' incident. President of Greek Chamber of Commerce handed the Armenian President a copy of Chamber's resolution adopted in the Spring of 1996 on the recognition of the 1915 Armenian genocide.[73]

The friendly overtures of Greece emboldened Armenia and made it feel more secure and strong with the Greek backing. However, in the regional context particularly the settlement of Karabakh conflict and co-operation in the matter of oil pipelines traversing the Armenian territory, these friendly statements instead of brightening the prospects of peace, hampered them, although Greece did not intend to do so.

Armenia is situated just at the doorsteps of Turkey. It needs Turkey's permission for using its airspace. Greece is situated quite far from Armenia. The reason for better understanding between Greece and Armenia is that both are followers of Greek Orthodox Church like the Slavic states of the region.

The Turkish Defence Minister, Sungurlu pointed out that "he does not know why Greece is seeking such relations with the Caucasian states . . . Armenia, on the other hand needs us because it depends on us for permission to use our airspace".[74]

Notwithstanding the perfect diplomatic gaugings Athens' perceptions are clear. The motive behind expanding ties with Armenia are obvious. It is seeking allies and influence not to challenge Turkish interests in the Caucasus but to seek accomodation for itself. Armenia on the other hand, appears to value relations with Greece as a way to destabilize the growing closeness between Ankara and Azerbaijan. Yerevan's isolation as a result of indifference of the major powers like the EU countries and the United States, has ended with the increasing Greek activity in Armenia. Greece, Iran, Syria Bulgaria and Russia all have become active in the protection of Armenian interests in the Nagorno-Karabakh conflict.

Turkey, on its part is satisfied with the statements made by the Greek President, diplomats and other responsible sources. Commenting on Greek-Armenian Defence Agreement, the Greek Foreign Ministry official said that Greece wanted peaceful relations with all regional countries and that these relations were based on international law to promote bilateral and multi-faceted cooperation.[75]

The Armenian President Ter Petrosyan also said that "the sooner Turkey takes its place in the European Union the better it will be for Armenia". Turkey expects Armenia to declare that it will not provide any help to the PKK and generate a climate of peace and security which would promote bilateral trade between Turkey and Armenia.

The Greek overtures in the Caucasus are motivated by a desire to restrain Turkey's hostile attitude towards Greece and discourage threatening declarations regarding the Aegean islands and its continental shelf. In order to enhance its own security, Athens wants to develop relations with Russia, Iran and Armenia within the framework of a tripartite cooperation agreement. Greece will exchange military intelligence with Armenia and expand their joint training programmes. The Greek side has made its real interest in the Caucasus public by saying that the main Greek interest is to secure stability and peace in the Caucasus in order to make possible the construction of an oil pipeline between Burgas-Bulgaria and Alexandroupolis Greece. The Burgas-Alexandroupolis pipeline was suggested by Russia in 1995 in order to reduce the amount of oil tanker traffic through the Bosphorus. Once completed, the pipeline would allow shipments of Caspian Sea oil exported *via* Russia's Black Sea port of Novorossisk to bypass Bosphorus. In nutshell, Greece's interest in Caucasus was created by the Russian proposal of Burgas-Alexandroupolis pipeline and it is still centering around it. Armenia cannot be of much help in this matter. If Turkey facilitates the construction of this pipeline perhaps Greece will drop all its hostility towards Turkey and may emerge as a highly useful neighbour. Had Armenia, agreed to the Baku-Tiblisi-Ceyhan pipeline's traversing through the Armenian territory and ensuring the safety of pipelines in the Karabakh region then friendly grouping of Turkey, Armenia, Azerbaijan, Georgia, Russia, Greece could emerge. Thus, the Azerbaijani oil could be exported to Europe by the pipelines (not only Baku-Tiblisi-Ceyhan and Burgas-Alexandroupolis but others as well) passing through the territories of Armenia, Iran-Turkey, or Baku-Georgia-Ukraine or others. Turkey may find overtures of Greece in the Caucasus intriguing but in the long run it may come to realize the advantage of having friendly understanding with an ally in NATO and in the EU which Turkey might be joining in due course.

GREECE IN AZERBAIJAN AND GEORGIA

Azerbaijan generated Greek interest for two reasons: (i) oil, and (ii) its Turkic character and ethno-linguistic and religious affinity with Turkey which Ankara could use in getting Azerbaijan's recognition to the Northern Turkish Republic of Cyprus. Greece was very much pleased when President Muttalibov said that "his country would follow the position of international community on the problem (occupied Cyprus's status).[76] This almost unexpected response heartened the Greeks. The Azerbaijani President and the Greece Foreign Minister, Karlos Papoulias met again during the conference of the Black Sea Economic Cooperation Zone (BSECZ) held in 1993. The issues prominent on the agenda were: (a) Cooperation between the two (Greece and Azerbaijan); and

(b) entering into contact with the European Union. Haider Aliev observed "our states have talked about the prospects for the development of bilateral relations".[77] Aliev tried to seek an assuring answer from the Greek Prime Minister on Nogorno-Karabakh dispute between Azerbaijan and Armenia but the Greek reply was just a usual diplomatic response. Papoulias maintained that Greece has always been a supporter of disputed questions being solved at the negotiating table, not with violence. We cannot be indifferent to the problems of refugees and offer our services for a halt to an escalation of the conflict. Greece as a sovereign state and as a country that heads the European Union is ready to cooperate with Azerbaijan".[78]

Azerbaijan was concerned about increasing involvement of Greece in Armenia. The Azeri newspaper *Zerkalo* logically argued that the developing relations between Turkey and Azerbaijan turned Athens towards Armenia. Greece is supporting Armenia just because Turkey is supporting Azerbaijan.[79] Besides, on the Burgas-Alexandroupolis pipeline, Athens wants to eradicate Armenia's apprehension that if Burgas-Alexandropoulis pipeline project is taken up for construction, the prospects of a future Caspian pipeline crossing Armenian territory will be marred.

However, in the context of the geopolitics of the region the oil pipeline projects are highly constrained. If a project is approved by Azerbaijan and Turkey it may be opposed by Armenia, Greece, Russia, Iran and so on. The Greek Foreign Minister Pangalos told Haider Aliev that "Greece is interested in Azerbaijani oil and is eager to take part in the projects to transport Baku's oil to Europe".[80] Aliev when asked: "Whether Baku favoured a Bulgarian-Greece pipeline that would bypass Turkey"? answered tactfully: "the route has not been decided. This is all speculation and do not believe everything you hear". During this meeting Pangalos and his Azeri counterpart,

Hasanov, signed three agreements on consular and cultural cooperation protocol between the two countries.[81]

The Greek-Georgian relations are based on better understanding about each other's interests and needs. Their relations in the economic and cultural sphere commenced soon after their interaction in the early years of Georgia's independence. Tourism is flourishing between the two countries. The Europe-Caucasus-Asia Transport Corridor Project (TRACECA) which is of universal significance is to be joined by Greece too, which has potential to contribute to its success.

The Greece-Georgia relationship is warming up since 1994. The Foreign ministers of both countries have concluded agreements in the sphere of postal communication and telecommunication.[82] In May 1997, the Greek Communication Organization (OTE) and the construction company Hellax, signed a $ 14 billion contract with Tiblisi to construct and operate fiber optic networks in Georgia.[83] In September 1997, Shevardnadze paid an official visit to Athens. He was accompanied by a ministerial delegation and businessmen as well as representatives of the 80,000 strong ethnic Greek community in Georgia which he called the "flesh and blood" of the economy. The issues related to security and stability in the Caucasus were discussed. Greek side maintained that "security and stability in the Caucasus region is of great interest to Greece".[84]

Athens envisages security in Caucasus through a four way partnership formula which includes Greece, Armenia, Georgia and Iran, collectively taking care of security and stability by combining their military strength and coordinating defence capabilities. However, Georgia's perception of four-way partnership includes Tiblisi, Baku, Ankara and Kiev.[85]

Georgia is eager to expand its relations with nations outside the Caucasus region but it cannot ignore the interests of its regional friends and allies either. Turkey is the largest trading partner of Georgia and along with Ukraine it shares Black Sea with Turkey which links them with Europe. Georgia is unlikely to endanger its relations with the two dependable allies in the region. However, at the same time it is committed to promote the project of creating a transport corridor linking Georgia, Azerbaijan, Central Asia and Europe *via* Turkey and Ukraine. Greece if desired to be accommodative can be a useful partner in the Georgian security formula. Yet, a meeting point in both the schemes may be found.

In fact security communities are formed around a "core" country or central power which can provide protection and inspiration to the surrounding countries. In that context Turkey and Russia are the two possible "core" countries. Iran has potential but not much following. Turkey alone is preferred more by the breakaway republics as they are not willing to be a camp follower of Moscow once again.

Greece's presence is definitely going to strengthen the independence and freedom of decision making of the regional countries but Athens neither has economic and military power, nor any easy access to the Caucasian-Caspian states. It can get desired favours in the Caucasus only by being accommodative to Turkey and developing mutuality of interests and complementarity in policies. A more rational course for Greece is to consider the Black Sea Economic Co-operation Zone as platform to strengthen security and stability in the Caucasian region. Athens can draw the EU towards the states of this region and offer them facilities to develop their economy and strengthen the sense of security.

As discussed in Chapter V the geo-political environment in the southern Caucasus is of competition rather than of co-operation. The behaviour of states is leading more to tensions than to peace. They are constantly harping on historical animosities and turning small issues into big challenge making the relations between them difficult.

The emerging geopolitical configurations are indicating towards competition even between the EU and the United States in the southern Caucasus. A series of geopolitical grouping are emerging in Eurasia, on the one side are Russia and Iran along with a number of smaller countries like Greece and Armenia and on the other side are Turkey, Azerbaijan, Georgia, Ukraine and possibly Israel. The EU and the United States are also expanding their own areas of influence as both seek to tap into the 'vast' energy reserves of the Caspian region. At times it appears that the talk about the "volume of oil and gas resources" has been initiated by states having stakes in the region and wish to dishearten others by raising doubts about the exact volume of oil and gas in the Caspian Basin.

However, one thing is clear that the small groupings that have been emerging in Central Asia-Trans-Caucasia too are prompted by the major contestants in the "great Game" which has become less severe during past few years. The chances of its revival now appear strong. The EU-US competition might provoke regional rivalry and aggravate tensions leading to bi-polarization of the region. With two international giants jumping in the Great Game (in case really revived) then Russia and China may not be far behind. The "new entrants" and old rivals, perhaps should think more in the interest of stability, security and development of the region and let the owners of oil and natural gas retain their right over the resources of the Caspian region.

The entry of Greece and Israel—the two extra-regional states in the politics of Central Asia-Trans-Caucasia is likely to draw the region in extra-regional problems which might again have an adverse effect on the stability of the region. Turkey needs Israel in resolving problems with Syria over the water of Tigris and Euphrates and with Iraq over the Kurds. Greece's presence in the region is likely to lessen the tensions for Turkey. Ankara is getting an opportunity of turning the "staunch" enemy into an "accommodative friend" and must make use of this opportunity in its own interest and interest of the region as a whole. The Burgas-Alexandroupolis oil pipeline will be useful not only to Greece but to all those that are interested in the prosperity of the Caucasian states. 'If' that is the primary objective then it would be easy to transform enemies into allies and "intruders" into the "insiders" in the Central Asian—South Caucasian region.

NOTES

1. Philip Robins, "The Middle East and Central Asia" in Peter Ferdinand (Eds.) *The New Central Asia and Its Neighbours* (London: Royal Institute of International Affairs (RIIA), 1994), p. 96.
2. Bulent Aras, *op.cit.*, p. 53.
3. *Ibid.*, p. 53.
4. Anoushiravan Ehteshami and Emma C. Murphy, "The Non-Arab Middle East States and the Caucasian Central Asia Republics: Iran and Israel", *International Relations*, 12 No. . (April 1994), p. 96.
5. See Martha Brill Olcott, *Central Asia's New States* (Washington: USIP, 1996), pp. 32-33.
6. Leon T. Hadar, "The Last days of Likud: The American-Israeli Big Chill", *Journal of Palestinian Studies*, 21, No. 4 (Summer, 1992), pp. 87-88.
7. Anoushiravan Ehteshami, "New Frontiers: Iran and GCC and the CCARs" in Anoushiravan Ehteshami, *From the Gulf to Central Asia: Players in the New Game* (Exeter: University of Exeter Press, 1994), p. 96.
8. Anoushiravan Ehteshami and Murphy, "The Non-Arab Middle East", *op.cit.*, p. 96.
9. Raphael Israeli, "Return to the Source: The Republics of Central Asia and the Return of the Middle East", *Central Asian Survey*, 13, No.1, (1994), p. 29.
10. Warren Chritopher, "The Strategic Priorities of American Foreign Policy", *Dispatch*, 4, No. 47, (1993), p. 797.
11. *Moscow Radio*, 8 November 1994.
12. Bulent Aras, *op.cit.*, p. 56.

13. John Pomfret, "Some Neighbourly Advice—Turkey Strengthens Its Ties to Israel", *Washington Post, National Weekly Addition*, 10-16 June 1997, pp. 16-17.
14. George E. Gruen, "Dynamic Progress in Turkish Israeli Relations", *Israel Affairs*, No. 4, (1995), p. 66.
15. Efraim Inbar, "The Strategic Glue in the Israeli-Turkish Alignment" in Barry Rubin and Kemal Kirisci, (Eds.), *Turkey in World Politics: An Emerging Multi-Regional Power* (Lynne Rienner Publishers: Boulder, London: 2001), pp. 115-116.
16. Syria is a common rival of both Turkey and Israel. With Turkey the quarrel is over territory. Syria claims district of Hatay, handed over to Turkey in 1939 by the mandatory power France. From Israel Syria claims the Golan Heights lost to Israel in the 1967 war—a territory to which Israel ascribes great strategic importance. Syria's relation with the PKK in Kurdish region of Turkey and connections with Arab militants in the PLO territory and Lebanon are the reasons of conflict between Syria and Turkey. (Euphrates and Tigris' water is also a bone of contention between Turkey and Syria).
17. Erfaim Inbar, *op.cit.*, p. 118.
18. *Defense News*, December 9-15, 1996, p.9.
19. Anoushiravan Ehteshami and Murphy, *The Non-Arab Middle East, op.cit.*, p. 97.
20. Henry J. Barkey, "Iran and Turkey" in Alvin Z. Rubinstein and Oles Smolansky (eds.), *Regional Power Rivalries in the New Eurasia, Turkey and Iran* (Armonk: M.E. Sharpe, 1995), p. 155.
21. Jane Hunter, "Israel and Turkey: Arms for Azerbaijan?" *Middle East International*, (23 October 1992, p. 12.
22. "Israeli Premier visits Azerbaijan", *Turan Analytical Review*, Turan News Agency, No. 357, 1 September 1997, (root @-turan.Azerbaijan.su).
23. SWB, 24 August 1996, SU/2699, F/6 and also see Turk Sanayici ve Isadamlari Beynelhalk Cemiyets (International Society of Turkish Industrialists and Businessmen), *Azerbaijan Handbook of Businessmen*, 1996 (Baku: Caglayan, 1996), p. 28.
24. Rafael Husainov, 'Netanyahu/Azerbaijan' *Voice of America*, 29 August 1997.
25. Jay Bushinsky, "PM Discusses Oil Pipelines in Baku", *Jerusalem Post*, 31 August 1997.
26. "Iran Radio Slams Azerbaijan for Hosting Israeli P.M.", *Reuters*, 30 August 1997.

27. "Armenian Foreign Minister: Turco-Israeli Co-operation Perilous for Region" *IRNA*, 10 September 1997.
28. *FBIS-LAT* 99-9-009, 12 January 1999.
29. Robert O. Freedman, "Israel and Central Asia: A Preliminary Analysis", *Central Asia Monitor*, No. 2 (1993), p.17.
30. *Al-Aalem*, 7 September 1993.
31. *Christian Science Monitor*, 25 September 1992.
32. "Dairy Cattle Husbandry Demonstration Project in Uzbekistan", via web page of Israeli Ministry of Foreign Affairs (http://www.israel-mfa.gov.il).
33. *Ibid.*
34. *Financial Times*, 6 May 1992.
35. Anoushiravan Ehteshami and Murphy, *op.cit.*, p. 101.
36. *Christian Science Monitor*, 25 September 1992.
37. "Fact Sheets: Central Asian Republics", *Dispatch* 5, No. 19 (1994), p.294; Also *Askabat Aksami* (Ashgabat), 7 February 1994.
38. *Turkmenistan* (Ashgabat), 27 March 1996.
39. *SWB*, 13 March 1995, Su 22.50 p. G/17; *Ashkabat Aksami*, 1 June 1995.
40. DEIK, *Turk ve Israil' li*, p. 3 (DEIK is Turkish Foreign Economic Relations Board).
41. Lowell Bezanis, "Niyazov in Egypt, Israel" *OMRI Daily Digest* (http://www.omri.cz) 26 May 1995 and *Turkmenistan*, 1 April 1995.
42. David Harris, "Sharon, Russians to Discuss Gas Deal", *Jerusalem Post* (http://www. Jposl.ci), 14 March 1997.
43. David Harris, "Merhav wins $ 500 m. Refinery Upgrade Deal in Turkmenistan", *Jerusalem Post* (http://www.jpost.corn), 26 Au;gust 1996; *Turkmanistan*, 8 October 1996.
44. George E. Gruen, "Dynamic Progress in Turkish-Israeli Relations", *Israel Affairs*, 1, No.4 (1995), p. 56.
45. *Financial Times*, 28 January 1993.
46. DEIK, *Turk Ve Israil 'li*, Istanbul, 10 December 1996, p. 6.
47. SWB, 4 October 1995.
48. Fact Sheets: Central Asian Republics, *Dispatch* 5, no. 19 (1994), p. 288.
49. Aluf Ben, "A Change in Israeli-Iranian Relations", *Ha' aretz*, 10 November 1996. quoted on the homepage of the Foreign Ministry of Israel on the Internet.
50. Anoushiravan Ehteshami and Murphy, *op.cit.*, p. 103.

51. Jay Bushinsky, "Russia's Role", *Jerusalem Post* (http://www.Jposi.com), 2 February 1997.
52. Lowell Bezanis, "Turco-Israeli Accord Aggrvates Regional Tensions", *OMRI Analytical brief* (http.//www.omri.cz), 18 April 1996.
53. The three historical traumas identified by Amikam Nachmani are: the fall of Constantinople (1453); the loss of Asia Minor (1922); and the partition of Cyprus (1974). See Amikam, Nichmani, "What says the Neighbor to the West? On Turkish Greek Relations", in Barry Rubin, Kemal Kirisci (eds.), *Turkey in World Politics: An Emerging Multiregional Power* (Boulder: Leiden, 2001), p. 72.
54. Constantinople Agreement (March 18, 1915), Treaty of London (April 26, 1915), Sykes-Picot Agreement (May 16, 1916) and the St. Jean de Maurienne Agreement (April 17, 1917).
55. Elaine Diana Smith, *Turkey: Origins of the Kemalist Movement and the Government of the Grand National Assembly* (1919-1923) (Washington D.C. 1959), pp. 7-8.
56. Vamik D. Volkan and Norman Itzkowitz, *Turks and Greeks—Neighbours in Conflict* (Huntington: Cambridgeshire, The Eothen Press, 1994), p. 167.
57. Amikam Nachmani, *op.cit.*, p. 73.
58. *Ibid.*, p. 73.
59. Athanasios Platias, "Greece's strategic Doctrine: In Search of Autonomy and Deterrance" in Dimitri Constans, (ed.), *The Greek Turkish Conflict in the 1990s* (London: Macmillan, 1991), pp. 97-98, 103.
60. *DNB* (*Daily News Broadcast*), March 8, 1996.
61. S. Victor Papacosma, "More than Rocks: The Aegean's Discordant Legacy", *Mediterranean Quarterly*, Vol. 7, No. 4, (Fall 1996), pp. 86-87.
62. *Ibid.*, pp. 87-88.
63. *DNB*, January 9, 1997.
64. John Sitilides, "Much Ado in the Eastern Mediterranean", *The Western Policy Centre*, September 15, 1999; Western Policy Centre, *The Strategic Regional Report*, 4, 7.
65. Bulent Aras, *op.cit.*, p. 27.
66. *Ibid.*
67. *Cyprus Mail* (Nicosia), 14 April 1995, p.7. Also *FBIS-WEU*, 14 November 1995, p. 73.

68. ITAR-TASS (Moscow in English), 23 July 1995, in *FBIS-SOV*, 7 November 1995, p. 141.
69. *Ibid.*
70. *FBIS-WEU*, 4 April 1996, p. 65.
71. *FBIS-WEU*, 21 June 1996, p. 120.
72. *FBIS-WEU*, 19 June 1996, p. 118.
73. Armenia's Radio First, in Armenia, 18 June 1996, in *FBIS-WEU*, 19 June 1996, p. 118.
74. Anatolia (Ankara, in Turkish), 18 June 1996, in *FBIS-WEU*, 21 June 1996, p. 120.
75. *FBIS-WEU*, 21 June 1996, p.120.
76. "Azerbaijan will not recognize Northern Cyprus", *Russian Press Digest*, 21 November 1991.
77. *FBIS-WEU*, 14 November 1995, p. 122.
78. *Ibid.*
79. *Zerkalo*, Baku, in Russian, No. 25, 22 June 1996, p. 23, in *FBIS-SOV*, 18 July 1997, p.138-S; See also "Instability No Stranger to the Trans Caucasus", *Jamestown Fortnight in Review*, 1, No. 1, 28 June 1996. Online.
80. *Athens News Agency* (Athens in English), 12 April 1997, in *FBIS-WEU*, 15 April 1997, p. 102.
81. *Turkish Daily News*, 2 November 1994, p. A3.
82. *FBIS-WEU*, 9 November 1995.
83. *FBIS-WEU*, 22 May 1997, p. 139.
84. *Athens News Agency* (Athens in English), 16 September 1997, in *FBIS-WEU*, 17 September 1997, p. 259.
85. *FBIS, UMA*, 23 July 1997, p.203.

CHAPTER 7

Whither Turkey?—Some Possible Options

Having examined the early ethno-linguistic, cultural, religious linkages of the Turks with the Turkic peoples of Central Asia and Southern Caucasus, and having gone through the historical and contemporary perspective of pan-Turkism which resurfaced on the political horizon of modern Turkey after remaining dormant for several decades since the World War II it is easier to understand the reasons for Ankara's renewed interest in Trans-Caucasus and Central Asia although it is still not easy to predict "how much of Turkey" is there and for how long it is "going to be there", notwithstanding the fact, that it is a Eurasian country having roots in that region.

Historically, the Ottoman Turkey was much closer to Europe not only geographically but also sentimentally as it was in awe with Europe's industrial, scientific and technological progress and wanted to import the entire European culture and civilization if it could be fitted in the Islamic framework of the Empire which was also the seat of the Caliphate—religious head of the Muslims of the world. The reforms undertaken by the Young Turks of all variations from time to time reflected their desire for Europeanization of their polity and society. The armed forces too fashioned on European pattern although the *Fez* continued to be symbol of Ottoman Turk.

Mustafa Kemal Ataturk as a young, thoughtful, ambitious and determined officer of Ottoman army imbibed into the tradition set by his predecessors—the Youth of Ottoman Empire. The circumstances of the post-World War I period compelled Ataturk to emerge as a leader of the nationalist movement organized to attain independence of Turkey from the allied occupation forces which had occupied Istanbul and several other regions of the Ottoman Empire and the Sultan Caliph was made a virtual prisoner of the foreign forces.

Having won the war of liberation against the Allied forces, Ataturk concentrated on reorganizing the Turkish state. He renounced all claims on the overseas territories of the Ottoman Empire, abolished Sultanate and Caliphate and thus put an end to Ottomanism and Islamism in modern Turkey. Renunciation of Ottoman and Islamic identity of the nation created a problem—a search for new identity for the Republic of Turkey. It is difficult to understand why the Turks of Turkey do not like to assume Turkish identity which is far more solid, glamourous, convincing and acceptable worldwide instead of running after the European identity. Ataturk imposed European-western identity on Turks unilaterally without considering that it needs to be "accepted" or recognized by the countries of the world. From 1923 onwards, the major preoccupation of the Republic of Turkey is "how to get recognized as European" and how to make Europeans realize that geographically, culturally, civilizationally and emotionally Turkey belongs to them.

Turkey has made tremendous sacrifices to get into the community of European Nations and to be known as a strong pillar of the west's security edifice. Ankara joined the western bloc during the era of cold war and bravely stood against the mighty Soviet Union as a bulwark of western security in Europe, Northern Tier, and West Asia.

Turkey sent a huge contingent to fight in the Korean war and earned the membership in NATO although several European countries, especially the Scandinavian and Benalux countries vehemently opposed inclusion of a Muslim country in the North Atlantic Christian Community of Nations. The objection was for its "Muslim" identity.

The recent denial of membership to Turkey in the European Community on the same ground, despite Turkey's long association with Europe not only in NATO but several other organizations formed to strengthen the security of Europe, Turkey is still treated as an "outcaste" and Europeans have reservations about its inclusion in the European Community. In the past, Turkey absorbed the hurt caused by the rejection of its European identity in view of several other advantages of belonging to the west, and the importance attached to Turkey by the United States. Currently, the collapse of the Soviet Union and emergence of a huge territory inhabited by the people of Turkic origin in its immediate neighbourhood exhilerated the Turks. They saw a whole new world emerging before their eyes which in every respect—culture, language, ethnicity, religion, geographical proximity, historical ties belonged to them.

The liberated Central Asia provided new opportunities to Ankara. It negated the depressing impact of the EU's denial of membership to Turkey. During the cold war, geo-strategic "value" of Turkey was largely limited to its role within the Atlantic Alliance, especially, its place within the NATO's southern flank. The collapse of Soviet Union enlarged Turkey's role in world affairs even without west's patronage.

Turkey belongs to many regions. It is Balkan, Aegean, Mediterranean, Black Sea, Middle Eastern and Central Asian all at the same time. In fact, barring the United States, Turkey is the only country which has operated and is still operating in many geographical regions even in the post-cold war world.

Obsessed by the denial of European identity on the basis of its having a different religion, Turkey while cultivating relations with the Central Asian states harped on ethno-linguistic, cultural, religious and other commonalties between the Central Asians and Turkey. The pan-Turkist euphoria in Turkey came to be seen as a "racist" approach to regional integration or establishing even the bilateral relations, although Turks did not intend to make "racial connections" a basis of their relations with the new republics. They in fact share common ancestry with the Turkic people although it was several centuries ago.

Turkey was quick to move in Central Asia-Trans-Caucasia, especially in Azerbaijan where Turkey's pan-Turkist political parties and members of the ruling elite, in view of presence of a large population of Turkic origin and speaking Turkish saw a great future for energy hungry Ankara. They wanted to make inroads in the polity and society, and outmaneuvering every other country, wanted to establish control over Azerbaijan's oil resources. This provoked the regional aspirants for power and influence in the region against Turkey. Iran and Russia along with Armenia opposed Turkey's intervention in internal affairs (Presidential Election) of Azerbaijan. With the backing of the West which was busy projecting Turkey as an ideal role model—a secular, democratic, republican and modern developed state—for the Central Asian republics, Turkey could establish its hold over Azeri oil and started negotiating pipeline routes to carry Baku's oil to Europe *via* Turkish territory. Ankara, managed to get the support of all concerned parties (except Iran and Russia) to its proposal for constructing the Baku-Tiblisi-Ceyhan oil pipeline bypassing Russia and Iran. In fact achieving the Baku-Tiblisi-Ceyhan pipeline is the only positive result of Turkey's frantic drive for allies and economic avenues in Central Asia–Trans-Caucasia. Turkey actually is having a bigger trade with its rivals—Iran and Russia, than any of the Central Asian regimes. Tehran and Moscow are the biggest exporters of natural gas to Turkey and are capable of solving its energy problem too provided it is able to get done with the US intransigence.

The major problem with Turkey in Central Asian–Trans-Caucasia and also in its relations with Iran and Russia is its "proxy" role. It is known to be politicking to protect the interests of the United states in Central Asia. Even Baku, in spite of tall claims of the West and the western companies, of turning Azerbaijan into a "largest oil exporter" of the world, is still dependent on Russia like Kazakhstan and is exporting oil to Europe *via* Russian pipelines. Now, quite a few new natural gas and oil exporting pipelines are in the process of coming up under China's patronage which might undermine BTC's future prospects.

Turkey has come to realize the negative aspects of its close association with the United States. Over the years Turkey has learned to rely on US for its security and well being. It cannot leave the US and the western camp altogether—it can simply assert its independence and make the US realize that Ankara needs to be given its own independent "space" to operate in freely.

Ankara does not agree with the repressive measures taken by the US against Iran and is convinced that Iran's "Islamic fundamentalism" has nothing to do with its foreign policy especially in Central Asia. Tehran has not made Islamic ideology a basis of its relations with the Central Asian republics, and Ankara is trying to convince the United States that new pipelines can not be constructed without involving Tehran which provides an inexpensive shortest route to caspian oil, and Moscow which alone is capable of guaranteeing safety to pipelines against the ethnic conflicts in the southern and northern Caucasus. The US is gradually coming to understand Turkey's difficulties. Recently, Washington has persuaded Israel to join Turkey in Central Asia and facilitate its objectives in the region—especially in Azerbaijan.

It is interesting to note that by tucking up Turkey to Azerbaijani oil and the pipeline, the United States has put Turkey in a political *quarantine*. Perhaps it does not want to give Ankara more leverage than what is considered fit for it by the United States. Israel's entry in the Central Asian region at the behest of America generates apprehensions about Turkey's long-term role in the Central Asian–Caucasian region. It appears that, once Turkey is given membership in the EU, it will not be interested in playing a major role in its backyard. Israel may be a future substitute for Ankara.

Turkey has cultivated good relations with Tehran and Moscow and is trying to strike a rapport which can facilitate long term association with Russia. Its role in the Black Sea region through the BSECZ is providing sufficient leverage to emerge as a regional power independent of West's dictates. Reviving the vitality of ECO can further strengthen its position in Central Asia and the neighbouring northern tier states. However, in order to prepare itself to emerge as a dependable, strong and 'independent' regional power (free from any proxy role) Turkey has to evaluate its foreign policy against the backdrop of existing international scenario and the future emerging scenario in which China may emerge more powerful than the Turkey's mentor, United States. In addition to that, Turkey should also try to reorganize its priorities and modes of attending to them. Several options have been offered by scholars and experts on Turkey's domestic and external policy.

William Hale, a well known historian has written extensively on Turkey's current problems and dilemmas. Turkey is an ancient country with a long experience in international politics. Notwithstanding this, Ankara does not have a well spelled out foreign policy except its "perpetual" slant towards the United States. It suffers from uncertainties—every action, decision and initiative in the field of foreign policy depends on how the United States looks at, and responds to them. In this context Turkey's relations with EU are important because "its inner urge" to be European is partly satisfied and more than that it provides an additional western platform where it can react without inhibition. Hale is of the opinion that Turkey should pay attention to Helsinki Summit's (December 1999) decisions. It has not put an end to Turkey's ever getting the EU membership but expects Turkey to meet the Copenhagen criteria (meeting held in June 1993) and settle its differences with Greece—a NATO ally and at the moment President of the EU. In order to accommodate Turkey the EU will have to make several structural changes and re-evaluate its policy. The Helsinki decision also made it clear that—an overall settlement with Greece of bilateral disputes, and the solution of the Cyprus problem would almost certainly be a *sine qua non* for Turkish accession.[1] Turkey needs to weigh the advantages and disadvantage of its venture in Cyprus and commitment to TRNC.

Turkey is showing some flexibility in its attitude towards Greece and the Republic of Cyprus (Greek Cypriots) and lately is accommodating Greece in Central Asia, although both are still working at cross purposes. Ankara is now willing to talk about the continental shelf, Aegean islands and Greece's rights in the Sea-bed and Ocean floor of the Aegean Sea.

Greece and Israel are the two new entrants in Central Asia. They have arrived after getting green signal from Washington. William Hale maintains that the possibility of a deal between Israel and Syria over Euphrates' water may be at the cost of Turkey's interest. Even if it is not the case, relaxed Syria can turn to be more aggressive towards Turkey. Although he himself has ruled out the occurrence of this kind of developments but warns Turkey against such eventualities.

However, Syria's own entry in Central Asia need not be ruled out.

In the coming years, it is possible that the US improves its relations with Iran and Iraq. It will certainly affect the status of Turkey and Israel in the Middle Eastern politics. Turkey will be required to keep its 'bridges' in tact and workable in case such a situation emerges.[2]

Instead of committing to "one side" in any regional dispute, Turkey can play the role of a "peace maker" or "mediator" and make mediation broad-based involving other interested and influential regional participants in the negotiations. William Hale has placed Turkey in the twenty first century as an emerging regional power which needs to be cautious and more 'balanced' in its international commitments.[3]

In the 1990s, after the collapse of the Soviet Union, China was seen as an emerging superpower which would in few decades surpass the United States. During the cold war period, the confrontation was between the USSR and the United States. In the twenty first century it is likely to be between China and the United States, which will have serious repercussions for Turkey as well.[4] As discussed earlier, China, by virtue of being a key country in the Shanghai Co-operation Organization (SCO) and having a 3700 kilometer long border with the three Central Asian partners in the SCO, is a Central Asian power. Turkey's Central Asia policy needs to be mindful of this fact as well.

In the 21st century, Turkey will be required to come out of its cold war mindset when it was supposed to act within the parameters of bi-polarization. It will be necessary to make choices out of available options, in case Ankara is willing to initiate some changes in its foreign policy and make it more receptive and responsive to the developments that are taking place in the international environment around it.

Turkey's attitude and activities in the southern Caucasus suggest that Ankara treats it as a region exclusively assigned to it and it is Turkey's exclusive domain. In fact, for Turkey perhaps the entire Central Asia–Trans-Caucasia has got submerged in Azerbaijan which is the focal point of Ankara's Central Asia policy. Turkey has to realize that Central Asian southern Caucasian—Caspian region is an international arena in which besides Turkey, several other states have serious stakes.

Ankara's Central Asia policy which is largely Baku-centered has been built on an understanding of rivalry with Iran and Russia. By and large, Turkey's Central Asia policy has become hostage to Kurdish problem and its concern for Azerbaijan. Some scholars define Ankara's Central Asia policy as "security first" policy with myopic view of Iran and Russia as main enemies of Turkey, among others providing a motivation for its overriding concern for security.[5]

Ankara's attitude towards Iran and Russia emanates from its Azerbaijan policy. The conflicting interests between Turkey and these two states mainly emerge from Turkey's loyalty to the Azeri side in all controversies, especially the legal status of the Caspian Sea, the pipeline politics, and the Karabakh conflict. It is difficult to say what exactly Turkey has gained by sticking to pro-Baku policy. It appears that in the entire region Azerbaijan is the only state which interests Ankara and perhaps its "energy need" is the major ground for its too much emphasis on relations with Azerbaijan.

The BTC pipeline appears to be the only gain for Turkey. The pipeline project was supported by the United States and its European allies who seriously desired to benefit Turkey. On completion of the BTC in June 2005 its length from Baku to Ceyhan is 1762 Km. and it is transporting about a million barrels of oil a day.

Having acquired the BTC, now Ankara should stop opposing proposals made by others for additional pipelines in the region. Instead of antagonizing the states of the Central Asian region, it should use the opportunity to befriend them and evolve relations with them in other areas of activity as well.

Kazakhstan is still exporting oil through Russian pipelines. BTC can become more lucrative if Ankara can make Kazakhstan agreeable to use BTC for its oil exports. However, Turkey's apathy has been encashed by China as it has undertaken a more ambitious pipeline project to carry Kazakh oil eastward. On December 15, 2006, the state-owned China National Petroleum Corporation (CNPC) inaugurated a new pipeline running from Kazakhstan to northwest China. It runs 962 Km. (598 miles) and will take China at least a one-third way to Kashagan in the Caspian Sea where one of the world's largest accessible oil reserves have been discovered.

According to known estimates Kazakhstan has 35 billion barrels of discovered oil reserves. Kazakhstan expects to produce 3.6 million barrels a day of oil from all its oil fields, on shore and off. By 2005 China has spent about $ 2.6 billion since 1997 on its pipeline projects from Kazakhstan to China. Although at the moment major oil export through this pipeline are from Russia until Kazakhstan is able to produce sufficient oil for this 200,000 barrels a day pipeline.

On the political side, this new pipeline will undercut the geo-political significance of the Washington—backed BTC oil pipeline which is presently exporting only the Azeri Oil.

The upcoming China-Kazakh-Russian energy cooperation may become a nightmarish scenario for all those who have been seeking a hold over oil and gas resources of the Caspian. Turkey will also be required to review its Central Asia policy and energy strategy in face of emerging new Asian Energy Corridor.

Turkey can initiate projects in which joint venture is required and regional states can be involved. Increasing communication and interaction with a large number of states will be more advantageous to Turkey than concentrating on Azerbaijan only.

Ankara can be helpful to Armenia and Azerbaijan both in solving the Karabakh dispute, provided it acts as a friend of both the countries. Its excessive slant towards Azerbaijan and policy of isolating Armenia on account of its close relations with Tehran and Moscow, which in fact is a geo-political necessity of Armenia, has made the solution of the problem even more difficult. Turkey being a stronger country and having had relations with Armenia can play a more positive role than just antagonizing the Armenians with the Azerbaijanis. If Turkey enjoys the trust of its neighbours it will be useful to it in its relations with the Central Asian regimes too, to which it is not able to pay much attention on account of its exclusive concentration on Baku and the BTC.

In Central Asia, Turkey's attention is on Turkmenistan for natural gas imports and construction of pipelines to carry Turkmen gas for export to Europe via Turkish territory. However, a project for an eastward pipeline from Turkmenistan to China has already been finalized by both the countries in April 2006. Ankara's interest in Kazakhstan is also mainly for oil and it wants Kazakh oil to be exported to Europe via Turkish territory. But with China's having acquired almost monopoly over the transport of Kazak oil eastward Turkey's chances of transporting the same to Europe via BTC are extremely bleak. Lately, after the formation of the BSEC, Turkey's interest in Ukraine has increased. Uzbekistan is another country, which owing to its pro-west attitude interests Ankara. Lately Uzbekistan has drifted away from the US after Washington's attempt to topple down the government in order to introduce western style democracy and install the leaders of their choice in power. However, with these two countries also Turkey has not widened its relations. People to people contact which is the most essential factor in bringing the two nations close to each other has yet not been initiated.

Ankara's other two business partners are Iran and Russia. Turkey is importing substantial quantity of gas from these two countries and several Turkish firms and private companies and businessmen are actively participating in the economy of Russia. However, here too, Turkey has not taken initiative in promoting interaction between the people of two countries. Ankara should try to make these trade relations long lasting by introducing economic reforms which can attract the businessmen from Moscow and Ukraine, Uzbekistan and other republics in Central Asia and seek similar reforms in these countries too.

Turkey's excessive concern for Azerbaijan and its total support to Baku in all controversies with Armenia and Russia has provided incentive for formation of conflicting geo-political configurations. Turkey, Azerbaijan, Georgia, Ukraine, Uzbekistan and Israel on one side and Russia, Iran, Armenia, Kazakhstan and possibly Greece, and Republic of Cyprus on the other are promoting bi-polarization in the region which may not be in the interest of stability and territorial integrity of the region. The participation of extra regional states would involve Central Asia into West Asian issues and controversies, thus bringing their problems to this region which has so far managed to stay unaffected by the Arab-Israeli conflicts and the conflict between Turkey and Greece over the Turkey-occupied northern Cyprus.

The entry of Israel, another pro-American state, in the Central Asian politics is welcomed by Turkey. However, in the long run Turkey may find Israel an obstruction in the way of its independent handling of the Central Asian politics. Israel being a non-Central Asian, non-Muslim and comparatively better equipped to give much needed armaments and technological and military know-how to Central Asian regimes might be able to carve a larger sphere of influence for itself in Central Asia than Turkey. With the arms transfers to the region militarization would increase and create several new problems for the Central Asian republics. Turkey will have to work out a plan of action with Israel which should be collaborative and not conflicting or contradictory.

The interest of Greece in Central Asia has emanated partly from its desire to counter Turkey's influence in the Central Asian region and dissuade the CARs from supporting Turkey on the Cyprus issue. Athens' intention is to get access to the region at this time when it is holding the presidency of the EU and Turkey's membership matter is still pending for final decision. Greece had given indication of being accommodative in case Ankara shows willingness to end hostility towards Republic of Cyprus and Greece and settles the problems related to the Aegean sea islands and Greece's rights in the continental shelf, sea bed and ocean floor. Ankara has got an opportunity to clear the misgivings and strike a fresh rapport with Athens which even if does not resolve the outstanding problems would certainly generate a climate of better understanding about each others' difficulties.

In its own interest and in the interest of the region in which Turkey is placed, it is necessary to strengthen the institutions and organizations where collective decisions are taken on regional problems and issues. It should promote the environment in which regional states prefer regional solutions to their problems instead of seeking intervention by foreign powers who generally, instead of solving the problem, complicate it further. The Nagorno-Karabakh problem today remains unresolved for the reason that it has been made an international problem in which America, Europe, OSCE, EU and other similar groupings of states have become interested.

Turkey should make the Black Sea Economic Co-operation (BSEC) more active and responsive to the needs and problems of the region. It should be utilized for addressing the problems of the region from a broader geo-political perspective and to mobilize support for relevant domestic actors. Generally speaking in most of the member states decision-making is in the hands of ruling elites and in the absence of democratic institutions and processes people's participation is almost missing. State policies are not decided by rational choices which would demand an end to the existing conflicts. Leaders, somehow remain interested in continuing the conflicting situations to keep the people drawn to them.

The Black Sea region has great potential and it is in the process of becoming a sub-region and assuming a distinct identity. In view of the state dominated approach to the BSECZ, nothing much can be expected. Yet, Turkey, a strong and influential country, can strengthen the organization by resorting to it for the solution of regional issues—whether big or small. The presence of a strong and stable country with sufficient resources to contribute, can make any organization work. Turkey can also activate both ECO and the BSECZ and persuade the regional countries to rely more on these regional organizations instead of seeking redressal to their grievances elsewhere.

For a successful foreign policy it is necessary that a legitimate mandate to its actions and performance is always available at the domestic front. There should be a proper co-ordination between the domestic and foreign policy because by and large, foreign policy is the extension of domestic policy and reflects the aspiration of its people in international politics. Turkey as a strong and stable democracy having an enlightened urban elite is fortunate in having democratic institutions and procedures of decision making. It can help in changing the cold war mind-set of the people which is primarily security oriented.

During these six years of this first decade of the 21st century, Turkey has performed well in Balkans, especially in the context of working according to the interests of its people instead of totally getting guided by the instructions from the western countries—EU and America. However, in the Gulf War, owing to its commitment to support the US, Turkey joined the United States in its war against Iraq. In the war against terrorism in Afghanistan too, Turkey acted as a pro-west country aligned to the United States. On several issues it was not in tune with the US policy but it worked according to the requirements of its commitment to support the United States.

In the aftermath of these two wars Turkey is evaluating its foreign policy choices and appears preparing for introducing changes in its choices and priorities. Notwithstanding the US pressure, Turkey is avoiding imposing sanctions against Iran and is continuing its bi-lateral relations with Tehran. Turkey succeeded in obtaining a tacit permission of the US to take military action against the Kurds in Northern Iraq in case of extreme necessity. It is also showing interest in establishing closer relations with the countries of Asia. However, before embarking upon an ambitious agenda of change Turkey needs to address some of its outstanding unresolved issues with countries like Syria, Greece and Iraq, which keep Ankara drawn to extra-regional political affairs.

Ankara has a serious problem with Syria over the water of the Euphrates besides the latter's links with the P.K.K. and its leaders. With Greece, in addition to the Cyprus problem it has several other outstanding issues which have kept relations between the two on hold. They are: problems of territorial sea, contiguous zone and economic zone in the Aegean sea, oil and minerals in the continental shelf, Greek support to Kurdish rebels, presence of minority groups in Greece's provinces of Xanthi, Rodepi and western Thrace (which are called Muslim minorities by Athens and Ankara calls them

Turkish minority groups) etc. Most outstanding problem is Turkish occupation of the territory of Cyprus by use of force in 1974 and it is still under the occupation of Turkey-sponsored government of Turkish Republic of Northern Cyprus. With Iraq, the Kurdish problem is most difficult one to be solved. Whatever happens to the Iraqi Kurds is likely to have immediate repercussions on the Kurds of Turkey.

WATER PROBLEM WITH SYRIA

Turkey's key water resources—Euphrates and Tigris rivers have been claimed by both Syria and Iraq. The Euphrates is 1675 miles long, 40% inside Turkey and Tigris is 1180 miles long and 20% inside Turkey. The major issue of conflict is sharing of water of these two rivers. Quality of the water is also an important aspect of the water issue as Turkey's hydroelectric projects and the Ataturk Dam (completed in 1990) consume more water and leave insufficient quantity of water for Syria and Iraq. The international rivers' use is determined by the international law which does not allow obstructing the cross border flow of water.

However, the problem has other aspects which are more complicated than permitting or obstructing the flow of water. During the cold war period both Syria and Iraq have been pro-Soviet countries with radical revolutionary governments. The PKK (Abdullah Ocalan's Kurdish Party) was supported by these two countries. Syria still supports the Kurdish rebels. Ocalan was hiding in Syria for some time. Later under international pressure Syria refused to give asylum to Ocalan and asked him to leave the country. Turkey had a *quid pro quo* in 1987 with Syria. In return of free flow of water to Syria, Demascus would stop all assistance to the Kurds of Turkey. Consequently Turkey also resumed normal water supply (500 cusecs per second) to Syria. In the post-Soviet period Syria is apprehensive that Turkey and Israel might resume their hostile attitude and take punitive measures against Demascus for supporting the *Hamas* and Abdullah Ocalan and in the new situation Moscow may not come to its rescue as it used to earlier. Hence Syria is keen on befriending the Central Asian regimes. It is exploring the possibility of joining the emerging power constellation under the leadership of Russia.

KURDISH PROBLEM WITH IRAQ

The problem between Ankara and Baghdad over the Kurds of northern Iraq is a thorny one. It had disturbed the relations between Turkey and the United States also during the Gulf War. Turkey wants that Iraq should adopt an accommodative attitude towards the Kurds and they need not be encouraged to the idea of seeking an independent state of their own outside Iraq and Turkey.

The Kurds are spread over the territories of a number of states. They are in Turkey, Iran, Iraq, Syria, Armenia and Azerbaijan but larger concentration is only in Turkey, Iran and Iraq. Affluent Kurds are settled in France, Germany and other European countries. Kurds are a mountainous tribe living in isolation, away from urban population as poor, uneducated and impoverished people. They are a militant race quite capable of handling the local governments through their violent methods.

Sadam Hussain treated Kurds of Iraq comparatively better and they also co-operated with him during the Iraq-Iran war. During the Gulf War I, America succeeded in dissuading them from Saddam Hussain by promising an independent Kurdish state.

Of all the Kurdish Organizations, PKK is the oldest Kurdish party which favours separation while other political parties—PUK, KDP prefer autonomy within the states of their residence. PKK is adherent of Marxist-Leninist ideology and takes help from the radical revolutionary regimes of West

Asia. It had supporters in Eastern Europe as well. Turkey is opposed to the PKK and its leader Abdullah Ocalan for concentrating the anti-Ankara Kurdish factions in northern Iraq—almost on the Turkish border. Turkey manages to have workable relations with PUK and KDP. Until 1980s, Turkey had kept PUK and KDP at arms length. KDP, the Kurdish Democratic Party of Masud Barzani, son of Mullah Mustafa Barzani and PUK, Patriotic Union of Kurdistan led by Jalal Talebani were in alliance until 1987. The situation radically changed in the aftermath of the Gulf War (1991) when a brief rebellion against Saddam Hussain broke out. Turkey tried to get in touch with the PUK and the KDP, invited their leaders to Ankara and put them in direct touch with the United States which was interested in toppling down Saddam Hussain.

By 1992, Turkish forces operating in Iraq were getting help from the Kurdish leaders in northern Iraq against the PKK which had tried to impose embargo between Turkey and northern Iraq. All through the war the KDP, PUK and PKK kept on shifting their loyalties by supporting or opposing Turkey's moves in Iraq. In 1994, a full-fledged war broke out between PUK and KDP allowing the PKK to establish military bases near the border with Turkey, in the area which is nominally controlled by the KDP.

Turkey launched a full scale attack with 35,000 troops against the PKK in 1995. It was the biggest military operation since the establishment of Republic of Turkey in 1923. The main purpose was to destroy PKK which was the most powerful organization of Turkih Kurds. In May 1996, Turkey again launched attacks against the PKK near the border. In the same year Barzani formed a brief alliance with Saddam Hussain against the PUK. Iran also had an alliance with the PUK against the anti-Iranian Kurdish forces of the KDP in Iran.

The Kurdish problem is so acute that notwithstanding the US opposition to any contacts with the government of Saddam, Turkey tried to revive the rapport with him. Bulent Ecevit the former Prime Minister of Turkey made a private visit to Baghdad and told Iraq to attack the US policy of supporting the UN economic embargo on Iraq and promised Turkey's support to "Operation Provide Comfort". Turkey's only interest is that Iraq, Syria and other Arab states do not propose formation of an independent Kurdish state. Turkey is opposed to the idea of having a Kurdish state in its neighbourhood. It must be having some valid reasons for that. But an ethnic unit with a total population of about 8 million and more scattered in several countries of West Asia, Central Asia and Europe cannot remain deprived of a place of their own which may be called a Kurdish state.

Major concentration of Kurds is in Iran, Turkey and Iraq and none of that three have taken measures to give them autonomy, provide better conditions of living or drawing them in the mainstream of nation's life. The Kurdish problem however, can not be solved by seeking *ad hoc* measures or temporary intervals in hostility towards the Kurds.

The EU had made it an important point of objection to Turkey's membership. Turkey must resolve the Kurdish issue before getting in the EU. The alleged human rights violations are also occurring on account of absence of a clear policy towards the Kurds of Turkey. Ankara has been asked to improve its human rights record in order to get membership in the European Union. Turkey cannot afford to ignore the Kurdish problem any longer in case it wants to be in the European Community.

ARMENIAN "GENOCIDE"

Another chronic issue is the alleged genocide of the Armenian population by Turkey in the late 19th century and also during the World War I. In the early stages of the First World War, Russian troops penetrated north eastern Anatolia. The Armenians acted in solidarity (may be they were compelled to act) with the intending Russian forces. They attacked the troops, massacred the civilians in Muslim villages in order to demoralize the Ottoman soldiers. The Sultan decided that the Armenians should be moved southwards in order to disperse them in Urfa, Mosul and Aleppo. This enforced migration, which was done during the war was utterly mismanaged. In the process of shifting the Armenian population several thousand died on the way from starvation, cold, diseases and lack of medical support. Thousands were killed by the Kurdish horsemen of the Ottoman army (Kurds have eternal enmity towards the Armenians). These events constitute the basis for Armenian accusation against the Turks of genocide. The EU has asked Ankara to settle the matter with the Armenians in order to get a seat in the European Union. The Armenians have a strong lobby in the American Congress and have large number of supporters in the European countries as well.

Ankara tried to draw Armenia in the pipeline projects in the Caspian region to show that it does not hold anything against its neighbour despite Armenian allegation of genocide against Turkey. However, the Nagorno-Karabakh conflict inhibited the financers and participating states from charting BTC's route via Armenia. At the official level Ankara has given up its antagonism and tried to play down its "nationalistic fervour" in favour of Azerbaijan. However, Armenians cannot be satisfied with such meager gestures especially the implacable Armenian diaspora. A dialogue been Turkey and Armenia under the supervision of a neutral international agency mutually accepted by both the parties might help in finding an amicable solution of this chronic problem.

Cyprus Problem

Cyprus is the another difficult problem which is obstructing Turkey's membership in EU. It has created tensions between Greece and Turkey both NATO members. EU has categorically asked Turkey to settle its differences with Greece over Cyprus. The decision taken at the Helsinki Summit in December 1999 also made it clear that an overall settlement with Greece of bilateral disputes and a solution to the Cyprus problem would almost certainly be a *sine qua non* for Turkish accession.

The small Mediterranean island state of Cyprus is inhabited by the Turkish and the Greek Cypriots. The Greek Cypriots constitute 80% and the Turkish Cypriots 18% of the total population (half-a million) of the Island.

Cyprus was granted independence by Britain in 1960. The Island was declared Republic of Cyprus and the constitution given to Cyprus was a part of the Independence Act. It has well-spelled out provisions regarding the rights of both the communities inhabiting the island. Since it was a part of the Tripartite Agreement between Britain, Greece and Turkey, the constitution could not be amended without the consent of the three.

In 1963 President Makarios tried to introduce some changes in the governance of the island and unitaterally sought amendments in the constitution. Turkey opposed the action of President Makarios and threatened to intervene militarily it necessary.

The United states warned Turkey against any military venture in Cyprus and disallowed Ankara from using any of the NATO weapons against Greece. The "Johnson letter" which conveyed the US directives to Ankara generated tension in US-Turkey relations as well as in relations between Turkey and Greece. Turkey, later in 1974 under the pretext of safeguarding the rights of the Turkish Cypriot population of

Cyprus, forcibly snatched 37% of its territory in the northern part of the Island. Notwithstanding the widespread opposition to Turkey's military intervention in Cyprus, Ankara has established the Turkish Republic of Northern Cyprus (TRNC) which till date has been recognized only by Turkey.

The forcible occupation of the territory of another state is a violation of the Charter of the United Nations and is against the international law. For a similar action (occupation of Kuwait by Iraq) the US with the UN mandate and support of the coalition forces had invaded Iraq. The apathy of the western bloc, especially of the United States emboldened Ankara. It started harrassing Greece on several other counts like territorial waters around the Aegean sea islands under the Greek territorial jurisdiction, continental shelf, seabed and ocean floor resources, use of airspace of the islands, rights of Turkish minorities living in Greece etc. which has further deteriorated the relations between the two states. Turkey's membership in the European Union is obstructed on account of these issues in addition to the Cyprus issue.

The several rounds of talks between Greece and Turkey and the Greek and Turkish Cypriots has made it clear that Ankara is adamant on retaining TRNC as an independent state. The other side (Greek Cypriots) has proposed to have a federal structure for Cyprus in which TRNC will be enjoying complete autonomy. But this too, has not been accepted by Ankara.

Turkey is placed in an advantageous position. It is a multi-regional State and has played its role in all those regions' affairs skillfully, but Ankara's almost total renunciation of its Asian identity, its excessive tilt towards the West, obsession for membership in the EU and its adamant stance on Kurdish and Cyprus issues are holding Ankara hostage to indecision and dissuading it from playing a constructive role in international politics.

An upcoming regional power, in order to gain wider acceptability and trust of other states in the region needs to come out of these chronic entanglements and evolve a clear perspective of its role and responsibilities in the emerging political scenario in the region and the world around.

NOTES

1. William Hale, *Turkish Foreign Policy: 1774-2000, op.cit.,* p. 335.
2. William Hale, *op.cit.,* p. 336.
3. *Ibid.*
4. *Ibid.,* p. 333.
5. Bulent Aras, *op.cit.,* p. 97.

APPENDICES

APPENDIX ONE

CASPIAN REGION STATISTICS

Table 1. Caspian Sea Region Oil and Natural Gas Reserves

	Proven Oil Reserves	*Possible Oil Reserves*	*Total Oil Reserves*	*Proven Gas Reserves*	*Possible Gas Reserves*	*Total Gas Reserves*
Azerbaijan	3.6-12.5 BBL	32 BBL	36-45 BBL	11Tcf	35 Tcf	46 Tcf
Iran*	0.1 BBL	15 BBL	15 BBL	OTcf	11 Tcf	11 Tcf
Kazakhstan	10.0-17.6 BBL	92 BBL	102-110 BBL	53-83 Tcf	88 Tcf	141-171 Tcf
Russia*	2.7 BBL	14 BBL	17 BBL	N/A	N/A	N/A
Turkmenistan	1.7 BBL	80 BBL	82 BBL	98-155 Tcf	159 Tcf	257-314 Tcf
Uzbekistan	0.3 BBL	2 BBL	2 BBL	74-88 Tcf	35 Tcf	109-123 Tcf
Total	18.4-34.9 BBL	235 BBL	253-270 BBL	236-337 Tcf	328 Tcf	564-665 Tcf

*only the regions near the Caspian are included.
BBL = billion barrels, Tcf = Trillion Cubic Feet.

Table 2. Caspian Sea Region Oil Production and Exports (thousand barrels per day)

	Production (1990)	*Est. Production J2000)*	*Possible Production (2010)*	*Net Exports (1990)*	*Est. Net Exports (2000)*	*Possible Net Exports (2010)*
Azerbaijan	259.3	290	1200	76.8	145	1000
Kazakhstan	602.1	660	2000	109.2	550	1700
Turkmenistan	124.8	150	200	69.0	100	150
Uzbekistan	86.2	170	200	–168.1	20	50
Iran*	0.0	0	0	0.0	0	0
Russia**	144.0	11	300	0.0	7	300
Total	1216.4	1281	3900	86.9	822	3200

*oniy the regions near the Caspian are included.
** includes Astrakhan, Dagestan, and the North Caucasus region bordering the Caspian Sea.

Table 3. Caspian Sea Region Natural Gas Production and Exports (billion cubic feet per year)

	Production (1990)	*Est. Production (2000)*	*Possible Production (2010)*	*Net Exports (1990)*	*Est. Net Exports (2000)*	*Possible Net Exports (2010)*
Azerbaijan	349.6	220	1100	-271.9	0	500
Kazakhstan	251.2	380	1100	-257.0	50	350
Turkmenistan	3099.5	1640	3900	2539.0	1170	3300
Uzbekistan	1439.5	2000	2400	102.5	100	200
Iran*	0.0	0	0	0.0	0	0
Russia**	219.0	30	N/A	N/A	N/A	N/A
Total	5358.8	4270	8500	2112.6	1320	4350

*only the regions near the Caspian are included.

** includes Astrakhan, Dagestan, and the North Caucasus region bordering the Caspian Sea.

Table 4. Oil Export Routes in the Caspian Sea Region

Name/Location	*Route*	*Crude Capacity*	*Length*	*Investment*	*Status*
AIOC - Main Export Pipeline	Baku-Tbilisi- Ceyhan	1.0 million bbl/d	1073 miles	$2.4 billion (other estimates as high as $3.7 billion)	Istanbul Accord signed November 1999 to build the line along the Baku-Tbilisi-Ceyhan route. Completion targeted 2004-2005. Commissioned.
AIOC - Early Oil Western Route	Baku (Azerbaijan) - Supsa (Georgia)	0.115 million bbl/d design capacity; upgrades by 2002 to 0.21 million bbl/d	515 miles	$600 million with no upgrade	Exports began April 1999
AIOC - Early Oil Northern Route	Baku (Azerbaijan) - Novorossisk (Russia) via Chechnya	0.1 million bbl/d capacity; possible upgrade to 0.3 million bbl/d	868 miles; 90 miles are in Chechnya	$600 million to upgrade to 0.3 million bbl/d	Exports began late 1997
AIOC Northern Route - Chechnya bypass with link to Mahachkala	Baku (Azerbaijan) via Dagestan to Tikhoretsk (Russia); connecting to Novorossisk (Russia)	2000 pipeline capacity -0.12 million bbl/d (rail and pipeline 0.16 million bbl/d) 2005 - 0.36 million bbl/d	204 miles	$140 million	Completed April 2000. 11 mile spur connects bypass with Russia's Caspian port of Mahachkala.

Atyrau -Samara	Atyrau (Kazakhstan) - Samara (Russia)	Current 0.21 million bbl/d; increase to 0.31 million bbl/d	432 miles	Increase would cost $37.5 million	Project modifies existing pipeline to Russia by adding pumping and heating stations. Upgrades began 1999.
Caspian Pipeline Consortium (CPC)	Tengiz (Kazakhstan) - Novorossisk (Russia)	0.56 million bbl/d Phase 1; 1.34 million bbl/d peak	930 miles	$2.4 billion for Phase 1; $4.2 billion total when completed	Construction has begun. Phase 1 flows begin October 2001; peak 2015
Gardabani-Batumi Pipeline	Gardabani Azerbaijan) -Batumi Georgia) oil refinery	N/A	Rebuild of an existing pipeline	N/A	The World Bank and the European Bank for Reconstruction and Development may provide financing
Iran -Azerbaijan	Baku (Azerbaijan) - Tebriz (Iran)	0.2 - 0.4 million bbl/d	N/A	$500 million	Proposed by Elf Aquitaine and Total Fina
Iran Oil Swap Pipeline	Iranian Caspian port of Neka - Tehran	175,000 bbl/d, rising to 370,000 bbl/d	208 miles	$400 - $500 million	Construction planned to begin 2000.
Kazakhstan - China	Aktyubinsk Kazakhstan) - Xinjiang (China)	0.4 - 0.8 million bbl/d	1,800 miles	$3.0 -3.5 billion	Agreement 1997; feasibility study halted September 1999 because insufficient Kazak oil Flows could be committed for the next 10 years.

(Contd.)

Table 4. (Contd.)

Name/Location	*Route*	*Crude Capacity*	*Length*	*Investment*	*Status*
Kazakhstan - Turkmenistan - Iran (KTI)	Kazakhstan - Turkmenistan - Kharg sland on Persian Gulf Iran)	1.0 million bbl/d	930 miles	$1.2 billion	Proposed completion date 2005
Khasuri-Batumi pipeline (Georgia)	Port of Dubendi (Azerbaijan) -Batumi	Initial 70,000 bbl/d, rising to 140,000 bbl/d.	Rail system and 144-mile Khasuri-Batumi pipeline	$70-$100 million for pipeline renovation	Chevron signed agreement September 1999 to rebuild the existing Khasuri-Batumi oil pipeline in 18-24 months
South Pipeline (Central Asia Oil Pipeline)	Kazakhstan - Turkmenistan - Afghanistan -Gwadar (Pakistan)	1 million bbl/d	1,040 miles	$2.5 billion	Memorandum of Understanding
Trans-Caspian (Kazakhstan Twin Pipelines)	kktau (western Kazakhstan coast) - Baku (Azerbaijan); could extend to Ceyhan (Turkey)	N/A	370 miles to Baku	$2 - $4 billion if to Ceyhan	Feasibility study agreement December 1998 Royal Dutch/Shell, Chevron, Mobil, Kazakhstan

Table 5. Natural Gas Export Routes in the Caspian Sea Region

Name/Location	*Route*	*Gas Capacity*	*Length*	*Investment*	*Status*
Baku-Tbilisi-Erzurum	Azerbaijan via Georgia to Erzurum (Turkey)	Initial 175 bcf/year rising to 350 bcf/year. Additional pipelines could raise capacity ko 565 bcf/year.	300 mile renovation Gazi Mahammad-Agdash-Gazakh pipeline Azerbaijan - Georgia; 174 miles extension to Erzurum (Turkey)	Renovation $82 million in Azerbaijan; extension Georgia - Erzurum $600-$700 million	Feasibility study done by Sofregas (France); completion target 2002-2003.
Centgas (Central Asia Gas)	Dauletad or Yashlar Fields (Turkmenistan) - Pakistan. May extend to India	700 bcf/year	900 miles to Multan, Pakistan (additional 400 miles to India)	$1.9 billion to Pakistan (additional $0.5 billion to India)	[Memorandum Understanding (Turkmenistan, Pakistan, Afghanistan & Uzbekistan. Project stalled with financing difficulties because of Afghan fighting.
Central Asia - Russia Europe	Turkmenistan-Kazakhstan -Russia	3.5Tcf	N/A - uses existing routes	Uses Existing route	Operational-uses existing Russian system. Turkmenistan signed an agreement to increase exports to Russia to 1.8-2.1 Tcf/year by 2005-2006.

(Contd.)

Table 5. (Contd.)

Name/Location	*Route*	*Gas Capacity*	*Length*	*Investment*	*Status*
China Pipeline	Turkmenistan - Xinjiang (China); may extend to Japan	1 Tcf/year	5,000 miles; more if to Japan	$10 billion China; more if to Japan	Preliminary feasibility study done by Exxon, Mitsubishi & CNPC
Trans-Caspian (Kazakhstan Twin Pipelines)	Caspian coast (Kazakhstan) - Baku (Azerbaijan) - Ceyhan (Turkey)	N/A	N/A	N/A	Feasibility study agreement December 1998 Royal Dutch/Shell, Chevron, Mobil, Kazakhstan
Trans - Caspian (Turkmenistan)	Turkmenbashi (Turkmenistan) - Baku (Azerbaijan) -Erzerum (Turkey)	1.1 Tcf/year	1054 miles	$2.0-S3.0 billion	Preliminary feasibility studies completed. PSG and Shell will be operators of the project Initial completion target date 2002 - may be delayed until 2006.
Trans-Georgian	Russia-Turkey via Georgia and Armenia	425 billion cubic feet/year	125 miles	$250 million	Gazprom's plans to complete preparations in 1999 were shelved

Turkmenistan - Iran	Korpeje (Turkmenistan) to Kord-Kui(Iran)	283 - 350 bcf/year; expansion proposed to 777 bcf/year by 2005; 1.1 Tcf/year 2010	90 miles	$190 million; 2005 expansion $300-$400 million	commissioned December 1997
Turkmenistan - Iran	Serakhs (Turkmenistan) - Teheran (Iran)	Initial 0.7 Tcf/year; expansion to 1.8 - 2.1 Tcf/year	N/A	$1.2-$1.5 billion	Proposed
Turkmenistan - Iran - Turkey	Ekarem (Turan - Tabriz	1 Tcf/year	1,350 miles	$3.8-4.0 billion	Feasibility study done by Royal Dutch/Shell; plan shelved

Table 6. Bosphorus Bypass Oil Export Routes (for Oil Transiting the Black Sea)

Name/Location	*Route*	*Crude Capacity*	*Length*	*Investment*	*Status*
Albanian - Macedonian - Bulgarian Oil (AMBO) trans-Balkan line	AMBO line from Burgas (Bulgaria) - Vlore (Albania)	750,000 bbl/d for AMBO line (could be expanded to 1 million bbl/d)	560 miles for the AMBO line	$1.13 billion for AMBO line to Vlore	Construction AMBO line proposed 2001-2002. Completion targeted for 2004-2005.
Burgas trans-Balkan line	Burgas (Bulgaria) - Alexandroupolis Greece)	600,000-800,000 bbl/d for the Burgas-Alexandroupolis line	200 miles for the Burgas line to Alexandroupolis;	$800 million for Burgas line to Alexandroupolis;	Initial agreement 1997 Bulgaria, Greece, Russia for Burgas line.
Constantza to Trieste Pipeline (CTPL); Romanian -Italian project version called South-East European Line (SEEL)	Constantza (Romania) - Trieste (Italy). Alternative destinations could include Omisalj (Croatia)	660,000 bbl/d	855 miles	$1.2-$1.6 billion	HLP-Parsons moving CTPL project forward after feasibility study completed end-1999. ENI (Italy) signed a cooperation agreement with Romania 2/98 for the SEEL.

Ukraine Odessa-Brodi-Gdansk	Odessa to Brody; optional spurs to the northern Druzhba line at Adamowa Zastawa Poland, or Schwechat, Austria.	180,000 bbl/d; ultimate capacity 600,000-800,000 bbl/d	415 miles	$400 -$450 million for pipeline and terminal; $140 million spent using revenues from the Friendship and Trans Dnieper pipelines	Yuzhnyi oil terminal near Odessa 15% complete; pipeline 75% finished with target competion 2001

Source: United States Energy Information Administration; 'Kazakhstan Country Analysis Brief, June 2000, USA.

Appendix Two

Table 1: Kazakhstan: Oil Production Joint Ventures

Name	*Foreign Partners*	*Reserves (proved + possible)*	*Invest-ment*	*Status*
Aktobe Preussag	Preussag Gmbh (Germany) 50.0%			Exploring near Zharkamys
Anako	Nafta a.s. (Slovakia)			Producing 1,390 bbl/d 8/98
Arman	Oryx (US) 50.0%. Oryx merged with Kerr-McGee			Producing 4,750 bbl/d 8/98; 5 new wells next 2-3 years
Uzen	Kazakhoil subsidiary Uzenmunaigaz(100%). CNPC won tender for joint development in 1997 but dropped out	Est. oil reserves 1.5 billion barrels	$1 billion 1st 5 years	Rehabilitating Uzen field
Aktobe	CNPC (60%), Aktobemunaigaz (40%)	Est. oil reserves 1 billion barrels	$4.1 billion	Developing Aktobe field
Demunai	Caesar Oil (US) 50.0%			Developing fields Aktobe Oblast

Embavedoil Onshore	MOL Rt, Vegyepszer (Hungary) combined 49.0%			Producing 220 bbl/d 8/98; Vegyepszer may pull out
Gyural	Urals Trading (Cyprus)			Producing 365 bbl/d 8/98
Hurricane-Kumkol	Hurricane (Canada)	Proved reserves: 442 million barrels of crude oil; 67.8 billion cubic feet of gas		Produced 51,000 bbl/d 1999
Karakudukmunai JV	American-Turkish Central Asia Guernsey 50.0% (JV with Chaparral/Turkish investors)	Est. oil reserves over 70 million barrels		Producing 220 bbl/d 8/98
KazakhOil-Telf	Telf AG (Switzerland)			Producing 580 bbl/d 8/98
Kazgermunai	Veba Oel (Germany) 25.0%; EEG (Germany) 17.5%; IFC 7.5%	Est. oil reserves 100 million barrels	$300 million	Producing 1,170 bbl/d 8/98
Kazpromstavba	Prumsylove Stavitelstvi (Czech Republic) 31.0%			Developing Kara-Arna field

(Contd.)

Table 1: (Contd.)

Name	*Foreign Partners*	*Reserves (proved + possible)*	*Invest-ment*	*Status*
Kazturkmunai	TPAO (Turkey) 49.0%			Producing 1,100 bbl/d 8/98
Kumkol-Lukoil	Lukoil (Russia)	Est. oil reserves over 600 million barrels		Producing 17,010 bbl/d 8/98
Kuatamlonmunai	Amlon (UK) 50.0%			Developing Bektas-Konys field
Matin	Matoil SA (50%)			Producing 3,360 bbl/d 8/98
Steppe Leopard	Snow Leopard Resources (Canada) 45%; Snow Leopard International (5%)	Est. oil reserves 100 million barrels		Developing Teplovsko-Tokareyev fields
Svetlandoil				Producing 290 bbl/d 8/98

Tasbulat Oil	Gendor (Cyprus)			Developing Tasbulat field
Tenge	Anglo-Dutch (US)	Est. oil reserves 500 million barrels; 1 trillion cubic feet gas		Developing Tenge field
TengizChevroil (TCO)	Chevron (US) 50%; Mobil (US), 25%; Kazakhstan 20%; LukArco (Russia), 5%	Est. oil reserves 6-9 billion barrels	$20 billion over 40 years	Produced 190,000 bbl/d 1999, projected rise to 240,000 bbl/d 2000. Adjacemt Korolevskoye field to be developed 2000.
Turan	Vega-D Geophysical (Canada) 25%; Technoeko (Canada) 25%			Developing Kzylkiya, Maybulak, Aryskum fields
Zhetbay-Quest	Quest (UK), Mannai (Qatar)			Well rehab at Zhetbay field

Table 2. Other Oil Projects in Kazakhstan

Name	*Foreign Partners*	*Reserves (proved + possible)*	*Invest-ment*	*Status*
American International Petroleum Corporation (AIPC) - Exploration License	AIPC (US) 70.0%	Est. oil/gas reserves 3.8 billion barrels oil equivalent		Seismic work done - drilling Altai No. 1 test well
American International Petroleum Corporation (AIPC)		Est. recoverable gas reserves 700 billion cubic feet		AIPC completed 2 wells in Shagyriy-Shomyshty gasfield in 1999; production in 2001
Caspian Pipeline Consortium (CPC)	Russia 24%; Kazakhstan 19%; Chevron (US) 15%; LukArco (Russia/United States) 12.5%; Mobil		$2.3 billion	Construction underway; 1st flows mid-2001. Ultimate capacity

	(US) 7.5%; Rosneft-Shell (Russia-U.K./Netherlands) 7.5%; Oman 7%, BG (U.K.) 2%;Agip(Italy)2%; Kazakhstan Pipeline Ventures (Kazakhstan) 1.75%; and Oryx (United States) 1.75%			1.34 million barrels/day
Ertismunai Onshore (NE Kazakhstan)	IPI (US) 50.0%; Kuat Holding (Kazakh) 50.0% Leah Industries has letter intent to buy IPI share	Est. oil reserves 4.0 billion barrels	$2 million invested through 1998	
Karachaganak Petroleum Operating	Agip (Italy) 32.5%; BG (UK) 32.5%; Texaco (US) 20.0%; Lukoil (Russia) 15%	Est. oil & condensate reserves 6 billion barrels; est. gas reserves 46 trillion cubic feet	$6 billion over 40 years; $600 million in 1999; $1.5 billion planned for 2000	Developing Karachaganak field; produced 0.127 Tcf gas in 1999. Condensate exported via CPC pipeline.

(Contd.)

Table 2. (Contd.)

Name	*Foreign Partners*	*Reserves (proved + possible)*	*Invest-ment*	*I Status*
Karazhanbasm unai	Nations Energy			Producing 10,300 bbl/d 8/90
OKIOC (Offshore Kazakhstan International Operating Company) PSA Signed November 1997	Agip (14.28%), BG (14.28%), BP/Statoil (14.28%), Mobil (14.28%), Royal Dutch/Shell (14.28%), Total (14.28%), Inpex (7.14%), Phillips (7.14%) BP Amoco (9.5%) plans to sell its shares.	Est. oil reserves 40 billion barrels at the Kashagan structures	$600 million spent since 1993	Drilling 1st well at the East Kashagan structure on the Caspian shelf began on August 12, 1999. Several more test wells through summer 2000
Mertvyi Kultuk PSA/ Ostrovnaya	Exxon (US) 50%; Oryx (US) 50%; Oryx merged with Kerr-McGee	Est. oil reserves 150 million barrels		Ostrovnaya prospect spudded due to lack of infrastructure

Munai NPTs				Producing 440 bbl/d 8/98
TemirPSA	Shell (UK/Netherlands) 60%; Veba Oil (Germany) 40%	Est. oil reserves 300 million barrels	$25 million	Veba bought out Elf s share in 1995
Tulparmunai	Mobil (US) 25%; Shell (UK/Netherlands) 25%; Japan Petroleum (Japan) 12.5%; Sumitomoto (Japan) 12.5%			Exploration blocks 2 & 3 Aktobe oblast
Exploration/Field Concession	Partex 50%; Oman Oil (Oman) 50%			Developing block in Mangistau Oblast
Exploration/Field Concession	Amoco (US); TPAO (Turkey)			Developing block in Aktobe Oblast
Exploration/Field Concession	Chinese Petroleum Corportion (Taiwan)	Est. oil reserves 90 million barrels		

(Contd.)

Table 2. (Contd.)

Name	*Foreign Partners*	*Reserves (proved + possible)*	*Invest-ment*	*I Status*
Exploration/Field Concession	ONGC (India)			Concession Pavlodar Oblast
Exploration/Field Concession	Repsol (Spain) 60%; Enterprise (UK) 40%			Concession Aktobe Oblast
Exploration/Field Concession	JIT (Japan/Indonesia)			Exploration Aral region
Exploration/Field Concession	Oman Oil, ARCO, Exxon			
Exploration/Field Concession	JNOC (Japan) 50%		$3.9 billion over 30 years	
Exploration/Field Concession	Texaco (US) 65.0%, Nimir (Saudi Arabia) 35.0%	Est. oil reserves 1.0-1.5 billion barrels	$800 million	Development North Buzachi; 3rd test well drilled

Sazankurak Summer 1997	FIOC(85%); Atyraumunaigazgeologiya (15%)	Total reserves over 70 million barrels; recoverable reserves 25 million barrels	$39 million invested to date	Test production 10 wells; field production in 2000
Field Rehablitation	Seneca Resources (US)			Rehab 7 fields Atyrau oblast

Source: United States Energy Information Administration; "Kazakhstan Country Analysis Brief, May 2001, USA.

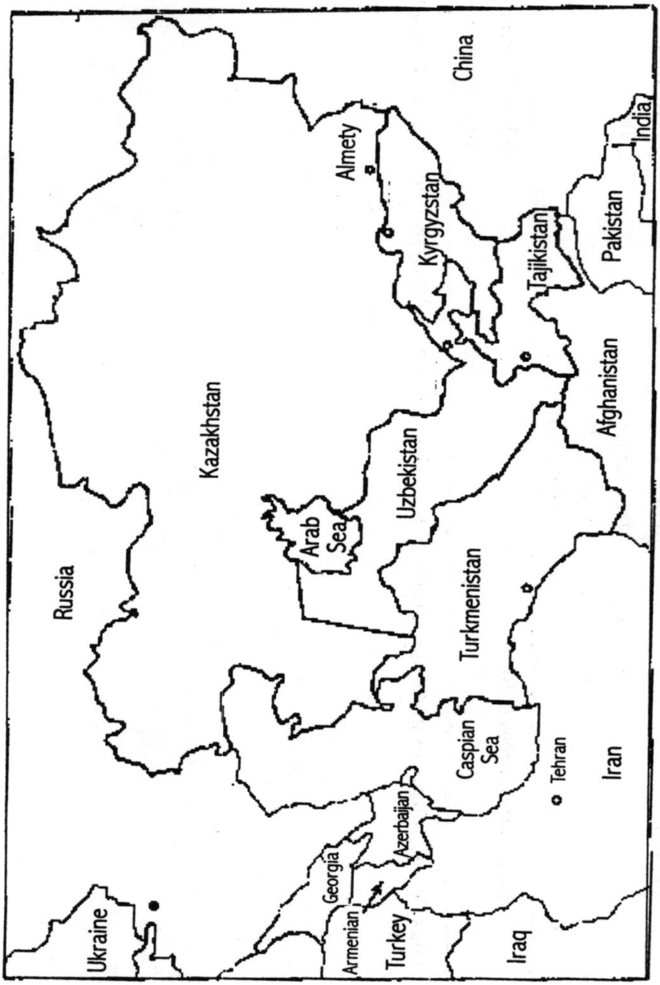

Map 1 : Contemporary Central Asia

Map. 2 : Central Asia consisting of Kazakhstan, Kyrgyzstan, Tajikistan, Turkmenistan and Uzbekistan and Turkey's proximity to Trans-Caucasia (Georgia, Armenia, Azerbaijan) and Central Asia

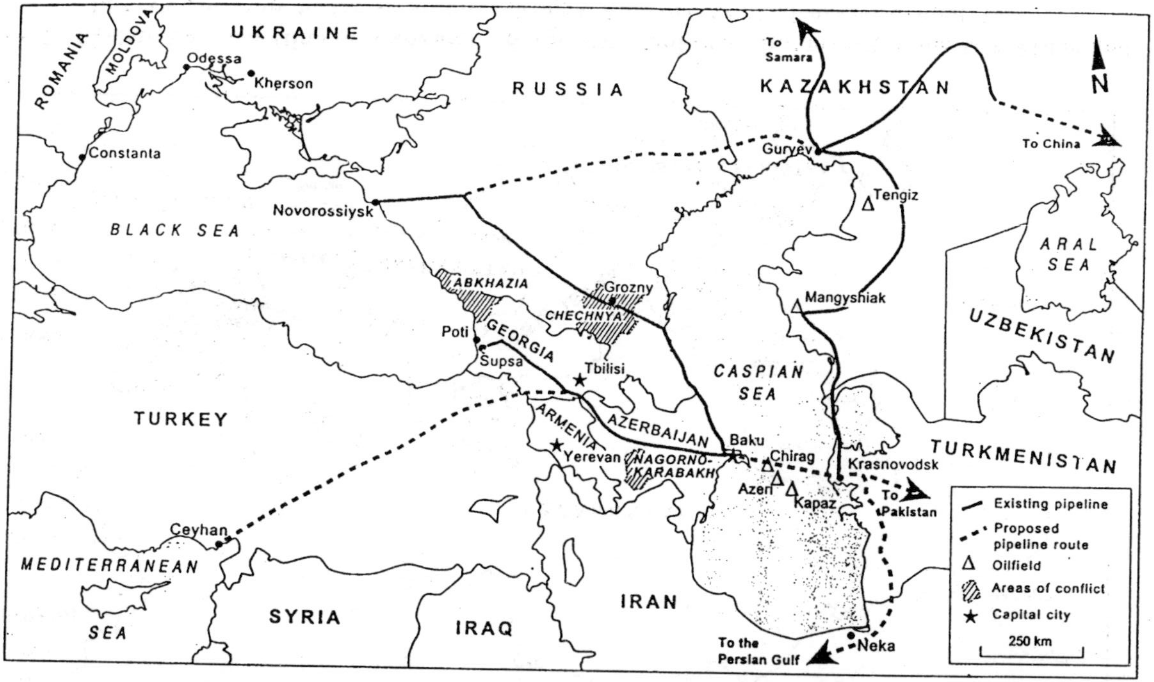

Map 3: Existing and Possible Future Oil Routes from Central Asia

Source : Russia and Asia : The Emerging Security Agenda Edited by Gennady Chufrin (SIPRI : Oxford University Press, 1999)

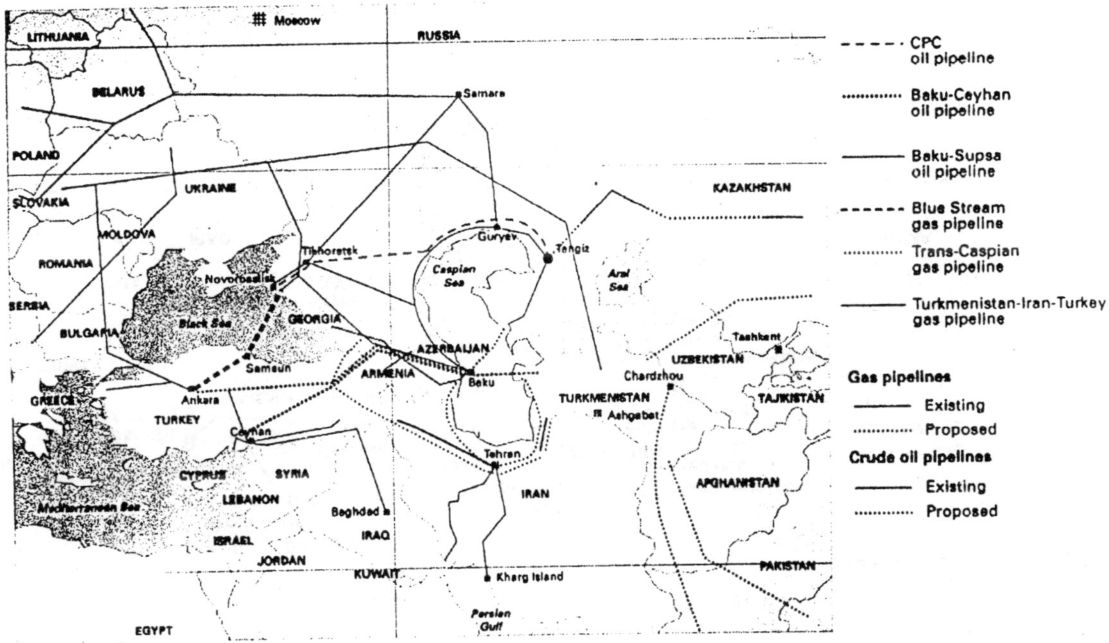

Source: International Energy Agency

Map 4: Crude-Oil Pipelines Around Caspian Sea

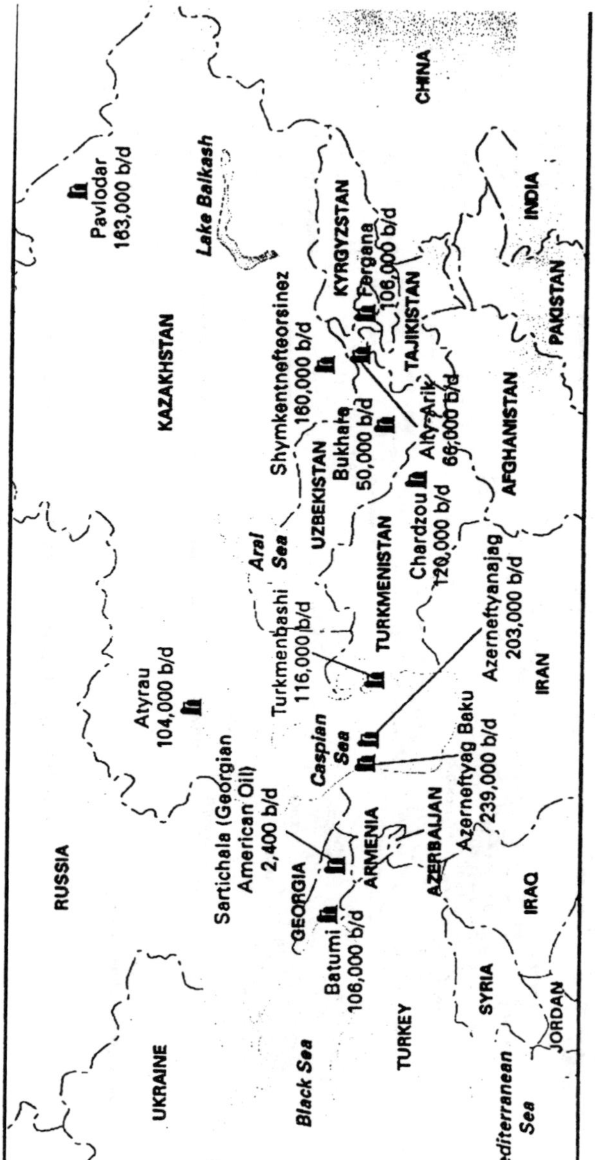

Map 5: Refineries in the Caspian Area

Map 6: Oil and Gas Infrastructure in Caspian Basin

Bibliography

Books

Akiner, Shirin (ed.), *Politics and Economic Trends in Central Asia.* (London, I.B. Tauris & Co. Ltd., 1992).

Akiner, Shirin, *The Islamic Peoples of the Soviet Union* (London, Keagan Paul International, 1983).

Allworth, E. (ed.), *Central Asia: A Century of Russian Rule* (London: Oxford Press, 1967).

Allworth, E., *Ethnic Russia in the USSR: The Dilemma of Dominance.* (New York, Pergamon, 1973).

———, *Nationality Group Survival in Multiethnic States: Shifting Support Patterns in the Soviet Baltic Region.* (New York, Praeger Publishers, 1977).

———, *The Modern Uzbeks* (Stanford, Hoover Institution Press, 1990.

———,*The Nationality Question in Soviet Central Asia* (New York & London, Praeger Publishers, 1973).

Allworth, Edward, *Central Asia: 120 Years of Russian Rule* (Durham, NC: Duke University Press, 1989).

Altstadt, A., The Azerbaijani Turks: Power and Identity Under Russian Rule (Stanford: Hoover Institution, 1992).

Alvin, Z., and Oles M. Smolansky (eds.), *Regional Power Rivalries in the New Eurasia: Russia, Turkey and Iran* (Armonk, N.H.: M.E. Sharpe, 1995).

Anderson, Benedict, *Imagined Communities: Reflection on the Origin and Spread of Nationalism*. (London, Verso Editions and New Left Book, 1983).

Anderson, John, *Kyrgyzstan: Central Asian Island of Democracy*. (Amsterdam, Hardwood Academic Publishers, 1999)

———, *Regime Change in Afghanistan: Foreign Intervention and the Politics of Legitimacy* (Boulder: Westview Press, 1991).

———, *The International Politics of Central Asia*. (London, Manchester University Press, 1997).

Arai, Masami, *Turkish Nationalism in the Young Turk Era*. (Leiden, New York, Kobenhavn, Koln: E.J. Brill, 1992).

Aydin, Turan and Olgan Bekar, *Turkey's Middle and Long Term Interests and Turco-Russian Relations*. (Ankara: Turkiye Ekonomik ve Sosyal Etudler Vakfi, 1997).

Azerbaijan: An Economic Profile. Springfield, V.A., Library of Congress Documents Expediting Project, 1995.

Bagis, A.I. (ed.), *Water as an Element of Cooperation in the Middle East* (Ankara: Hacettepe University, 1994).

Balim, Cigdem, et.al., Turkey: Political, Social and Economic Challenges in the 1990s (Leiden: E.J. Brill, 1995).

Balkir, Canan, and Algan M. Williams (eds.), *Turkey and Europe* (London and New York: Pinter, 1993).

Banuazizi, Ali and Weiner (eds.), *The New Geopolitics of Central Asia and its Borderlands* (Bloomington: Indiana University Press, 1994).

Barchard, D., T*urkey and the European Union* (London: Centre for European Reform, 1998).

———, *Turkey and the West*. (London, Boston and Henley: Routledge and Kegan Paul, 1985).

Barkey, Henri J. (ed.), *Reluctant Neighbor: Turkey's Role in the Middle East* (Washington D.C.: U.S. Institute for Peace Press, 1996).

Bennigsen, A. & Quelquejay, C.L., *Islam in the Soviet Union* (London, Pall Mall Press, 1967).

Bennigsen, A. & S.E. Wimbush, *Muslim National Communism in the Soviet Union: A Revolutionary Strategy for Colonial World*. (Chicago, 1980).

Bennigsen, Alexandre & Marie Broxup, *The Islamic Threat to the Soviet State*. (London, Croom Helm Ltd., 1983).

Barry Rubin, Kemal Kirisci, *Turkey in World Politics: An Emerging Multiregional Power* (Lynne Rienner Publishers, London, 2001).

Bialer, Seweryn (ed.), *Politics, Society and Nationality inside Gorbachev's Russia*. (Boulder Colo, 1989).

Blank, S.J., et.al., (ed.), *Turkey's Strategic Position at the Crossroads of World Affairs* (Strategic Studies Institute, U.S. Army War College, 1993).

Bourdeaux, Michael (ed.), *The Politics of Religion in Russia and New States of Eurasia*. (London, M.E. Sharpe, 1995).

Bozdaglioglu, Yucel, *Turkish Foreign Policy and Turkish Identity: A Constructivist Approach* (Routledge, New York and London, 2003).

Bozdogan, Sibel and Resat Kasaba (eds.), *Rethinking, Modernity and National Identity in Turkey*. (Seattle, University of Washington Press, 1997).

Brass, Paul, *Ethnicity and Nationalism: Theory and Comparisons*. (New Delhi, Sage Publications, 1991).

Brown, Michael E. (ed.), *Ethnic Conflict and International Security*. (Princeton, Princeton University Press, 1995).

Bruce, Parrot (ed.), *The Dynamics of Soviet Defense Policy* (Washington DC: The Wilson Centre Press, 1990).

Bugra, A., *State and Business in Modern Turkey: A Comparative Study* (New York: State University of New York Press, 1994).

Bulent Aras, *The New Geoplitics of Eurasia and Turkey's Position* (Grank Cass: London, 2002).

Buttino, Marco (ed.), *In a Collapsing Empire: Underdevelopment, Ethnic Conflict and Nationalism in the Soviet Union.* (Milano, Fondazione Giangiacomo Fentrinelli, 1993)

Celik, Yasemin, *Contemporary Turkish Foreign Policy.* (Westport, Connecticut, London: Praeger, 1999).

Chinn, Jeff & Others, *Russians as the New Minority: Ethnicity and Nationalism in the Soviet Successors States* (New York: Westview Press, 1996).

Chufrin, Genaddy (Ed.), *Russia and Asia: The Emerging Security Agenda.* (Sipri, Oxford Press, 1999).

Confield, Robert L. (ed.), *Turko-Persian in Historical Perspectives* (London: Cambridge University Press, 1991).

Constans, Dimitri (ed.), *The Greek-Turkish Conflict in the 1990s* (London: Macmillan, 1991).

Cooperation in the Middle East (London and New York: Routledge Press, 1998).

Dani, A.H., *New Light on Central Asia* (Lahore: Sange-e-Meel Publications, 1993).

Dawisha, Karen & Others, *Russia and the New States of Eurasia* (London: Cambridge University Press, 1994).

Dawisha, Karen and Parrot Bruce (eds), *Conflict, Cleavage and Change in Central Asia and the Causes* (New York: Cambridge University Press, 1994).

———, *Russia and the New States of Eurasia: The Politics of Upheaval* (New York: Cambridge University Press, 1994).

———, *The International Politics of Eurasia* (New York: M.E. Sharpe Press, 1995).

D'Encauese, Helene Carrere, *The End of Soviet Empire, the Triumph of the Nations.* (New York/London, Harper Collins, 1993).

Diloram, Ibrahim, *The Islamisation of Central Asia: A Case Study of Uzbekistan* (Leicester, The Islam Foundation, 1993).

Dodd, Clement H. (ed.), *Turkish Foreign Policy: New Prospects.* (Cambridgeshire; The Eastern Press, 1992).

Dodd, Clement H., *The Cyprus Imbroglio* (Cambridgeshire: The Eothen Press, 1998).

Ehteshami, Anoushirvan, *From the Gulf to Central Asia: Players in the New Great Game* (Exeter: University of Exeter Press, 1994).

Eickelman, Dale F. (ed.), *Russia's Muslim Frontier: New Directions in Cross-Cultural Analysis* (Bloomington: Indian University Press, 1993).

Encausse, H. Carrere-d', *The Great Challenge* (New York: Holmes & Meir, 1992).

Esposito, John L., *The Islamic Threat: Myth or Reality?* (New York, Oxford University Press, 1995).

Ferdinand, Peter (ed.), *The New Central Asia and its Neighbours* (London: The Royal Institute of International Affairs, 1994).

Fierman, William, *Soviet Central Asia: The Failed Transformation.* (Oxford, Westview Press, 1991).

Fuller, G.E. and I.O. Lesser, (eds.), *Turkey's New Geopolitics: From the Balkans to Western China.* (Boulder: Westview Press, 1993).

Fuller, Graham E., *Turkey Faces East: New Orientations toward the Middle East and the Old Soviet Union* (Santa Monica, CA: RAND, 1992)

Fuller, Graham, *Central Asia: The New Geopolitics* (New York: Defence Press, 1992).

Gibb, H.A.R., *Arab Conquest in Central Asia* (New York: AMS Press, 1970).

Glenn, John, *The Soviet Legay in Central Asia* (Macmillan Press, London,1999).

Gokey, Bluent and Others, *Turkey and the New States of the Caucasus and Central Asia* (London: HMSO, 1996).

Gross, Jo-Ann (ed.), *Muslims in Central Asia: Expressions of Identity and Change.* (Durham, NZ, Duke University Press, 1992).

Haghayeghi, Mehrded, *Islam and Politics in Central Asia* (London, Macmillan Press, 1995),

Hale, William, *Turkish Politics and the Military* (New York and London, Routledge, 1994).

Hale, William, *Turish Foreign Policy: 1774-2000* (Frank Cass London, 2000).

Herzig, Edmund, *Iran and the Former Soviet South* (London: Royal Institute of International Affairs, 1995)

Hiro, Dilip, *Between Marx and Muhammad: The Changing Face of Central Asia* (London, Harper Collins Publishers, 1994).

Hoshirk, Peter, *The Great Game: The Struggle for Empire in Central Asia* (New York: Kodansha International Press, 1992).

Hudson, George (ed.), *Soviet National Security Policy Under-Perestroika* (Cambridge: The University Press, 1990).

Hunter, Shireen T., *Central Asia Since Independence* (Washington DC: CSIS, 1996).

Karimov, Islam, *Uzbekistan on the Threshold of the Twenty-First Century: Threats to Security, Condition of Stability and Guarantee for Progress* (Tashkent, 1997).

Kaushik, Devendra, *Central Asia in Modern Times: A History from the Early 19th Century* (Moscow: Progress Publications, 1970).

Kedourie, Sylvia (ed.), *Turkey Before and After Ataturk: Internal and External Affairs* (London and Portland, Ore: Frank Cass, 1999).

Kedourie, Sylvia (ed.), *Turkey: Identity, Democracy, Politics* (Frank Cass, London: 1998).

Kinross, Patrick B., *Ataturk: A Biography of Mustafa Kemal, Father of Modern Turkey*. (New York: William Morrow and Company, 1965).

Kirisci, Kemal, and Gareth M. Winrow, *The Kurdish Question and Turkey: An Example of a Trans-State Ethnic Conflict* (London: Frank Cass, 1997).

Kolars, J., and R. Mitchell, *The Euphrates River and the Southeast Anatolia Development Project* (1991).

Kolstoe, Paul, *Russians in the Former Soviet Republics* (London: C. Hurst & Co.,1995).

Kramer, Heinz, *A Changing Turkey: Challenges to Europe and the United States* (Washington D.C.: Brookings Institution Press, 1999).

Kruger, K., *Kemalist Turkiye ve Ortadogu*. (Ankara: Altin Kitaplar Basimevi, 1981).

Kushner, David, *The Rise of Turkish Nationalism, 1876-1908*. (London, Billing & Sons. Ltd., 1977).

Landau, Jacob M. (ed.), *Ataturk and Modernization of Turkey*. (Boulder, Westview Press, 1984).

Landau, Jacob M., *Pan Turkism: From Irredentism to Cooperation* (Bloomington: Indiana University Press, 1995).

Larrabee, Stephen, *The Troubled Partnership: Turkey and Europe*. (Santa Monica, CA: Rend, 1998).

Lesser, Ian, *Bridge or Barrier? Turkey and the West After the Cold War*. (Santa Monica, CA: Rend, 1992).

Levy, Avigdor, "Preface", in *The Jews of the Ottoman Empire*, ed. by Avigdor Levy. (New Jersey. The Darwin Press, 1994).

Lewis, Bernard, *The Emergence of Modern Turkey*. (London, New York, Toronto: Oxford University Press, 1961).

Makovsky, Alan, and Sabri Sayari (eds.), *Changing Dynamics of Turkish Foreign Policy* (Washington D.C.: Washington Institute for Near East Policy).

Mandelbaum, M. (ed.), *Central Asia and the World* (New York: Council on Foreign Relations, 1994).

Mandelbaum, Michael, *Central Asia and the World: Kazakhstan, Uzbekistan, Tajikistan, Turkmenistan, Kyrgyzstan* (New York: Foreign Relations Press, 1994).

Manz, Beatrice F. (ed.), *Central Asia in Historical Perspective.* (Boulder, Colorado and Oxford, UK, Westview Press, 1994).

Mastny, Vojtech and R. Craig Nation (eds.), *Turkey Between East and West: New Challenges for a Rising Regional Power* (Boulder, Colo. Westview, 1996).

McGhee, G., *The US-Turkish-NATO Middle East Connection: How the Truman Doctrine and Turkey's NATO Entry Contained the Soviets* (New York, St. Martin"s Press, 1990).

Melvin, Neil, *Russian Beyond Russia: The Politics of National Identity* (London: Royal Institute of International Affairs, 1995).

Menashri, David, *Central Asia Meets the Middle East* (Frank Cass, London: 1998).

Menon, Rajan, Yuri E. Fedorov and Ghia Nodia (eds.), *Russia, the Caucasus and Central Asia.* (East-West Institute, NY, 1999).

Middy-Weitzman, Bruce and Efraim Inbar (eds.), *Religious Radicalism in the Greater Middle East* (London: Frank Cass, 1997).

Mouritzen, Hans (ed.), *Bordering Russia: Theory and Prospects for Europe's Baltic Rein* (England: Aldershot Press, 1998).

Muftuler-Bac, Meltem, *Turkey's Relations with a Changing Europe* (Manchester: Manchester University Press, 1997).

Nachmani, Amikam, *Israel, Turkey and Greece: Uneasy Relations in the East Mediterranean* (London: Frank Cass, 1987).

Nas, T.F. and M. Odekon (eds.), *Liberalization and the Turkish Economy* (Hamden, Conn: Greenwood Press, 1988).

Ohlsson, Leif (ed.), *Hydropolitics: Conflicts over Water as a Development Constraint* (London: Zed Books, 1995).

Olson, Robert, *The Kurdish Question and Turkish-Iranian Relations: From World War I to 1998* (Costa Meta, Calif: Mazda Publishers, 1998).

Onuf, Nicholas, *World of Our Making*. (Colombia University of South Corolina Press, 1989).

Ozal, Turgut, *Turkey in Europe and Europe in Turkey*. Nicosia: K. Rustem and Brother, 1991.

Panarin, Sergei A. Nlavmkin, Vitly, *State Religion and Society in Central Asia: A post-Soviet Critique*. (Reading, Ithaca Press, 1993).

Patnaik, Ajay (ed.), *Commonwealth of Independent States: Problems and Prospects* (New Delhi: Konark Publishers, 1995).

Patnaik, Ajay, *State Building in Tajikistan*. (Research Monograph, Maulana Abul Kalam Azad Institute of Asian Studies, Calcutta, 2000).

Peimani, Hooman, *Regional Security and the Future of Central Asia: The Competition of Iran, Turkey and Russia* (London: Praeger Publishers, Westport, 1998).

Pierce, Richard A., *Russian Central Asia, 1867-1917: A Study in Colonial Rule* (Berkley: University of California Press, 1960).

Pinakney, R., *Democracy in the Third World* (Buckingham, Open University Press, 1993).

Pipes, R., *The Formation of the Soviet Union* (Cambridge MA: Harvard University Press, 1954).

Rahul, Ram, *Central Asia: Major Perspectives* (New Delhi: Vikas Publication House, 1995).

Rahul, Ram, *China, Russia and Central Asia* (New Delhi: Vikas Publication House, 1995).

Rahul, Ram, *Modern Central Asia* (New Delhi: Vikas Publication House, 1991).

———, *Politics of Central Asia* (New Delhi: Vikas Publication House, 1971).

Rashid, Ahmad, *Taliban: Islam Oil and the New Great Game in Central Asia*. (I.B. Tauris Publishers, London, 2001).

———, *The Resurgence of Central Asia: Islam or Nationalism?* (Karachi, Oxford University Press, 1994).

Robins. Philip J., *Turkey and the Middle East* (London: Royal Institute of International Affairs, 1991).

Rubinsein, Alvin Z., and Oles M. Smolansky (eds.), *Regional Power Rivalries in the New Eurasia: Russia, Turkey and Iran* (New York, M.E. Sharpe, 1995).

Ro'i, Yaacov (ed.), *Muslim Eurasia Conflicting Legacies*. (London, Frank Cass, 1995).

Ro'i, Yaacov, *Islam in the Soviet Union: From World War II to Perestroika*. (London, Hurst and Company, 2000).

Rubin, Bernett R. & Jack Snyder (eds.), *Post-Soviet Political Order Conflict and State Building*. (London & New York, Routledge, 1998).

Rubinstein, Alvin Z. & Others, *Regional Power Rivalries in the New Eurasia: Russia, Turkey and Iran* (New York: ME Sharpe, 1995).

Rubinstein, Alvin Z., *Soviet Foreign Policy Since World War II: Imperial and Global* (New York: Harper Collins, 1992).

Rywkin, Michael, *Moscow's Muslim Challenge: Soviet Central Asia* (New York: Armonk, 1990).

Sagdeev, Ronald Z. & Others (eds.), *Central Asia: Conflict, Resolution and Change* (Maryland: CPSS Press, 1995).

Sahni, Kalpana, *Crucifying the Orient: Russian Orientalism and the Colonization of Caucasus and Central Asia* (Bangkok: White Orchid Press, 1997).

Saikal, Amin & Others (eds.), *Russia in Search of its Future* (London: Cambridge University Press, 1995).

Sander, Oral, *Turkiye'nin Dis Politikasi.* (Ankara: Imge Kitabevi, 1998).

Senses, F. (ed.), *The Recent Industrialization Experience of Turkey in Global Context* (Greenwood Press, 1994).

Shashenkov Maxim, *Security Issues of the Ex-Soviet Central Asian Republics* (Brassey, London: Defence Studies Kings College Press,, 1996).

Shaw, Stanford J., *The Jews of the Ottoman Empire and the Turkish Republic.* (New York: New York University Press, 1991).

Shearman, Peter (ed.), *Russian Foreign Policy Since 1990* (New York: Westview Press, 1995).

Sheykh-Attar, Ali-Reza, *The Roots of Political Behaviour in Central Asia and the Caucasus* (Tehran: C, CA & CRIPIS, 1992).

Shirazi, Abolhassan, *The Nations of Central Asia* (Tehran: The Institute for Political and International Studies, 1991).

Smith, Anthony D., *National Identity.* (Reno, Las Vegas. London: University of Nevada Press, 1991).

Smith, Graham, Vivian Law, Andrew, etc. (eds.), *Nation Building in the Post Soviet Borderlands: The Politics of National Identities.* (Cambridge, Cambridge University Press, 1998).

Stephen, J. Blank & others, *Turkey's Strategic Position at the Crossroads of World Affairs* (Pennsylvania: Carlisle Barracks, 1993).

Synder, Jed C., *After Empire: The Emerging Geopolitics of Central Asia* (Washington DC: National Defence University Press, 1995).

Thomson, John M., *Russia and the Soviet Union.* (Boulder, Westview Press, 1994).

Tishkov, Vallery, *Ethnicity and Nationalism and Conflict in and after the Soviet Union.* (London, Sage Publications, 1997).

Tplstov, S.P. (ed.), *The Russian in Central Asia* (Moscow, 1992).

Turkish Foreign Policy Institute (TFPI), *Turkey and European Union: Nebulous Nature of Relations*. Ankara: Hacettepe University, 1996.

Tursunov, H.T., *National Delimitation in Central Asia* (Tashkent: 1957).

Ugar, Mehmet, *The EU and Turkey: An Anchor/Credibility Dilemma* (London: Ashgate Press, 1999).

Vaasilyeva, O., *Central Asia: One Year After the Putch* (Moscow, 1993).

Vaidyanath, R., *The Formation of the Soviet Central Asian Republics: 1917-1936* (New Delhi: People's Publication House, 1967).

Vali, Ferenc A., *Bridge Across the Bosphorus*. (Batimore and London: The Johns Hopkins Press, 1971).

Vassiliev, Alexi (ed.), *Central Asia: Political and Economic Challenges in the Post-Soviet Era*. (London, Saqui Book, 2001).

Walker, Edward W. (ed.),*Minorities, Mullah and Modernity: Reshaping Community in the Former Soviet Union* (Berkeley: University of California Press, 1997).

Warikoo, K. (ed.), *Central Asia: Emerging New Order* (New Delhi: Har Anand Publishers, 1995).

Warikoo, K. and Norbu, D. (eds.), *Ethnicity and Politics in Central Asia*. (New Delhi, South Asia Publishers Pvt. Ltd., 1992).

Webber, Mark, *CIS Integration Trends: Russia and the Former Soviet South* (London: Royal Institute of International Affairs, 1995).

Weiker, Walter F., *The Modernization of Turkey*. (New York and London: Holmes and Meier Publishers, Inc., 1981).

Weisbrode, Kenneth, *Central Eurasia: Prize or Quciksand? Contending Views of Instability in Karabakh, Ferghana and*

Afghanistan. (Adelphi Paper 338, Oxford University Press, 2001).

Wetz, Richard (ed.), *The National Security of Russia* (Harvard University, 1997).

Wheeler, G., *The Modern History of Soviet Central Asia* (West Part, CT: Greenwood Press, 1975).

William, Fierman (ed.), *Soviet Central Asia* (New York: Westview Press, 1991).

Winrow, Gareth M., *Turkey and Caspian Energy* (Abu Dhabi: Emirates Center for Strategic Studies and Research, 1999).

———, *Where East Meets West: Turkey and the Balkans* (Exeter: Institute for European Defence and Strategic Studies, 1993).

Winrow, Gareth, *Regional Security and National Identity: The Role of Turkey in Former Soviet Central Asia* (Leiden: E.J. Brill, 1999).

———, *Turkey in Post-Soviet Central Asia*. (London: The Royal Institute of International Affairs, 1995).

Yalcin, Soner, *Hangi Erbakan?* (Ankara: Oteki Yayinevi, 1995).

Yuriy, Kulchik and Others, *Central Asia After the Empire* (London: Pluto Press, 1996).

Zbigniew, Brzezinski, *The Grand Chessboard: American Primacy and Its Geostrategic Imperatives*. (Basic Books, NY, 1997).

Zhang, Yongjin & Others (eds.), *Ethnic Challenges Beyond Borders: Chinese and Russian Perspectives of the Central Asian Conundrum* (New York: Oxford Press, 1998).

Zurcher, Erik J., *Turkey: A Modern History*. (London and New York: I.B. Taurais & Co.Ltd., 1995).

Zviagelskaia, Irina, *The Russian Policy Debate on Central Asia* (London: Royal Institute of International Affairs, 1995).

Articles

Abazov, Rafis, "Central Asia's Conflicting Legacy". *Nationalism and Ethnic Politics*, Vol.5, No.2, Summer 1999.

Abidi, A.H.H., 'Iran and Central Asian States". *World Focus* (New Delhi), 14(34), 1993.

Abromowitz, M., "Turkey After Ozal", *Foreign Policy*, No. 91 (Summer 1993).

Adams, T. and Rich, G., "Great Power Politics and the Azerbaijan Oil Pipeline", *Washington Institute of Near East Policy: Policy Watch*, 24 February 1997.

Ahmad, Feroz, "Politics and Islam in Modern Turkey", *Middle Eastern Studies* 27 (January 1991).

Ahmad, Feroz, "The Political Economy of Kemalism", in Ali Kazancigil and Ergun Ozbudun (eds.), *Ataturk: Founder of a Modern State*, Hamden: Archon Books, 1981.

Ahmad, Rashid, "The Fires of Faith in Central Asia". *World Policy Journal*, Spring 2001.

Ahmar, Moonis, "Conflict Resolution and Confidence Building in Central Asia". *Strategic Studies* (Islamabad), 16(43), Spring 1994.

Ahmar, Moonis, "Ethnic Factor in Contemporary Central Asia: Pakistan's Perspective". *Eurasian Studies*, 2(4), Winter 1995-96.

Ahmar, Samina, "Political Implications of Ethnicity in Central Asia". *Regional Studies* (Islamabad), 13(2), 1995.

Ahrari, M.E., "Dynamics of the New Great Game in Muslim Central Asia". *Central Asian Survey* (London), 13(4), 1994.

Aidaraliev, A.A., "Problems and Ways of Providing Human Activities in the Mountains of Central Asia". *Himalayan and Central Asian Studies*, 2(3-4), 1998 (July-Dec.).

Akarslan, Mediha, "Uzbek Khanates and the Emergence of the Uzbeks in the 15th Century". *Eurasian Studies*, 2(4), Winter 1995-96.

Akbarzadeh, Shahram, "Nation-Building in Uzbekistan". *Central Asian Survey*, 15(1), Mar.96.

———, "Political Shape of Central Asia". *Central Asian Survey*, 16(4), Dec. 97.

———, 'Why Did Nationalism Fail in Tajikistan?" *Eurasian Studies*, (4), Winter 1995-96.

Akural, Sabri, "Kemalist Views on Social Change", in *Ataturk and Modernization of Turkey*, ed. by Jacob M. Landau, (Boulder, CO Westview Press, 1984).

Akzali, Pinar, "Islam as a Common Bond in Central Asia: Islamic Renaissance Party and the Afghan Mujahideen". *Central Asian Survey*, Vol.17, No.2, 1998.

Alemdar, Zeynep, "Ideology Behind Turkish Army", *Washington Post*, 14 June 1997.

———, "Turkish Military on Anti-Islam Offense", *Washington Post*, 10 June 1997.

Alexeyer, Valery, "Islam and Politics: Muslims in the Commonwealth of Independent States in the Post-Communist World". *Social Science Quarterly Review* (Moscow), 24(2), 1993.

Altunisik, Meliha Benli, "Turkish-Israeli Rapproachement in the Post Cold War Era", *Middle Eastern Studies 10* (April 2000)

Amin, Tahir, "Pakistan and the Central Asian States". *Strategic Studies*, 16(4), Summer 1994.

Anderson, Jennifer, "Central Asia and Mongolia". *Adelphi Paper*, (31), 1997.

Anderson, John, "Authoritarian Political Development in Central Asia: The Case of Turkmenistan". *Central Asian Survey*, 14(4), 1995.

———, "Constitutional Development in Central Asia". *Central Asian Survey*, 16(3), Sept. 97.

Apostolou, A., "New Players in an Old Game", *The Middle East*, No.213 (July 1992).

Aras, B., "Azerbaijan's Far Eastern Friends", *Middle East International 570*, 13 March 1998.

Aras, Bulent,"Turkish-Israeli-Iranian Relations in the Nineties: Impact on the Middle East", *Middle East Policy 7* (June 2000).

Ataee, Farhad, "Iran and Turkey in Post-Soviet Central Asia". *Discourse: An Iranian Quarterly*, Vol.2, No.1 (Summer 2000).

Ataov, Turkkaya, "Central Asia on the Threshold of the 21st Century". *Himalayan and Central Asian Studies*, 1(3); Oct.97.

Ayata, Sencer, "The Rise of Islamic Fundamentalism and Its Institutional Framework", in *The Political and Socio-economic Transformation of Turkey*, ed. by Atila Eralp, Muharrem Tunay and Birol Yesilada. (Westport, Connecticut, London: Praeger, 1993).

Aydin, Mustafa, "Turkey and Central Asia: Challenges of Change". *Central Asian Survey*, 15(2), June 96.

Aykan, Mahmut Bali, "The Palestinian Question in Turkish Foreign Policy from the 1950s to the 1990s", *International Journal of Middle Eastern Studies 25* (1993).

Baghayeghi, Mehradad, "Islamic Revival in the Central Asian Republics". *Central Asian Survey*, 13(2), 1994.

Bakshi, G.D., "Central Asian Cauldron: Conflict Prognostication". *Strategic Analysis*, 19(3), June 96.

Bakshi, Jyotsna, "Central Asian Republics Today'. *Strategic Analysis*, 17(5), 1994.

———, "No Single Power or Power Centre can have exclusive sway over Central Asia: A Geo-political Analysis". *Strategic Analysis*, 22(1), Apr.98.

———, "Russia, India and the Central Asian Republics: Geo-political Convergence". *Strategic Analysis*, 19(5), Aug.96.

———, "Security and Nuclear Issue". *World Focus*, 14(3), 1993.

Banerjee, D., "Recent Development in Central Asia and Their Security Implications". *Strategic Analysis* (New Delhi), 15(6), September 1992.

Barkey, Henri J., "The Silent Victor: Turkey's Role in the Gulf War", in *The Iran-Iraq War: Impact and Implications*, ed. by Efraim Karsh. (London: The Macmillan Press, 1989).

———, "Turkey, Islamic Politics and the Kurdish Question", *World Policy Journal 13* (Spring 1996).

Batu, Hamit, "The Cultural Board", *Studies on Turkish Arab Relations 6* (1991).

———, "Turkish Foreign Policy in a Changing World", *Studies on Turkish-Arab Relations 6* (1991).

Belokrenitsky, "Central Asia in the New Eurasian Geopolitics Implications for Pakistan and Russia". *Pakistan Horizon*, 48(3), July 1995.

Belokrenitsky, U., "Russia and Greater Central Asia". *Central Asian Survey*, 13(2), 1994.

Bennigsen, Alexandre, "Mullahs, Mujahideen and Soviet Muslims". *Problems of Communism* (March-April, 1980).

Bhatty, Maqbool A., "Pakistan's Perspectives on Central Asia". *Strategic Studies*, 16(3), Spring 1994.

Birand, Mehmet Ali, "Is There a New Role for Turkey in the Middle East", in *Reluctant Neighbor: Turkey's Role in the Middle East*, ed. by Henry J. Barkey. Washington D.C.: US Institute of Peace Press, 1996.

Bishku, Michael B., "Turkey and its Neighbors since 1945", *Journal of South Asian and Middle Eastern Studies 15* (Spring 1992).

Black, Ian, "Turkey Blocks NATO Deal on EU Force, *The Guardian*, December 15, 2000.

Blank, S.J., "Turkey's Strategic Engagement in the Former USSR and US Interests", in Stephen J. Blank, *Turkey: Strategic Position at the Crossroads of World Affairs*, ed. by Stephens J. Blank et.al. (Carlisle Barracks, PA: Strategic Studies Institute, 1993).

Blank, Stephen, "Central Asia: 120 Years of Russian Rule". *Central Asian Survey*, 8(4), 1989.

———, "Energy, Economics and Security in Central Asia: Russia and its Rivals". *Central Asian Survey*, (3), 1995.

B'Olivier, "Tajikistan's Elusive Peace". *World Today* (London), 52(2), February 1996.

Boljurova, I.S., "Central Asia: Search for Priorities". *Contemporary Central Asia*, 11(2), Sept. 98.

Bolukbasi, S., "The Controversy Over the Caspian Sea Mineral Resources: Conflicting Perception, Clashing Interests", *Europe-Asia Studies 50*, No.3 (May 1998).

Boquerat, Gilles, "Evolution of India's Perception of Central Asia in the Twentieth Century". *Strategic Analysis*, 19(5), Aug.96.

Bremmer, Ian & Welt, Cory, "Trouble with Democracy in Kazakhstan". *Central Asian Survey*, 15(2), June 96.

Bremmer, Ian, "Nazarbaev and the North: State Building and Ethnic Relations in Kazakhstan". *Ethnic and Racial Studies*, Vol.17, No.4, October 1994.

Brenninkmeijer, Oliver, "Tajikistan's Elusive Peace". *World Today*, 52(2), Feb. 96.

Brown, Bess, "Central Asia: The First Year of Unexpected Statehood". *RFE/RL Research Report*, 2/1 January 1993.

Broxup, Marie, "USSR: The Islamic Threat". *Immigrants and Minorities*, 9(3), 1990.

Bruno, Werner, Firouzeh, "Central Asian Region in a New International Environment", *NATO Review* (Brussels), Sept. 1996.

Budak, Mustafa, "Origins of Ottoman-Uzbek Relations". *Eurasian Studies*, 2(4), Winter 1995-96.

Chakravorty, Sumit, "Russia and Central Asia". *World Focus*, 14(3-4), 1993.

Chandra, Amiya, "Turkmen-India Cooperation for Peace and Development". *Strategic Analysis*, 19(), Dec. 96.

Chang, Felix K., "China's Central Asian Power and Problems" *Orbis*, 41(3), Summer 1997.

Chang, Felix K., "China's Central Asian Power and Problems" *Strategic Digest*, 27(8), Aug. 97, 1149-67.

Chebotarev, A., "In Web of Uzbek Clan". *Central Asia: Politics and Economics*, No.2, November 2000.

Chenoy, Anuradha M., "Islam, Women and Identity in Contemporary Central Asia". *Economic and Political Weekly*, 32(9), 1966 (2 March).

Chenoy, Anuradha, "Geo-Strategies and Foreign Policies". *World Focus*, 14(3-4), 1993.

Coppieters, Bruni & Others, "Central Asian Region in a New International Environment". *NATO Review*, 44(5), Sept.96.

Cordier, Brune De, "Economic Cooperation Organization: Towards a New Silk Road on the Ruins of the Cold War?" *Central Asian Survey*, 15(1), Mar., 96.

Critchlow, J., "Islam in Public Life: Can this be Soviet Uzbekistan?" *Report on the USSR*, 16 March 1990.

Croissant, M.P., "Turkey and NATO After the Cold War", *Strategic Review* 23, No.4 (Fall 1995).

Daanvander, Schriek, "The Central Asian Taliban". *The Times of Central Asia*, 18 October 2001.

Dadwal, Shebonti Ray, "Politics of Oil: Caspian Imbroglio". *Strategic Analysis* (August 1998).

Dannreuther, Roland, "Creating New States in Central Asia". *Adalphi Paper* (London), 288, March 1994.

Dannreuther, Roland, "Russia, Central Asia and the Persian Gulf". *Survival* (London), 35(4), Winter 1993-94.

Dave, Bhavna, "National Revival in Kazakhstan: Language Shift and Identity Change". *Post-Soviet Affairs*, 12(1), Jan.-Mar. 96.

Devereux, John and Roberts, Bryan, "Direct Foreign Investment and Welfare in the Transforming Economies: The Case of Central Asia". *Journal of Comparative Economics*, 24(3), June 1997.

Dieter, Herbert, "Regional Integration in Central Asia: Current Economic Position and Prospectus". *Central Asian Survey*, 15(3-4), Dec. 96.

Dietl, Gulshan, "Quest for Influence in Central Asia: India and Pakistan'. *International Studies*, 34(2), Apr-June 97.

Dixit, Abha, "Tajikistan: Engulfed by Flames of Afghanistan Civil War". *Strategic Analysis*, (9), 1992.

Djalili, Mohammad Reza, "In Search of New Friends: Iran and Central Asia". *World Affairs*, 1(1), Jan.-Mar. 97.

Dorian, James P. & Others, "Central Asia and Zinjiang China: Emerging Energy, Economic and Ethnic Relations". *Central Asian Survey*, 16(45), Dec. 97.

Duran, Khalid, "Rivalries over the New Muslim Countries". *Aussen Politik*, (Bielefeld, Germany), 43(4), 1992

Economist Intelligence Unit Country Report: Azerbaijan, London: *The Economist*, 1998.

Fanisovich, Abazov Rafis, "Balkanization of the Economy of the Central Asian Republics and its Impact on the non-State Sector". *International Journal of Urban and Regional Research*, 20(4), 1996.

Federov, Y., "Russia's Policies Toward Caspian Region Oil: Neo Imperial or Pragmatic II?" *Perspective on Central Asia* (October 1996).

Fierman, William, "Religion and Nationalism in Soviet Central Asia". *Problem of Communism*, 38(4), July-Aug. 89.

Firdous, Tabassum, "Central Asia, Security, Stakes and Strategies". *World Focus*, 4(1), June 1995.

Foltz, Richarad, "Cultural Contacts between Central Asia and Mughal India". *Central Asiatic Journal*, 42(1), 1998.

Foltz, Richarad, "Tajiks of Uzbekistan". *Central Asian Survey*, 15(2), June 96.

Forstythe, R., The Politics of Oil in the Caucasus and Central Asia: *Adelphi Papers, No.40*, (Oxford: International Institute for Strategic Studies, 1996).

Frank, Andre Gunder, 'The Centrality of Central Asia". *Bulletin of Concerned Asian Scholars*, 24/2, 1992.

Freij, Hanna Yousif, "State Interests vs the Umma: Iranian Policy in Central Asia". *Middle East Journal*, 50(1), Winter 1996.

Fuller, G.E., "Turkey's New Eastern Orientation", in Graham E. Fuller and lan O. Lesser (eds.), *Turkey's New Geopolitics: From the Balkans to Western China*, (Boulder, Westview Press, 1993).

Gidadhubli, R.G., "Russia: Oil Politics in Central Asia". *Economic and Political Weekly*, 34(5), 1999 (Jan.30-Feb.5).

Gidadhubli, R.G., "Turko-Lingual States make Common Cause". *Economic and Political Weekly*, 31(50), 14 Dec. 96.

Gleason, Gregory, "Independence and Decolonization in Central Asia". *Asian Perspective*, 21(2), Fall 1997.

Gleason, Gregory, "Independent Muslim Republics in Central Asia: Legacy of the Past, Shape of the Future". *Journal of the Institute of Muslim Minority Affairs*, 12(2), July 1991.

Goetz, Roland, "Political Spheres of Interest in the Southern Caucasus and in Central Asia". *Aussen Politik*, 48(3), 1997.

Gokay, Bulent, Turkish Settlement and the Caucasus, 1918-20. *Middle Eastern Studies*, 32(2), Apr. 96.

Goldstein, L., "Conflict in the Caucasus may Escalate", *Harvard International Review*, 16, No.1 (Fall 1993).

Goldsmith, Ben R., "Victory to Fear or a Source of Hope?" *World Today*, 53(7), July 97.

Gultekin, N.B. and Mumcu, A., "Black Sea Economic Cooperation", in Vojtech Mastny and R. Craig Nation (eds.), *Turkey Between East and West*, (Boulder, Westview, 1996).

Haghayeghi, Mehrdad, "Islamic Revival in Central Asian Republics". *Central Asian Survey*, 13(2), 1994.

Halbach, Owe, "The Caucasus as a Region of Conflict". *Aussen Politik*, No.4, 1997.

Halbach, Owe, Tiller, Heinrich, "Russia and Its Southern Flank". *Aussen Politik*, No.11 (1994).

Hale, W., "Turkey, the Black Sea and Transcaucasia", in John F.R. Wright, Suzanne Goldenberg and Richard Schofield (eds.), *Transcaucasian Boundaries*, (New York: St. Martin's, 1996).

Harrish, Lillian, "Xinjiang, Central Asia and the Implications for China's Policy in the Islamic World". *China Quarterly* (Beijing), (133), March 1993.

Hauner, Milan, "Central Asian Geopolitics in the Last Hundred Years: A Critical Survey from Gorchakov to Gorbachev". *Central Asian Survey*, Vol. 8, No.11, 1989.

Heleniak, Tim, "Changing Nationality Composition of the Central Asian and Trans-Caucasian States". *Post-Soviet Geography and Economics*, 38(6), June 97.

Hetmanek, Allen, "Islamic Revolution and Jihad Came to the Former Soviet Central Asia: The Case of Tajikistan". *Central Asian Survey*, 12(3), 1993.

Hiro, Dilip, "Beyond the Fringe". *New Statesman and Society*, 6/234, 8 January 1993.

Horsman, Stuart, "Uzbekistan's Involvement in the Tajik Civil War 1992-97: Domestic Considerations". *Central Asian Survey*, Vol.18, No.1, 1999.

Hostler, Charles, "The Turks and Soviet Central Asia". *Middle East Journal*, 12 Summer, 1958.

Howell, Jude, "Coping with Transition: Insights from Kyrgyzstan". *Third World Quarterly*, 17(1), Mar.96.

Howell, Jude, 'Poverty and Transition in Kyrgyzstan: How Some Households Cope". *Central Asian Survey*, 15(1), Mar.96.

Hunter, Shireen T., "Forging Chains Across Eurasia". *World Today*, 52(12), Dec.96.

Hussain, Mushahid, "Iran and Turkey in Central Asia: Complimentary or Competing Roles'. *Middle East International*, (444), February 19, 1993.

Hyman, Anthony, "Moving out of Moscow's Orbit: The Outlook for Central Asia". *International Affairs* (London), 69(2), April 1993.

Hyman, Anthony, "Power and Politics in Central Asia's New Republics". *Conflict Studies* (London), (273), August 1994.

Hyman, Anthony, "Russian Minorities in the Near Abroad'. *Conflict Studies*, (299), May 1997, 1-25.

Imart, Guy, "Kirgizia-Kazakhstan: A Hinge or a Faultline". *Problems of Communism*, 39, September-October 1990.

Iskit, T., "Turkey: A New Actor in the Field of Energy Politics", *Perceptions 1*, No.1 (March-May 1996).

Janabel, Jiger, "When National Ambition Conflicts with Reality: Studies on Kazakhstan's Ethnic Relations". *Central Asian Survey*, 15(1), Mar.96.

Joshi, Nirmala, "Russia and Central Asia: The Strategic Dimension". *Strategic Analysis*, 18(9).

Kamrava, Mehran, 'State Building in Azerbaijan: The Search for Consolidation". *Middle East Journal*, Vol.55, No.2 (Spring 2001).

Kartha, Tara, "Light Weapon Proliferation and Regional Instability in Central Asia". *Strategic Analysis*, 19(9), Dec. 96.

Kasenov, O., "Russia, Transcaucasia and Central Asia: Oil, Pipelines and Geopolitics", in Ronald Z. Sagdeev and Susan Eisenhower (eds.), *Central Asia: Conflict, Resolution and Change*, (Chevy Chase: CPSS Press, 1997).

Kasenov, O., 'Central Asia: National, Regional and Global Aspects of Security". *Himalayan and Central Asian Studies*, 1(1), Apr.-June 97.

Kaser, Michael, "Economic Transition in Six Central Asian Economies". *Central Asian Survey*, 16(1), Mar.97.

Kaushik, Devendra, "India and Central Asia: Past and Present Realities and Future Hopes". *Contemporary Central Asia*, 1(1), 1997.

———, "India and Central Asia: Renewing a Traditional Relationship". *South Asian Survey*, 5:2 (1998).

———, "Islamic Fundamentalism in Central Asia". *Himalayan and Central Asian Studies*, Vol.4, No.3-4, July-dec. 2000.

———, "The Central Asian Republics: the Balance Sheet of a Decade of Ozodi". *Eurasian Studies*, Summer 2001.

Keller, Shosana, "Islam in Soviet Central Asia'. *Central Asian Survey*, Vol.11, No.1, 1992.

Khan, Rashid Ahmad, 'Pakistan's Relations with the Central Asians Republics: Problems and Prospects". *Bliss Journal*, 15(3), 1994.

Khazanov, Anatoly, "The Ethnic Problems of Contemporary Kazakhstan". *Central Asian Survey*, Vol.14, No.2, 1995.

Kirisci, K., "New Patterns of Turkish Foreign Policy Behavior", in Cigdem Balim, et.al. (eds.), *Turkey: Political, Social and Economic Challenges in the 1990s*. (Leiden: E.J. Brill, 1995).

Klatt, Martin, "Russians in the 'Near Abroad'". *REF/RL Research Report*, 332. 19 August 1994.

Knyazev, Alexander, "International Terrorism in Central Asia". *Aakrosh*, Vol.4, No.12, July 2001,

Kosmarskaya, Natalya, "Russian Women in Kyrgyzstan: Coping with New Realities". *Women's Studies International Forum*, 19(1-2), Jan.-Apr. 96.

Kozyrev, Andrei, "New Russia and the Atlantic Alliance". *NATO Review*, 41(1), February 1993.

———, "Partnership of Cold Peace". *Foreign Policy* (Washington DC), No.99, Seminar 1995.

———, "Russia and NATO: A Partnership for United and Peaceful Europe". *NATO Review*, 42(4), August 1994.

Kramer, Heinz, "Turkey and the European Union: A Multi-Dimensional Relationship with Hazy Perspectives", in *Turkey Between East and West*, ed. by Vojtech Mastny and R. Craig Nation. (Boulder: Westview Press, 1996).

Krause, Joachim, "Risk of Nuclear Proliferation Following the Dissolution of the Soviet Union". *Aussen Politik*, 43(4), 1992.

Kubicek, Paul, "Authoritarianism in Central Asia: Curse or Cure?" *Third World Quarterly*, 19(1), 1998.

———, 'Regionalism, Nationalism and Real Politik in Central Asia". *Europe-Asia Studies*, 49(4), June 97.

Kuniholm, Bruce R., "The Geopolitics of the Caspian Basin". *Middle East Journal*, Vol.4, Fall 2000.

Kuniholm, Bruce, "Turkey and the West", *Foreign Affairs 70* (Spring 1991).

Kushner, David, "Self Perception and Identity in Contemporary Turkey", *Journal of Contemporary History 32* (1997).

———, "Westernism in Contemporary Turkey", in Ataturk and *The Modernization of Turkey*, ed. by Jacob M. Landau. (Boulder CA, Westview Press, 1984).

Lange, Keely, "Do Borders make a Nation?: New Analysis of Identities with a Focus on Central Asia". *Regional Studies*, 15(4), Autumn 1997.

Legro, Jeffrey W., "Culture and Preferences in the International Cooperation Two-Step", *American Political Science Review 90* (March 1996).

Lerman, Zvi & Others, "Land and Water Politics in Uzbekistan". *Post-Soviet Geography and Economics*, 37(3), 1996.

Lesser, I.O., "Bridge or Barrier? Turkey and the West After the Cold War", in Graham E. Fuller and Ian O. Lesser (eds.), *Turkey's New Geopolitics: From the Balkans to Western China*, Boulder, Westview Press, 1993.

Lewin, Anat, "Turkey and Israel: Reciprocal and Mutual Imagery in the Media, 1994-1999", *Journal of International Affairs 54* (Fall 2000).

Lewis, David C., "Ethnicity and Religion in Tatarstan and the Volga-Ural Region'. *Central Asian Survey*, 16(1), June 97.

Lewis, G.L., "Ataturk's Language Reform and Modernization", in *Ataturk and the Modernization of Turkey*, ed. by Jacob M. Landau. Boulder CO: Westview Press, 1984.

Lipovsky, Igor P., "Central Asia: In Search of a New Political Identity", *Middle East Journal 50*, No.2 (Spring 1996).

———, "Russian Problem in Central Asia". *Orient*, 36(3), 1995 (Sept.).

———, "Awakening of Central Asian Islam". *Middle Eastern Studies*, 32(3), July 96.

———, "Middle East and Central Asia". *Survival*, 35(4), Winter 1993-94 (Series of Articles).

———, 'Deterioration of the Ecological Situation in Central Asia: Causes and Possible Consequences". *Europe-Asia Studies*, 47(7), 1995 (Nov.).

Lloyd, John, "Turkey's closeness to the Islamic bloc causes problems for the West, but it need not shatter our confidence in it", *New Statesman*, August 30, 1996.

Mackenzie, K., "Azerbaijan and the Neighbors", *World Today 48*, No.1 (January 1992).

Magnus and Naby, "Afghanistan and Central Asia: Mirrors and Models". *Asian Survey*, 35(7), July 1995.

Mahmood, Annice, "Collapse of the Soviet Union and its Implications for Central Asia". *Strategic Studies*, 16(3), Spring 1994.

Makovsky, Alan, "Israeli-Turkish Relations: A Turkish 'Periphery' Strategy", in *Reluctant Neighbor: Turkey's Role in the Middle East*, ed. by Henri J. Barkey. (Washington: United States Institute of Peace Press, 1996).

Malashenko, Alexei, "Islam in Central Asia: Dynamism of its Influence". *Vostok*, M, 1996, No. 5. Reproduced in *Russia and the Moslem World*, No.3(57), 1997.

Mango, Andrew, "A Speaking Turkey", *Middle Eastern Studies 33* (January 1997).

———, "Testing Time in Turkey", *The Washington Quarterly 20* (1996).

———, "The Turkish Model", *Middle Eastern Studies 29* (October 1993).

———, "Turkey and the Enlargement of the European Mind", *Middle Eastern Studies 34* (April 1998).

———, "Turkish Policy in the Middle East", in *Turkish Foreign Policy: New Prospects*, ed. by Clement H. Dodd. Cambridgeshire: The Eothen Press, 1992.

Mark, David E., 'Eurasia Letter: Russia and the New Trans-Caucasus". *Foreign Policy*, (105), Winter 1996-97.

Martin, Keith, "Tajikistan: Civil War without End". *REFRL Research Report*, 2/33, 20 August 1993.

Matin, Abdul, "Fostering Linkages with Central Asia". *Journal of Rural Development and Administration*, 25(1), 1993.

Mehrotra, O.N., "Commonwealth of the Former Soviet Republics". *Strategic Analysis*, 14(11), 1992.

Menon, Rajan, "In the Shadow of the Bear, Security in Post-Soviet Central Asia". *International Security*, Summer 1995, 20(1).

Mesbahi, Mohiaddin, "Russia and the new Muslim States: Change or Continuity". *Central Asian Survey*, (1), 1993.

———, "Russian Foreign Policy and Security in Central Asia and Caucasus". *Central Asian Survey*, (2), 1993.

Mishra, Rajesh Kumar, "Throbbing State of the Central Asian Republics". *Bliss Journal*, 17(4), 1996.

Mohsenin, Mehrdad, 'Iran's Relations with Central Asia and the Caucasus". *Iranian Journal of International Affairs*, 7(4), Winter 1996.

Moustakis, Fotis, "Turkey's Entry into the EU: Asset or Liability", *Contemporary Review 273* (September 1998).

Mufti, M., "Daring and Caution in Turkish Foreign Policy", *Middle East Journal 52*, No.1 (Winter 1998).

Muftuler, Meltem, "Turkey: A New Player in Middle Eastern Politics", *Mediterranean Quarterly 6* (Fall 1995).

Muftuler-Bac, Meltem, "Turkey's Predicament in the Post-Cold War Era", *Futures 28* (1996).

Nation, Craig R., "The Turkic and Other Muslim Peoples of Central Asia, the Caucasus and the Balkans", in *Turkey Between East and West*, ed. by Vojtech Mastny and R. Craig Nation. Boulder: Westview Press, 1996.

Neumann, Iver B., "Identity and Security", *Journal of Peace Research* 29 (1992).

Nodia, Ghia, "How Different are post-Communist Transitions". *Journal of Democracy*, Vol.7, No.2, 1996.

Nurhan, Aydin, "Turkey and Middle Eastern Stability: Iraq, Iran, Israel and the Kurdish Question", *Vital Speeches 63* (December 1996).

Nuri, Maqsudul Hasan, "Tajikistan in the 1996". *Regional Studies*, 14(4), Autumn 1996.

Ogutcu, Mehmet, "Islam and the West: Can Turkey Bridge the Gap", *Futures 26* (1994).

Okyar, Osman, "Ataturk's Quest for Modernism", in *Ataturk and Modernization of Turkey*, ed. by Jacob M. Landau. (Boulder CO., Westview Press, 1984).

Olcott, Martha Brill, "Central Asia on Its Own". *Journal of Democracy*, 4/1, January 1993

———, "Central Asian Independence". *Foreign Affairs*, Summer, 1992.

———, "Central Asia's Islamic Awakening". *Current History*, Vol.93, No.589, April 1994.

———, "Perestroika in Kazakhstan". *Problems of Communism*, 39/4, July-August 1990.

———, "The Caspian's False Promise". *Foreign Policy* (Summer 1998).

———, "The Soviet (Dis)union". *Foreign Policy*, 82, Spring 1991.

Olson, Robert, "The Kurdish Question and Chechnya: Turkish and Russian Foreign Policies since the Gulf War", *Middle East Policy 4* (March 1996).

Omestad, Thomas, "Israel's Intriguing Turkish Ties", *US News and World Report 127* (August 2, 1999).

Onis, Ziya, "Turkey in the Post-Cold War Era in Search of Identity", *Middle East Journal 49* (Winter 1995).

Onuf, Nicholas and Frank F. Klink, "Anarchy, Authority, Rule", *International Studies Quarterly 33* (1989).

Orbudun, Ergun, "The Nature of the Kemalist Political Regime", in *Ataturk: Founder of a Modern State*, ed. by Ali Kazancigil and Ergun Ozbudun. (Hamden: Archon Books, 1981).

Ozbudun, Ergun and Ali Kazancigil, "Introduction", in *Ataturk: Founder of a Modern State*, ed. by Ali Kazancigil and Ergun Ozbudun. (Hamden: Archon Books, 1981).

Ozdag, U., "Kuzey Irak ve PKK" (Northern Iraq and PKK), *Avrasya Dosyasi 3*, No.1 (Spring).

Ozel, Soli, "Of Not Being a Lone Wolf: Geography, Domestic Plays and Turkish Foreign Policy in the Middle East", in the *Powder Keg in the Middle East: The Struggle for Gulf Security*, ed. by Geoffrey Kemp and Janice Gross Stein, (Lanham: Rowman and Littlefield Publishers, Inc. 1995).

Page, Stephen, "Creation of a Sphere of Influence in Russian and Central Asia". *International Journal* (Toronto, Canada), 49(4), 1994.

Palat, Madhavan K., "Emergence of Central Asia". *Indian Historical Review*, 18(1-2), July 1991 & Jan. 1992.

Pande, Savita, "Prospects of Nuclear Weapon-free Zones: South-East and Central Asia'. *Strategic Analysis*, 22(6), Sept. 98.

Pasha, S.A.M., "Turkey and the Republics of Central Asia: Emerging Relations and Dilemmas". *International Studies*, 34(3), 1997 (July-Sept.).

Patnaik, Ajay, "Central Asia since Soviet Disintegration". *World Focus*, Vol.22, No.2, February 2001.

———, "Ethnicity, Culture and Migration in Central Asia". *Labyrinth*, Vol.1, No.3, 1994.

———, "Russian Minority as a Factor in Russo-Central Asia Relations". *World Focus*, May 1998.

Pelletiere, Stephen C., "Turkey and the United States in the Middle East: The Kurdish Connection", in *Turkey's Strategic Passion at the Crossroads of World Affairs*, ed. by Stephen J. Blank et.al. (Carlisle, PA: Strategic Studies Institute, US Army War College, 1993).

Picard, Elizabeth, "Relations Between Iraq and its Turkish Neighbor: From Ideological to Geo-Strategic Constraints", in *Iraq: Power and Society*, ed. by Derek Hopwood, Habib Ishow and Thomas Koszinowski (Oxford Ithaca Press, 1993).

Pipes, Richard, "Muslims of Soviet Central Asia: Trends and Prospects". *Middle East Journal*, 9, Spring and Summer 1958.

Pompfret, R., "The Economic Cooperation Organization: Current Status and Future Prospects", *Europe-Asia Studies 49*, No.4 (June 1997).

Poorsoltan, Keramat, "Western Asia in Turmoil and Rivalry Between Iran and Turkey", *Contemporary Review 262* (May 1993).

Powell, Robert, "Anarchy in International Relations Theory: The Neorealsit-Neoliberal Debate", *International Organization 48* (Spring 1994).

Puri, Madan Mohan, "Central Asian Geopolitics: The Indian View". *Central Asian Survey*, 16(1), June 97.

Qzuye, O., "Black Sea Economic Cooperation", *Mediterranean Quarterly 3*, No.3 (Summer 1992).

Ramchandran, Sita Gopalan, "India's Relations with Erstwhile Soviet Union and Russia". *Strategic Analysis* (October 1995).

Rashid, Ahmad, "Islam and Nationalism in Pakistan and Central Asia: An Address". *South Asia*, 18(2), Dec. 1996.

Richter, Anthony, "Spring Time in Tajikistan". *World Policy Journal*, 2, 1994.

Richter, James G., "Perpetuating the Cold War: Domestic Sources of International Patterns of Behavior", *Political Science Quarterly, 107* (1992).

Risse-Kappen, Thomas, "Collective Identity in a Democratic Community: The Case of NATO", in The Culture of National Security, ed. by Peter J. Katzenstein, (New York: Columbia University Press, 1996).

Robins, P., "Between Sentiment and Self-Interest: Turkey's Policy Toward Azerbaijan and the Central Asian States", *Middle East Journal 47,* No.4 (Autumn 1993).

Robins, Philip J., "Avoiding the Question", in *Reluctant Neighbor: Turkey"s Role in the Middle East,* ed. by Henri J. Barkey. (Washington D.C.: US Institute of Peace Press, 1996).

———, "Turkish Foreign Policy under Erbakan", *Survival* 39 (Summer 1997).

———, "Turkish Policy and the Gulf Crisis: Dynamic or Adventurist", in *Turkish Foreign Policy: New Prospects,* ed. by Clement H. Dodd, (Cambridgeshire: The Eothen Press, 1992).

Ro'i, Yaacov, "The Islamic Influence on Nationalism in Soviet Central Asia". *Problems of Communism,* 39/4, July-August 1990.

Roulean, Eric, "The Challenges to Turkey", *Foreign Affairs* 72 (Nov.-Dec. 1993).

———, "Turkey Beyond Ataturk", *Foreign Policy* (Summer 1996).

Roy, Olivier, "Islam and Central Asia". *Seminar* (New Delhi), (393), May 1992.

Rubin, Barnett, "The Fragmentation of Tajikistan". *Survival,* Vol.35, No.4, Winter 1993-94.

Ruggie, John Gerard, "Continuity and Transformation in the World Polity: Toward a Neorealist Synthesis", in

Neurealism and its Critics, ed. by Robert O. Keohane. (New York: Columbia University Press, 1986).

Rumer, B.Z., "The Gathering Storm in Central Asia", *Orbis 37*, No.1 (Winter 1993).

Rustow, Dankwart A., "Ataturk as an Institution Builder", in *Ataturk: Founder of a Modern State*, ed. by Ali Kazancigil and Ergun Ozbudan. (Hamden: Archon Books, 1981).

Rustow, Dankwart A., "Turkey's Liberal Revolution", *Middle East Review 17* (Spring 1985).

Rywkin, Michael, "Central Asia and the Challenge of the Soviet Legacy'. *Central Asian Survey*, Vol.4, No.1, 1985.

Sabol, Steven, "The Creation of Soviet Central Asia: The 1924 National Delimitation". *Central Asian Survey*, 14(2), 1995.

Sachdeva, Gulshan, "Economic Transformation in Central Asia". *International Studies*, 34(3), 1997 (July-Sept.).

Sadri, Houman, A., "Integration in Central Asia: From Theory to Policy'. *Central Asian Survey*, 16(4), Dec. 97.

Sajjadpour, K. Kazim, "Relationship Between Security and Development in Central Asia and the Caucasus'. *Iranian Journal of International Affairs*, 6(3-4), 1994-95.

Salt, Jeremy, "Nationalism and the Rise of Muslim Sentiment in Turkey", *Middle Eastern Studies 31* (January 1995).

Saltmarshe, Douglas, "Civil Society and Sustainable Development in Central Asia". *Central Asian Survey*, 15(3-4), Dec. 1996.

Sayari, Sabri, "Turkey and the Middle East in the 1990s", *Journal of Palestine Studies 26* (Spring 1997).

———, "Turkey: The Changing European Security Environment and the Gulf Crisis", *Middle East Journal 46* (Winter 1992).

———, "Turkish Foreign Policy in the Post-Cold War Era: The Challenges of Multi-Regionalism", *Journal of International Affairs 54* (Fall 2000).

Schilling, Walter, "Return of Geopolitics in the Caucasus and Central Asia". *Aussen Politik,* 49, 1998 (4th Quarter).

Sengupta, Anita, "Beyond Boundaries: Identity, Nationality and Consciousness in Central Asia". *Contemporary Central Asia,* 11(1), March 1998.

———, "Minorities and Nationalizing States in Central Asia". *International Studies,* 34(3), 1997 (July-Sept.).

Sever, Aysegul, "The Arab-Israeli Peace Process and Turkey since the 1995 Interim Agreement", *Turkish Review of Middle East Studies* (1996-97).

———, "The Compliant Ally: Turkey and the West in the Middle East, 1954-58", *Middle Eastern Studies 34* (April 1998).

Shahrani, Nazif, "Central Asia and the Challenge of the Soviet Legacy". *Central Asian Survey,* Vol.12, No.2, 1993.

Sheinbaum, Stanley K., "Israel Plays Turkey", *New Perspectives Quarterly 13* (Summer 1996).

Shoumikhin, A., "Economics and Politics of Developing Caspian Oil Resources", *Perspective on Central Asia* (November 1996).

Shoumikhin, A., New Developments Related to Caspian Oil" *Perspectives on Central Asia* (December 1996).

Singh, Rai, "Russian and Its Southern Flank". *India Quarterly* (New Delhi), 50(3), 1994.

Smith, Anthony D., "The Origins of Nations", *Ethnic and Racial Studies 12* (July 1989).

Smith, Dianne L., "Central Asia: A New Great Game?" *Asian Affairs: An American Review* (Fall 1996).

Snyder, Jack, "Nationalism and the Crisis of the Post-Soviet State". *Survival,* Vol.35, No.1, Spring 1993.

Sokolsky, Richard & Tanya Charlik-Paley, "Look Before NATO Leaps into the Caspian". *Orbis,* Vol.43, No.2, Spring 1999.

Soysal, Ismail, "The Middle East Peace Process and Turkey" *Turkish Review of Middle East Studies 8* (1994-95).

Spoor, Max, "Aral Sea Basin Crisis: Transition and Environment in Former Soviet Central Asia". *Development and Change*, 29(3), July 98.

Stars, S. Frederick, "Making Eurasia Stable'. *Foreign Affairs*, 75(1), Jan.-Feb.96.

———, "United Nations Activities and Regional Cooperation in the Republics of Central Asia and the Caucasus". *Iranian Journal of International Affairs*, 6(3-4), 1994-95.

Steinbach, Udo, "The Impact of Ataturk on Turkey's Political Culture since World War II", in *Ataturk and Modernization of Turkey*, ed. by Jacob M. Landau. (Boulder CO: Westview Press, 1984).

Stobdan, P., "Central Asia in Geo-political Transition'. *Strategic Analysis*, 22(1), Apr.98.

———, "China's Central Asia Dilemma". *Strategic Analysis*, 22(3), June 98.

———, "Emergence of Central Asia: Strategic Implications". *Strategic Analysis*, 18(3), 1995.

———, "Islamic Reawakening in Central Asia: Towards Stability or Conflicts". *Strategic Analysis*, 15(6), September 1992.

Sukhjov, Alexey, "Hizb-ul-Tahrir in Kyrgyzstan". *The Times of Central Asia*, 25 October 2001.

Tachau, Frank, "Turkish Foreign Policy: Between East and West", *Middle East Review 17* (Spring 1985).

Tadjbakhsh, Shahrbanou, "National Reconciliation: The Imperfect Whim". *Central Asian Survey*, 15(3-4), Dec. 96.

Talbott, S., "US-Turkish Relations in an Age of Independence", Speech to the Washington Institute for Near East Policy, Willard Inter Continental Hotel, Wednesday, 14 October 1998.

Tang, Shiping, "Economic Integration in Central Asia". *Asian Survey*, Vol.40, No.2 (2000).

Tarock, Adam, "Iran's Policy in Central Asia". *Central Asian Survey*, 16(1), June 1997.

Tashan, Seyfi, "Contemporary Turkish Policies in the Middle East: Prospects and Constraints", *Foreign Policy 17* (Ankara, June 1985).

Tashan, Seyfi, "Turkey Between Europe and the Arab World", *Studies on Turkish-Arab Relations* 2 (1987).

Tazmini, Ghoneheh, 'The Islamic Revival in Central Asia". *Central Asian Survey*, Vol.20, No.1, 2001.

Teller, Heinrich, "Russia and its Southern Flanks". *Strategic Digest*, 24(9), 1994.

Tirman, J., "Improving Turkey's Bad Neighborhood", *World Policy Journal 15*, No.1 (Spring 1998).

Tirman, John, "The Ankara-Jerusalem Axis", *The Nation 268* (January 4, 1999).

Turk, Hikmet Sami, "NATO's Evolution in the 21st Century and Turkey", *Centre for Strategic & International Studies (Speeches and Transcripts)* (April 26, 1999). Internet Address: www.csis.org.

Usmanov, Lerman, "Will the Islamic Factors Decide the Future of Uzbekistan?" *Nezavisimaya Gazeta*, Moscow, 1994, January1994, reproduced in *Russia and Moslem World*, No. 2, 1994.

Ustugov, Michael, "Will Kazakhstan be a Federated State". *Central Asian Forum*, 15, 1994.

Versan, Vakur, "The Kemalist Reform of Turkish Law and its Impact", in *Ataturk and the Modernization of Turkey*, ed. by Jacob M. Landau. (Boulder, CO: Westview Press, 1984).

Vladimir, Mesamed, "Inter Ethnic Relations in the Republic of Uzbekistan". *Central Asia Monitor*, No.6, 1996.

Vora, Batuk, "American Strategy in the Caucasus and Central Asia". *Mainstream*, 37(17), 1999 (April 17).

Wallace, William, "Foreign Policy and National Identity in the United Kingdom", *International Affairs 67* (1991).

Walsh, J. Richard, "China and the New Geopolitics of Central Asia". *Asian Survey*, 33(3), 1993.

Wilkens, Katherine A., "Turkey: Emerging Regional Power or State in Crisis", *Great Decisions* (1998).

Winrow, G.M., "Turkey's Role in Asian Pipeline Politics", *Jane's Intelligence Review 9*, No.2 (February 1997).

Winrow, Gareth, "Regional Security and National Identity: The Role of Turkey in Former Soviet Central Asia", in *Turkey: Political, Social and Economic Challenges in the 1990s*, ed. by Cigdem Balim et.al. (New York and Kol: E.J. Brill, 1995).

Yapp, M.E., "Europe in the Turkish Mirror", *Past and Present* (November 1992).

Yavuz, M. Hakan, "Turkey's Relations with Israel", *Foreign Policy* (Ankara, 1991).

———, "Turkish-Israeli Relations through the Lens of the Turkish Identity Debate", *Journal of Palestine Studies 27* (Autumn 1997).

Zurcher, Erik J. *Turkey: A Modern History* (London and New York: E.B. Tauris & Co. Ltd. 1995).

Index